SLOW T

T0004291

Suffolk

Local, characterful guides to Britain's special places

Laurence Mitchell

EDITION 3
Bradt Guides Ltd, UK
The Globe Pequot Press Inc, USA

Third edition published September 2023
First published April 2014
Bradt Guides Ltd
31a High Street, Chesham, Buckinghamshire, HP5 1BW, England
www.bradtguides.com
Print edition published in the USA by The Globe Pequot Press Inc,
PO Box 480, Guilford, Connecticut 06437-0480

Text copyright © 2023 Bradt Guides Ltd
Maps copyright © 2023 Bradt Guides Ltd; includes map data © OpenStreetMap contributors
Photographs copyright © 2023 Individual photographers (see below)
Project Manager: Emma Gibbs
Cover research: Pepi Bluck, Perfect Picture

The author and publisher have made every effort to ensure the accuracy of the information
in this book at the time of going to press. However, they cannot accept any responsibility
for any loss, injury or inconvenience resulting from the use of information contained in this
guide. All rights reserved. No part of this publication may be reproduced, stored in a retrieval
system, or transmitted in any form or by any means, electronic, mechanical, photocopying,
recording or otherwise without the prior consent of the publisher.

ISBN: 9781804690499

British Library Cataloguing in Publication Data
A catalogue record for this book is available from the British Library

Photographs
© individual photographers credited beside images & also those from image libraries
credited as follows: Alamy Stock Photo (A); AWL Images (AWL); Dreamstime.com (DT);
Shutterstock.com (S); SuperStock (SS)
Front cover Southwold pier at sunset (eye35.pix/A)
Back cover Flatford Mill, East Bergholt (RAMBO80/S)
Title page The River Stour in Constable Country (Travelling-light/DT)

Maps David McCutcheon FBCart.S

Typeset by Ian Spick, Bradt Guides
Production managed by Zenith Media printed in the UK
Digital conversion by www.dataworks.co.in

AUTHOR

Laurence Mitchell has at various times worked as an English teacher in Sudan, surveyed farm buildings in Norfolk, pushed a pen in a local government office and taught geography in a rural secondary school. Having finally settled for the uncertain life of a freelance travel writer and photographer, he specialises in places like the Balkans, central Asia and the Middle East, although these days he tends to spend most of his time wandering around his home patch of East Anglia. As well as writing several guides for Bradt, his work has appeared in publications like *Geographical*, *Walk*, *Discover Britain*, *Wild Travel* and *hidden europe*. Laurence is a member of the Outdoor Writers and Photographers Guild. His blog can be found at ⊘ eastofelveden.wordpress.com.

AUTHOR'S STORY

Give or take a year here or there, I have lived in East Anglia for over four decades now. Admittedly my home has always been over the border in Norfolk, but Suffolk has long been a feature of my life too. As an incomer originating from the West Midlands, I like to think I can view either county with equal magnanimity. I do not have any particular tribal loyalty or county allegiance to affect my judgement and so hopefully I am able to be fair-minded about what lies on either side of the River Waveney.

As a keen birdwatcher, the Suffolk coast with its marshes and reedbeds has always been a draw. The Waveney Valley with its lovely countryside has long been a natural magnet too. In the Waveney Valley, no-one really seems to bother too much about which side of the county border they are on. I liked

that: identifying with a region rather than an artificial political entity – surely that is what 'sense of place' is all about? And 'sense of place' is really what *Slow Suffolk* is all about.

In *Slow Suffolk* I have tried to seek out those places that make Suffolk special – towns, villages and hamlets that have a uniqueness about them, an identity forged by the people who live there and the landscape that shapes them. Researching this book, as well as revisiting old familiar haunts, I have discovered many places that hitherto had just been names on the map. Villages especially – wonderful little places that I hardly knew existed like Westleton, Middleton, Mendham and Hartest, to name just a few. I am happy in the knowledge that there are still plenty more such places waiting to be discovered.

ACKNOWLEDGEMENTS

I would like to thank all the team at Bradt, in particular Sue Cooper, Emma Gibbs, Kate Howard, Anna Moores, Claire Strange and Jennifer Wildman. My gratitude goes to those who contributed boxes – Anne Locke, Hilary Bradt and Janice Booth – and thanks go too to Wendy Ellis of Boydell & Brewer for permission to quote from John Seymour's *Companion Guide to East Anglia*, and to Helen Sibley for her information on Thornham Walks. For this edition, I am grateful for helpful feedback from readers Jean Johnson and Vanessa Mitchell. I would also like to thank Nicola Miller for her suggestions regarding Bury St Edmunds and Newmarket. As always, I must also pay tribute to the unstinting support of my wife Jackie, a Norfolk native who admits to quite liking Suffolk too.

FEEDBACK REQUEST

At Bradt Guides we're aware that guidebooks start to go out of date on the day they're published – and that you, our readers, are out there in the field doing research of your own. You'll find out before us when a fine new family-run hotel opens or a favourite restaurant changes hands and goes downhill. So why not tell us about your experiences? Contact us on ✆ 01753 893444 or ✉ info@bradtguides.com. We will forward emails to the author who may post updates on the Bradt website at ⬙ bradtguides.com/updates. Alternatively, you can add a review of the book to Amazon, or share your adventures with us on social:

🅕 BradtGuides   🅘 BradtGuides
𝕏 BradtGuides & @eastofelveden

CONTENTS

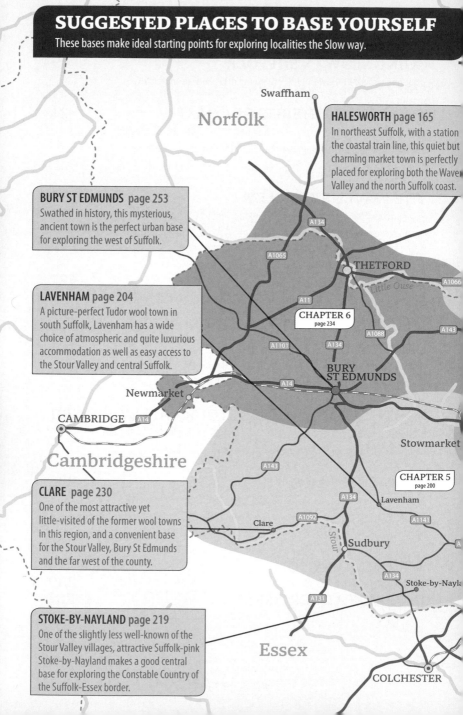

SUGGESTED PLACES TO BASE YOURSELF

These bases make ideal starting points for exploring localities the Slow way.

Swaffham

Norfolk

HALESWORTH page 165

In northeast Suffolk, with a station
the coastal train line, this quiet but
charming market town is perfectly
placed for exploring both the Wave
Valley and the north Suffolk coast.

BURY ST EDMUNDS page 253

Swathed in history, this mysterious,
ancient town is the perfect urban base
for exploring the west of Suffolk.

THETFORD

Little Ouse

A134

A1065

A11

CHAPTER 6
page 234

A1088

A143

LAVENHAM page 204

A picture-perfect Tudor wool town in
south Suffolk, Lavenham has a wide
choice of atmospheric and quite luxurious
accommodation as well as easy access to
the Stour Valley and central Suffolk.

A1101

A134

A14

BURY
ST EDMUNDS

Newmarket

CAMBRIDGE

A14

Stowmarket

Cambridgeshire

A143

CHAPTER 5
page 200

A134

Lavenham

CLARE page 230

One of the most attractive yet
little-visited of the former wool towns
in this region, and a convenient base
for the Stour Valley, Bury St Edmunds
and the far west of the county.

Clare

A1092

A1141

Stour

Sudbury

A134

Stoke-by-Nayla

STOKE-BY-NAYLAND page 219

One of the slightly less well-known of the
Stour Valley villages, attractive Suffolk-pink
Stoke-by-Nayland makes a good central
base for exploring the Constable Country of
the Suffolk-Essex border.

A131

Essex

COLCHESTER

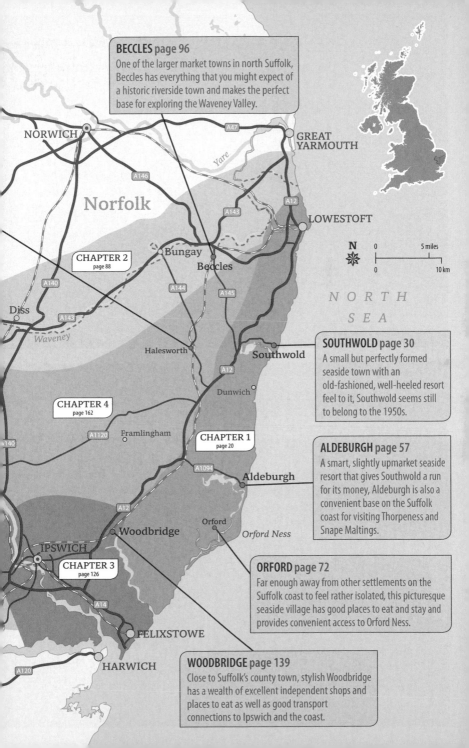

BECCLES page 96
One of the larger market towns in north Suffolk, Beccles has everything that you might expect of a historic riverside town and makes the perfect base for exploring the Waveney Valley.

NORWICH

GREAT YARMOUTH

Yare

Norfolk

LOWESTOFT

CHAPTER 2 page 88

Bungay

Beccles

Diss

Halesworth

Waveney

N O R T H
S E A

N 0 — 5 miles
0 — 10 km

Southwold

SOUTHWOLD page 30
A small but perfectly formed seaside town with an old-fashioned, well-heeled resort feel to it, Southwold seems still to belong to the 1950s.

CHAPTER 4 page 162

Framlingham

Dunwich

CHAPTER 1 page 20

Aldeburgh

ALDEBURGH page 57
A smart, slightly upmarket seaside resort that gives Southwold a run for its money, Aldeburgh is also a convenient base on the Suffolk coast for visiting Thorpeness and Snape Maltings.

Woodbridge

Orford

Orford Ness

IPSWICH

CHAPTER 3 page 126

ORFORD page 72
Far enough away from other settlements on the Suffolk coast to feel rather isolated, this picturesque seaside village has good places to eat and stay and provides convenient access to Orford Ness.

FELIXSTOWE

HARWICH

WOODBRIDGE page 139
Close to Suffolk's county town, stylish Woodbridge has a wealth of excellent independent shops and places to eat as well as good transport connections to Ipswich and the coast.

PINK SPITFIRE/S

ALAN COPSON/AWL

GOING SLOW IN
SUFFOLK

Slow Suffolk? What does that mean exactly? Well, it's not a slur on the character of the people of that county for a start. Sometimes referred to as 'Silly Suffolk', it is easy to assume that the term is just a mild pejorative that refers to the natives of the county as being a bit slow on the uptake. It doesn't mean anything of the sort of course: 'Silly Suffolk' is simply a corruption of the expression 'Selig' Suffolk, selig meaning 'holy' or 'blessed' in Old English, on account of the vast number of churches in the county. The majority of the churches that stand today were erected at a time when Suffolk was one of the richest counties in England thanks to profits from the wool trade. It was this wool wealth that paid for both the construction of the churches and the fine timber-framed houses that still stand proud, if sometimes a little crookedly, in Suffolk towns like Lavenham today.

Like Norfolk, its neighbour to the north, Suffolk was largely bypassed by the Industrial Revolution. And like Norfolk, the county's heyday was not in the 19th century but much earlier, in the medieval period. Suffolk's medieval history is second to none, and the material evidence is still there to be seen – an abundance of fine Tudor buildings in many towns and villages, an enormous wealth of medieval churches and a good showing of castles too.

The county is distinguished in terms of geography too. The landscape is low-lying but rarely flat, and it is surprisingly varied. Take a transect across the county and you'll find sand and shingle beaches, saltings, spits, estuaries, muddy tidal creeks and reedbeds, Sandlings heaths, river valleys and the sandy wastes of the Brecks. Among these landscapes is a countryside filled with rolling farmland, tracts of ancient woodland, stands of modern forestry, a handful of market towns and countless small villages, each with its church. More than anything, it is

◄ 1 Framlingham Castle, page 178. 2 The picturesque village of Lavenham, page 204.

THE SLOW MINDSET
Hilary Bradt, Founder, Bradt Guides

> We shall not cease from exploration
> And the end of all our exploring
> Will be to arrive where we started
> And know the place for the first time.
>
> T S Eliot, 'Little Gidding', *Four Quartets*

This series evolved, slowly, from a Bradt editorial meeting when we started to explore ideas for guides to our favourite part of the world – Great Britain. We wanted to get away from the usual 'top sights' formula and encourage our authors to bring out the nuances and local differences that make up a sense of place – such things as food, building styles, nature, geology, or local people and what makes them tick. Our aim was to create a series that celebrates the present, focusing on sustainable tourism, rather than taking a nostalgic wallow in the past.

So without our realising it at the time, we had defined 'Slow Travel', or at least our concept of it. For the beauty of the Slow movement is that there is no fixed definition; we adapt the philosophy to fit our individual needs and aspirations. Thus Carl Honoré, author of *In Praise of Slow*, writes: 'The Slow Movement is a cultural revolution against the notion that faster is always better. It's not about doing everything at a snail's pace, it's about seeking to do everything at the right speed. Savouring the hours and minutes rather than just counting them. Doing everything as well as possible, instead of as fast as possible. It's about quality over quantity in everything from work to food to parenting.' And travel.

So take time to explore. Don't rush it, get to know an area – and the people who live there – and you'll be as delighted as the authors by what you find.

the villages that make the county what it is and Suffolk has villages in spades. With the exception of Ipswich, which is by far the largest urban area though not a city, there are only a few towns of any size in the county. Suffolk has no motorways either and, despite being home to a number of bomber bases during World War II, there is also no airport to speak of.

The way I see it, the essence of Slow is to find the extraordinary in the commonplace. It is to identify the unique patina created by history, landscape and custom that makes a place a bit special. Everywhere has these qualities to some extent; it is just that Suffolk probably has more than its fair share.

But Slow is about slowing down too; it's taking the time to look closely and savour something, to not hurry too much, to not get too caught up with the need for instant gratification that seems to dominate the current zeitgeist. As the Welsh poet (and tramp) William Henry Davies (1871–1940) once put it:

**What is this life if, full of care,
We have no time to stand and stare.
No time to stand beneath the boughs
And stare as long as sheep or cows**.

There's plenty of scope for staring in Suffolk.

SAVOURING SUFFOLK

Suffolk is primarily an agricultural county and it prides itself on the foodstuffs it produces – directly or indirectly – from its fertile soil. As well as the obvious cereal, sugar beet and oilseed rape crops, there are plenty of fresh seasonal vegetables to be had from smallholdings throughout the county. Suffolk also has its fair share of orchards and a large number of varieties of apple, pear and plum, some of which are rare and hard to find or absent elsewhere in the country. A good example of this is the sweet black cherry variety found at Polstead (page 222). Apple varieties are prolific and a number of Apple Day celebrations are held at several locations throughout the county in October. Fruit can be purchased either directly from the orchard, such as at High House Fruit Farm at Sudbourne near Orford (page 72), or at one of the many farmers' markets held regularly in towns and villages throughout Suffolk.

There is plenty of grazing too and the county has a number of rare breed farms that stock specialties like Red Poll cattle. Many of the better pubs and restaurants have locally reared meat on the menu and it can also be bought for home consumption at butchers, delis and farmers' markets all over Suffolk. There's also game and venison aplenty available from large estates like Elveden (page 252). Good places for food shopping are the Suffolk Food Hall near Ipswich (page 152), which as well as meat products has an excellent selection of breads, cheese and fish, and Emmett's of Peasenhall (page 181), a deli and smokehouse that has a variety of smoked meat products that include sweet-cured Suffolk hams and bacon from free-range pigs.

While Lowestoft is not the fishing port it once was, the waters of the North Sea off the Suffolk coast continue to provide plenty of fish. The former ports of Southwold and Aldeburgh still have a small number of fishermen who make their living from the sea. To buy bright-eyed ultra-fresh fish direct from a fisherman's hut next to the water is a pleasure that outdoes supermarket shopping any day. To eat locally caught fish and chips next to the sea is an even greater delight: the Aldeburgh Fish & Chip Shop (page 63) is considered by many to be the best in the country... just be aware that its popularity always means that there's a queue.

SUFFOLK SUPPING

The county is well known for the beer it produces: Greene King from Bury St Edmunds (page 256) is pretty ubiquitous, and Adnams from Southwold (page 35) can be found more or less throughout the county (and even in Norfolk and beyond). Suffolk also boasts a number of smaller-scale breweries like those at St Peter's in the Waveney Valley (page 108), the Earl Soham Brewery in Debenham (page 192) and Old Cannon Brewery in Bury St Edmunds (page 257). Hardly surprising considering the number of orchards in the county, it is good to discover that cider – or rather, cyder – is not just a product from the West Country. One fairly large producer in the county is Aspall Hall near Debenham, which makes delicious apple juices too. Last but not least, there's also Suffolk-produced wine to be savoured. A number of quite select whites are produced from a handful of vineyards in the county, such as those at Wyken near Ixworth (page 264) and Giffords Hall near Hartest (page 271).

HOW THIS BOOK IS ARRANGED

This book divides Suffolk into six fairly distinct geographical areas starting with the Suffolk Heritage Coast and ending with the Brecks and the area around Bury St Edmunds in the west of the county. *Chapter 1* covers the Suffolk coast from Lowestoft down as far as

---

1 Suffolk's landscape features great stretches of cereal fields. **2** Stock up on fresh produce in Lavenham, page 204. **3** There's plenty of seafood to enjoy in Aldeburgh, page 57. **4** Adnams Brewery looks over Southwold, page 35. ▶

NIGEL WALLACE/S

LAVENHAM
BUTCHERS
Winners of
The East Anglian Award and
The Countryside Alliance Award 2011
Local
Lamb · Beef · Chicken
Blythburgh FREE RANGE **Pork**
Homemade

ALENAKRAVCHENKO/DT

THESUFFOLKCOAST.CO.UK

ADNAMS/ANTHONY CULLEN

the north bank of the River Orwell, and also includes the coastal hinterland between the sea and the A14. This includes much of the area of the Suffolk Coast and Heaths AONB (Area of Outstanding Beauty), the remainder of which is covered in *Chapter 3*. *Chapter 2* deals with the most northerly region of Suffolk – the stretch along the Waveney Valley between the coast and the river's source at Redgrave Fen. This chapter also occasionally veers across the river into Norfolk as the Waveney Valley sits astride both counties. *Chapter 3* focuses on the southern part of the Suffolk coast that includes the Felixstowe and Shotley peninsulas as well as the county town of Ipswich and its immediate surroundings. *Chapter 4* moves further inland to cover the eastern and central part of Suffolk that is centred upon the market towns of Halesworth, Framlingham and Stowmarket. *Chapter 5* deals with the Stour Valley and its hinterland – the southern part of the county that lies close to the Essex border. Finally, *Chapter 6* concludes with the west of the county – the Brecks of northwest Suffolk near Brandon, the region of 'high' west Suffolk that has Bury St Edmunds at its centre, and Newmarket in the far west, next to the border with Cambridgeshire.

MAPS

Each chapter begins with a map with **numbered stopping points** that correspond to numbered headings in the text. The featured walks have maps accompanying them.

Suffolk is a fairly large county and requires a total of seven 1:50,000 Landranger OS maps to cover it fully. Another useful map for the Waveney Valley is the double-sided 1:25,000 scale OS Explorer OL40 The Broads, which shows much interesting detail and has plenty of walker- and cyclist-friendly information.

FOOD & DRINK

I've listed some of my favourite pubs, cafés, tea rooms and places to eat at the relevant points in the book, favouring those places that serve local produce or are worth a visit for some other reason, such as appealing quirkiness or distinctive character. In a few cases I have listed an establishment simply because it is a convenient option in a place that offers few alternatives. In places where there are no food and drink facilities at all I have suggested options nearby.

ACCOMMODATION

Accommodation has been recommended on the basis of location and because it embraces a Slow approach in its 'green' ethos or its overall feel. Hotels and B&Bs are indicated by the symbol 🏠 after town and village headings, self-catering options by 🏡 and campsites by ⛺, with a cross-reference to the listing under *Accommodation*, page 276. For full descriptions of these listings, visit ⊘ bradtguides.com/suffolksleeps.

GETTING AROUND

Cycling and walking make the ideal methods of Slow travel. I'd like to encourage people to visit without a car wherever possible but I appreciate that this can be difficult in some parts of Suffolk, particularly if attempting to travel up and down the coast where progress is impeded by river estuaries that need to be circumnavigated (it is the same for cars too).

Details of how best to get around are given in detail at the beginning of each chapter. Below is a brief overview with suggestions of how to reach Suffolk from other parts of the country.

A useful website for **planning journeys by bus or train**, or a combination of the two, is ⊘ traveline.info.

TRAINS

You have several options for getting around by train within the county, with regular Greater Anglia rail services between Ipswich, Stowmarket and Norwich, Ipswich and Felixstowe, Ipswich and Lowestoft, and between Ipswich, Stowmarket, Bury St Edmunds and Newmarket. Ipswich is connected to London by frequent direct trains from Liverpool Street station and to the Midlands and North by means of a change at Ely or Peterborough. Lowestoft can also be reached by direct trains from Norwich. Greater Anglia has timetables online at ⊘ greateranglia.co.uk.

Greater Anglia offers a range of **Anglia Plus tickets** valid throughout Suffolk, Norfolk and parts of Cambridgeshire. These include One Day Rangers and 'Three Days in Seven' Flexi Rover tickets, both allowing travel for up to four accompanied children for a little extra payment. East Suffolk Line Day Ranger tickets allow one day's unlimited travel between Lowestoft, Ipswich and Felixstowe. Duo tickets are another option, which save 25% on weekend travel for two travelling together.

MARK STAPLES

CRISTINA GRANENA/DT

MARK STAPLES

MIKE KENNELLY/S

BUS & COACH

Ipswich has long-distance coach services with National Express that connect the county with London. Ipswich also has daily coach services to Stansted and Heathrow airports. Newmarket has fairly regular coach connections with London and Norwich. Several different bus companies provide routes within the county, most notably First Bus, Borderbus, Ipswich Buses, Galloway, Konectbus, Stephensons of Essex, Beestons and Simonds. Bus travel details for a locality are given at the beginning of each chapter. Suffolk County Council produces booklets of bus timetables that helpfully combine all the various routes in each area and come in useful for planning; they are widely available in shops, pubs and tourist centres and can be downloaded from ⊘ suffolkonboard.com.

CYCLING

Suffolk has plenty to offer cyclists, from quiet country lanes and disused railway lines to off-road routes that follow bridleways and forest tracks. Details of suggested routes and areas with good potential for cycling are outlined at the start of each chapter, as are local outlets for cycle hire. The website ⊘ cycle-route.com has many good suggestions for routes in the county, as does ⊘ discoversuffolk.org.uk. The website ⊘ suffolkonboard.com also has useful town cycle maps. For off-road cycling probably the best part of the county to head for is Breckland where a large number of routes criss-cross Thetford Forest.

WALKING

Suffolk abounds with walking potential, from windswept coastal strolls to circular walks through forest and open farmland. As well as walking suggestions made at the beginning of each chapter, a number of personal favourites are offered throughout the book together with a sketch map and directions for the walk. Walking in Suffolk is rarely very demanding thanks to the reasonably flat topography. The going is mostly easy and so walkers just need to decide how far they are prepared to walk if attempting a route. Any obstacles, such as they are, are limited to nuisances like overgrown nettles, hungry mosquitoes, obstructing

◀ **1** St Peter's Church in Freston, page 154. **2** Canoeing near Nayland, page 223.
3 A murmuration of starlings at RSPB Minsmere, page 46. **4** Snake's head fritillaries growing near Framsden, page 189.

herds of cows or the occasional cropped field that bears no trace of the footpath marked on the OS map. Otherwise, it's ideal, especially when a walk takes in a country pub and/or an interesting village church to explore en route.

Several notable **long-distance paths** run through the county. Longest of all is the **Suffolk Way**, a 113-mile route that begins at Flatford and crosses central Suffolk to finish at Lowestoft. The best known though is probably the **Suffolk Coast Path** between Lowestoft and Landguard Fort at Felixstowe. This route connects with the **Stour and Orwell Walk** to continue around the Orwell and Stour estuaries to reach Cattawade near Manningtree. This, in turn, is the starting point of the **Stour Valley Path** that threads through the Constable Country of the Stour Valley to end at Newmarket. Another long-distance route in the coastal region that follows a route a little way inland from the coast itself is the **Sandlings Walk** between Ipswich and Southwold. Away from the coast, the **Mid Suffolk Footpath** runs for 20 miles between Hoxne and Stowmarket. In west Suffolk, the **St Edmunds Way** connects Bury St Edmunds with Manningtree in Essex via the Stour Valley. In the Waveney Valley of north Suffolk, the **Angles Way** that runs between Great Yarmouth and Thetford uses paths on both sides of the River Waveney and the Norfolk–Suffolk border. Shorter trails include the 14-mile Brecks Trail, the 19-mile Bury to Clare Walk through west Suffolk, the ten-mile Fynn Valley Path between Woodbridge and Westerfield, the 13-mile Lark Valley Path between Bury St Edmunds and Mildenhall, and the six-mile Sailors' Path along the coast from Snape to Aldeburgh.

The Discover Suffolk website (⊘ discoversuffolk.org.uk) has details of a number of walking routes in the county, both the long-distance routes listed above and shorter, 'easy going trails'.

JOIN

THE TRAVEL CLUB

THE MEMBERSHIP CLUB FOR SERIOUS TRAVELLERS
FROM BRADT GUIDES

Be inspired
Free books and exclusive
insider travel tips
and inspiration

Save money
Special offers and
discounts from our
favourite travel brands

Plan the trip
of a lifetime
Access our exclusive concierge
service and have a bespoke
itinerary created for you
by a Bradt author

Join here:
bradtguides.com/travelclub

Membership levels to suit all budgets

Bradt GUIDES
TRAVEL TAKEN SERIOUSLY

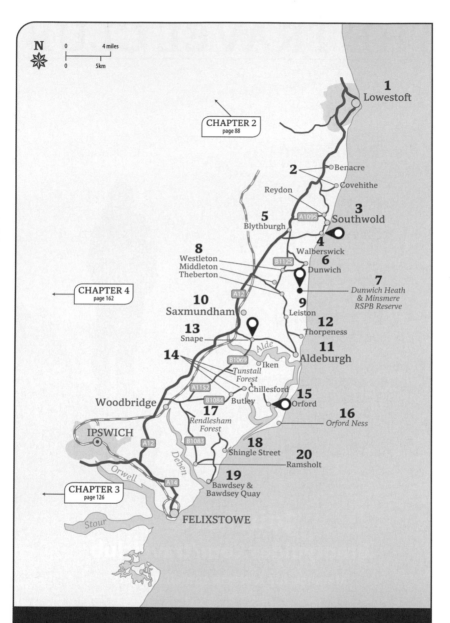

CHAPTER 2
page 88

CHAPTER 4
page 162

CHAPTER 3
page 126

N

0   4 miles

0   5km

1 Lowestoft

2 Benacre

Covehithe

Reydon

3 Southwold

5 Blythburgh

A1095

4

Walberswick

8 Westleton

Middleton

Theberton

B1125

6 Dunwich

7 Dunwich Heath & Minsmere RSPB Reserve

A12

10 Saxmundham

9 Leiston

12 Thorpeness

13 Snape

Alde

11 Aldeburgh

14

B1069

Iken

Tunstall Forest

A1152

Chillesford

B1084

Butley

15 Orford

16 Orford Ness

Woodbridge

17

Rendlesham Forest

B1083

18 Shingle Street

20 Ramsholt

19 Bawdsey & Bawdsey Quay

IPSWICH

A12

Deben

Orwell

A14

Stour

FELIXSTOWE

THE SUFFOLK HERITAGE COAST

1

THE SUFFOLK HERITAGE COAST

Swoul, and Dunwich, and Walderswick
All go in at one lousie creek.
Suffolk coastal rhyme

It may be tempting to think that the workaday town of Lowestoft typifies this coastline. This couldn't be further from the truth, as the port is an exception and, from Kessingland all the way down to Bawdsey, the Suffolk coast is mostly rural and peaceful, with a couple of old-fashioned resorts interspersed by tiny villages up against the shingle. It is not an undiscovered coastline – far from it – but somehow Suffolk's unhurried, gentle pace of life has managed to persist without too much intrusion from the 21st century. Some things have changed quite dramatically over the past half century, of course, particularly the economy of the region and the incomers who have come to live here, but overall its character has survived without it ever becoming too much of a museum piece.

This coast has always attracted outsiders. The Scottish Art Nouveau architect and designer Charles Rennie Mackintosh came here to paint flowers when his architectural career was in the dumps. Benjamin Britten, having taken leave of his home town of Lowestoft, made his home at Aldeburgh and wrote an opera about a fisherman, *Peter Grimes*. Southwold and Walberswick have always been popular with BBC television producers, authors and politicians, and you might even catch a glimpse of a vacationing rock star or Hollywood royalty at Aldeburgh's better hotels and restaurants. There is no doubt about it: the Suffolk coast exudes a certain type of understated glamour – classy and comfortable, like a pair of old but expensive shoes.

Between Lowestoft and Felixstowe, various inlets and estuaries punctuate the coastline. The rivers Blyth, Dunwich, Minsmere, Alde, Ore, Deben, Orwell and Stour all flow into the North Sea along this stretch, and the larger of these once brought trade and prosperity to the wool villages of the Suffolk hinterland. These rivers were once far more important than they are today, and far more navigable too. Look at the River Ore that flows through Framlingham – a mere brook these days – and shake your head in disbelief that stone for building the town's castle was once shipped here all the way from the coast.

As well as the coast itself, this chapter also covers the immediate hinterland, roughly east of the A12 Lowestoft to Ipswich road. A good chunk of that terrain constitutes what's known as **The Sandlings**, which has light sandy soil akin to that of the Brecks in the west of the region. The Sandlings has a similar history to the Brecks too: early settlement by Neolithic peoples thanks to easily workable soil; medieval overgrazing by sheep; widespread gamekeeping and forestry in the first part of the 20th century; arable crops in the second half. Today, it is an area characterised by sandy heaths, forestry plantations and wide fields of grain.

The urban centre, **Lowestoft**, by far the biggest place along this stretch of coast, gets a mention but is hardly representative of the rest. However, if you are at all interested in Southwold sailors, bedevilled Blythburgh or disappearing Dunwich, or are curious to experience the sensation of 'orfordness', then read on. I start by working down the coast north to south, detouring inland as seems appropriate. Away from the comfortable respectability of resorts like **Southwold** and **Aldeburgh** are some real oddities. **Dunwich**, now little more than a pub, café and car park, was one of England's great ports back in the 12th century. **Orford Ness** was a top-secret military research site that was firmly off-limits until the National Trust bought it in 1993, while **Snape Maltings**, now an extensive arts and music complex, was a working maltings until not so very long ago.

GETTING AROUND

There is no coast road as such. Away from the busy A12, plenty of minor roads veer off towards the sea, although travelling between places along the coast itself, say between Aldeburgh and Orford for example, often involves circuitous journeys to get round estuaries. Southwold to Walberswick, which is really just a pleasant stroll on foot using the footbridge across the River Blyth, is a case in point and driving involves a long detour around the estuary to Blythburgh. Really, it's best to park up somewhere convenient and get your hiking boots on.

PUBLIC TRANSPORT

This is so-so: quite good in the north but progressively worse as you head south along the coast. Lowestoft is well connected to Norwich by a regular **train service** and frequent buses – the X2 and X22 operated by First in Suffolk & Norfolk runs every 20 minutes or so, as does the X1 that runs between Peterborough and Lowestoft via King's Lynn, Norwich and Great Yarmouth. The East Suffolk Line railway, run by Greater Anglia, connects Lowestoft with Ipswich at roughly two-hour intervals stopping at Halesworth, Darsham, Saxmundham, Wickham Market and Woodbridge along the way. You need the local **bus service** to reach the coast itself. The First Eastern Counties 99 service connects Southwold with Lowestoft, while Borderbus service 146 connects Southwold with Beccles and Norwich. The Borderbus 524 service connects Southwold with Bungay, Beccles and Halesworth, and the Borderbus 521/522 service connects Haleswoth with Saxmundham and Aldeburgh. First Eastern Counties services 63/64/65 connect Aldeburgh with Snape, Woodbridge and Ipswich. With a bit of judicious timetable juggling you should be able to travel around the coast as long as you avoid Sundays. First Eastern Counties service 71 runs throught the day between Woodbridge and Sutton Hoo but only one (inconveniently timed) of the buses connects Woodbridge and Orford. Coastal Accessible Transport (✐ 01728 635 938 ⌀ cats-paws. co.uk ☉ 08.30–16.00 Mon–Fri) provides a demand-responsive local service between villages that have no regular bus service. These operate east of the A14 from Walberswick to Orford and in the triangle from Woodbridge down to Orford and Bawdsey, and must be booked in advance either online or by phone.

CYCLING

Cycling is generally enjoyable away from the A12. Although the narrow roads to the coast can get pretty busy in the summer months, most of the traffic is tourist vehicles that are not in any great hurry and are generally respectful to those on bikes. There are some excellent bridleways to explore too. The OS Landranger 156 map covers the area.

If you are arriving by train, bicycles may be picked up at Darsham station by arrangement with Byways Bicycles ($\mathcal{D}$ 01728 668764). Suffolk Cycle Hire ($\mathcal{D}$ 07851 402587 $\mathcal{O}$ suffolkcyclehire.co.uk) will deliver and collect bikes to and from anywhere within a ten-mile area from Yoxford. You can also transport your own bike using the Greater Anglia rail services although, as there is usually only provision for four bikes per train and it's on a first-come first-served basis, there is a slight risk you won't be able to take it aboard. Darsham is perhaps the best station to use as a base, as it has both Dunwich and Minsmere within easy pedalling distance. Saxmundham station is reasonably convenient for Snape, Aldeburgh and Thorpeness. Bear in mind that at as a cyclist you can also make use of some of the passenger ferry services outlined on page 25, which could save some quite considerable detours. For those without their own bike, there is also the convenient Eastbridge Cycle Hire Company ($\mathcal{D}$ 01728 830154) based at the Eel's Foot Inn in Eastbridge near Minsmere.

WALKING

This is very special country for walkers. As well as beach walks and quiet country lanes, the coastal region is criss-crossed by footpaths. Some of the most enjoyable hikes are along estuaries, such as that of the rivers Blyth and Alde, and you'll find plenty of scope for forest walks too, especially to the south in the extensive Tunstall and Rendlesham plantations. Those areas notated on the map as 'walks', such as The Walks near Leiston or Westleton Walks near Dunwich, refer to the old sheep 'walks' that ranged on the coastal hinterland but you can still walk there, even without a white woolly coat. There's a good and varied selection of

---

i **TOURIST INFORMATION**

Self-service visitor information points with leaflets and guides can be found at the following locations:

Aldeburgh 161 High St
Lowestoft Lowestoft library, Clapham Road South
Southwold Southwold Library, North Green
Suffolk Coast & Heaths AONB $\mathcal{O}$ suffolkcoastandheaths.org
Suffolk Coastal $\mathcal{O}$ eastsuffolk.gov.uk
The Suffolk Coast $\mathcal{O}$ thesuffolkcoast.co.uk

FOOT FERRIES ON THE SUFFOLK COAST

Three foot ferries operate along the Suffolk coast, all are seasonal and operate between Easter and October; all can take bicycles. A small charge is made for people and bicycles, dogs travel free.

Bawdsey Ferry ✆ 01394 282173 (boatyard), 07709 411511 (ferry operator). Crossing the River Deben between Bawdsey Quay and Felixstowe Ferry, the Bawdsey Ferry operates daily from May to the end of September 10.00–17.00 and also at weekends 10.00–17.00 during April and October.

Butley Ferry ✆ 07913 672499. Running between the Capel and Gedgrave banks of the River Butley, this claims to be the smallest licensed ferry in Europe. Run by volunteers, this operates between Easter Saturday and mid October 11.00–16.00 on weekends and bank holidays.

Walberswick Ferry ⌂ walberswickferry.com. This family-run ferry, one of the UK's last remaining rowed ferries, between Southwold and Walberswick at the mouth of the River Blyth, operates weekends only in late March, then daily 10.00–17.00 between 1 April and 29 October.

downloadable walks at ⌂ suffolkonboard.com/train/east-suffolk-line-walks that begin and end at the stations along the East Suffolk Line.

As a walker (or a cyclist) rather than a driver, you have a distinct advantage in the Suffolk coast region in being able to make use of the **passenger ferries** across some rivers that flow to the coast. There is a rowing-boat ferry across the Blyth between Southwold and Walberswick (although walking via the pontoon bridge is not so much of a detour), another across the Butley River west of Orford and a third one across the River Deben between Bawdsey Ferry and Felixstowe Ferry.

Two long-distance walks pass through the Suffolk Coastal region. The **Suffolk Coast Path**, sometimes referred to as the Suffolk Coast and Heaths Path, is a 100-mile route between Lowestoft and Landguard Point at Felixstowe. Much of this walk follows the coast itself, with some long optional stretches of beach walking. The **Sandlings Walk** is a meandering 60-mile route between Southwold and Ipswich that, as its name implies, traverses the dry heathland of the Sandlings region just inland from the coast. Both of these routes connect with a third one, the **Stour and Orwell Walk** that follows the edge of the Stour and Orwell estuaries that are covered in *Chapter 5*.

THE SUNRISE COAST: LOWESTOFT TO COVEHITHE

The Suffolk coast begins in the north at **Corton**, more or less a suburb of Lowestoft, which distinguishes itself by having a naturist beach. Lowestoft sprawls north and south of Britain's most easterly point, Lowestoft Ness, and extends as far as Pakefield, a village that is effectively a southern suburb of the town. The Suffolk Coast Area of Outstanding Natural Beauty (AONB) begins shortly beyond here at Kessingland, a small holiday resort. Further south along this stretch of coast lies Benacre Broad, a national nature reserve, and the tiny hamlet of Covehithe, which has a church built within the walls of an older demolished one. All of the north Suffolk coast is particularly vulnerable to severe sea erosion.

1 LOWESTOFT

Lowestoft has probably seen better days, although it still possesses a fine sandy beach. In his book *The Rings of Saturn* W G Sebald describes being 'disheartened' by the town's deserted streets but, there again, he was always a writer whose glass was considerably less than half full. Like Great Yarmouth, just across the county boundary to the north, Lowestoft has seen service as both a fishing port and a resort and, rather like Cromer and Sheringham in Norfolk, the two towns have always been great rivals. Lowestoft's fleet of trawlers was decommissioned in 2002 and, like Yarmouth, the town saw tourist numbers dwindle during the last quarter of the 20th century. William A Dutt, in his *Highways and Byways in East Anglia* published in 1900, writes of 'Clapham and Brixton primly disporting themselves on the south beach or placidly promenading the pier' back in the days when Brixton was a solidly middle-class part of London.

Much has changed, and these days 'Loos-toff', as East Anglians tend to call it, is redolent of faded memories. If you are curious, you might want to check out **Lowestoft Ness**, close to the Birds Eye fish-finger factory, which is the most easterly point in the British Isles. Gaze out to sea here and you can satisfy yourself in knowing that, temporarily at least, you

---

1 The shingle beach at Kessingland. **2** Covehithe's church within a church. **3** Lowestoft's First Light Festival. **4** The Walberswick rowed ferry. ▶

SUXXESPHOTO/S

LAURENCE MITCHELL

CHEDKO/S

I WEI HUANG/DT

are the most easterly person in the United Kingdom. The giant compass-like piece of artwork known as the *Euroscope* that marks the spot will inform you of the bearings and distances to various points in the British Isles and Europe. Both of Britain's southern and northern extremities are evocatively distant: The Lizard, the British mainland's most southerly point, lies 352 miles away, while Dunnet Head, the most northerly, even further, some 465 miles distant. It might seem a shame that, given its longitudinal importance, the Ness occupies such an unprepossessing setting. Bear in mind, though, that both The Lizard and John O'Groats (which has unashamedly usurped the 'most northerly' claim for many years now) are little more than windswept headlands with overpriced car parks, so the lack of romance at such places is nothing unusual. For

"In recent years, Lowestoft has done its utmost to exploit its location as the most easterly town in the UK."

a taste of the town's maritime history you might want to visit the **Scores**, a series of steep narrow lanes – 11 in total – created by people passing between the High Street and the former beach village by way of the soft cliffs. The word probably comes from a corruption of 'scour'. A leaflet describing a 1.5 mile-long Scores Trail is available from the tourist information centre.

Lowestoft has several 'most easterlies' it can boast of. There's **Christ Church**, Britain's most easterly church; a modest Victorian building that served a poor fisherman's parish, which suffered Zeppelin raids in World War I, aerial bombing in World War II and devastating floods in 1953 – there is a sign to this effect outside. On a less spiritual note, the town also has the Green Jack Brewery, the nation's most easterly brewery, which produces some splendidly hoppy and appositely named ales, like Trawlerboys Best Bitter and Rising Sun Pale Ale. Close to the bus station stands the Catholic church of **Our Lady of The Star**, the most easterly Catholic church in the United Kingdom, decorated in tasteful Arts and Crafts style and probably the grandest Catholic church in all Suffolk, in which the Virgin Mary is represented as a guiding star for seafarers. Seafaring was always the mainstay here and, although burly fishermen in oilskins are a rare sight these days, there is a reminder of former times on the swing bridge over the harbour, where a monument of a trawlerman in full seafaring attire gazes wistfully out to sea.

If you wish to get a taste for what life aboard a fishing trawler was like you could always visit the *Mincarlo* (lydiaevamincarlo.com ⊙ 10.00–

15.30 Mon–Thu & Sat) at Heritage Quay in Lowestoft harbour. The last vessel of its kind to be made in the town, it now serves as a boat museum owned by the same charitable trust that owns the *Lydia Eva* just up the road in Great Yarmouth.

In recent years, Lowestoft has done its utmost to exploit its location as the most easterly town in the UK. The **First Light Festival** (⌗ firstlightlowestoft.com) was initiated in 2019 in an effort to help regenerate the town and after a brief hiatus during the Covid years has now become an annual event. Taking place on the beach and at various locations around town, First Light celebrates the midsummer solstice (and Lowestoft's unique location as the first place in the UK to greet the longest day) with an array of music, dance, comedy and literature events that take place during the weekend that falls closest to midsummer. Entry is free, although some of the sundown events are ticketed. Wild beach camping is available for those who wish stay overnight.

ᵗ⃦ FOOD & DRINK

Triangle Tavern 29 St Peters St ⌀ 01502 582711 ⌗ green-jack.com. Probably the best pub in Lowestoft and undoubtedly the best place to sample the range of Green Jack ales. No food, live music on Friday nights.

2 BENACRE & COVEHITHE

Head a little way south of the town along the 'Sunrise Coast' (a recent marketing ploy) and you reach **Kessingland** with its holiday village and Africa-themed Suffolk Wildlife Park. Just south of Kessingland is where the Suffolk Coast & Heaths Area of Outstanding Natural Beauty (AONB) begins – a broad swathe of deservedly acclaimed coastal landscape that, with the exception of the urban enclaves of Felixstowe and Ipswich, stretches all the way to the Essex border at Manningtree. The shingle beach at Kessingland is an excellent place to admire attractive salt-tolerant plant species like sea holly, sea pea and yellow-horned poppy. At low- or mid-tide it is possible to beach walk all the way to Southwold, about seven miles in total. Although Kessingland and Southwold can be busy in summer, much of the territory that lies between them is often surprisingly deserted and you may well have the beach to yourself.

A little way beyond Kessingland you reach **Benacre**, which until recently was home to an isolated freshwater broad of the same name, a national nature reserve managed by Natural England. In recent years regular incursions of seawater have breached the shingle bank that separated the broad from the sea and as a result its ecosystem has changed dramatically. Dead trees killed by salt spray and saltwater inundation litter the beach here – highly photogenic but in an apocalyptic sort of way. It is only a matter of time before the last vestiges of Benacre Broad are engulfed and reclaimed by the sea.

South of Benacare, you soon encounter further evidence of a rapidly disappearing coast. **Covehithe** was a small town in the medieval period but has been whittled down by North Sea erosion to a mere village these days, with the oddity of the partly dismantled church of St Andrew having a later, smaller church built within it. The road that leads past the church to what would have once been more of the village ends abruptly at a cliff, its tarmac surface severed and recycled by the North Sea. The coastline has retreated over a quarter of a mile here in the past two centuries and offers a taste of what is to come at Dunwich, beyond Southwold, a far more dramatically reduced place.

SOUTHWOLD, DUNWICH & AROUND

3 SOUTHWOLD

🏠 **The Swan** (page 276) ⛺ **Harbour Camping & Caravan Park** (page 276)

It's hard to imagine anyone not being seduced by Southwold: that this most bewitching of seaside towns manages to exude such easy charm without much trace of smugness is to its great credit. George Orwell (real name Eric Blair), who lived in the town with his family in the 1930s (you can see his plaque at Montague House on High Street), may have been critical of Southwold's comforting gentility, but for most this is actually its draw. Southwold seems still to belong to the 1930s (in the nicest sense) in many ways.

A lighthouse stands right in the middle of town, and there's a pier, lines of colourful beach huts and a brewery where, until 2006, casks were delivered locally by horse and cart. Despite all this, the town has more than enough grit to keep it real, and deeper layers exist here beneath the shiny veneer of cream teas, overpriced real estate, gleaming 4x4s and metropolitan accents. There are retired folk licking ice-cream cornets, kids making sandcastles on the beach, wet fish for sale at fishermen's huts along the Blyth River, and even a reading room for sailors.

The town's genteel feel is partly serendipitous thanks to a devastating fire that tore many of its buildings down in 1659. This created a handful of open areas that were left as fire breaks and never rebuilt upon, and it is these **greens** that contribute towards the town's wholesome air of uncluttered space. The best known of these is above the beach at Gun Hill, where cannon commemorate the Battle of Sole Bay fought just offshore from here, a rare contretemps in which the English and French fleets combined forces to fight the Dutch.

The town's ultimate landmark is its **lighthouse**, built in 1887 to replace three lighthouses threatened by coastal erosion. Tours are possible at certain times of year or you could simply contemplate its white pepper-pot form from one of the outside tables at the Sole Bay Inn just across the road. The lighthouse was automated in 1938 but, before this, the keeper must have had the least lonely posting in the land, with the option of enjoying a pint in one of the town's hostelries whenever the fancy took him. The lighthouse's close neighbour, the **Adnams Sole Bay Brewery** was built in the same year (1890) that the lighthouse first went into operation. This replaced an earlier brewery on the same site, so the legend 'established 1660' that you see on bottles of Adnams ales is not mere hyperbole. The town is peppered with splendid Adnams houses all serving up delicious, well-hopped beer, a phenomenon that in this instance at least gives the word 'monopoly' a newfound respectability. The Sole Bay Inn is perhaps the best known but the Lord Nelson, Harbour Inn and others are equally good places to sup a pint. Sometimes I do wonder why a pint of Adnams bitter costs quite a bit more here at a pub right next to the brewery than it does at my local in Norwich 35 miles away. But this is Southwold and it would be simply vulgar to ask. Besides, the sea view and the briny air come absolutely free of charge.

"The town is peppered with splendid Adnams houses all serving up delicious, well-hopped beer."

Southwold Pier (⏁ southwoldpier.co.uk) reopened for business in 2001 but the original structure dates from 1900 and stood until 1934 when a gale virtually destroyed it. The pier – promoted as '623 feet of fun for everyone' – is proudly claimed to be the first to be built in Britain for over 45 years, which in itself is quite something. Take a stroll

ADNAMS/ANTHONY CULLEN

ADNAMS/ANTHONY CULLEN

I WEI HUANG/S

ELLEI/S

along it and you will find that it is not quite as run-of-the-mill as you might first have imagined. Thanks to the wacky and inventive mind of engineer Tim Hunkin, the pier's machine arcade has a wealth of bizarre but charming Heath Robinson-like slot machines that put a smile on even the most serious of faces. Here at the **Under the Pier Show** you can enjoy playing 'Whack a Banker', help old ladies cross the road (usually unsuccessfully) in the face of murderous traffic in 'Help the Old Lady' and even get to decide the fate of a lovable lamb in a game of 'Pet or Meat'. The arcade is worth half an hour and a couple of pounds' worth of change of anyone's money. You might also wish to be present for the rather rude, half-hourly chiming of Hunkin's water clock, although it rarely seems to go off exactly when it should. As well as the arcade, you'll find a couple of gift shops and cafés. And if it is not too windy there are also some rather stylish benches to sit on and ponder the giant white golf ball of Sizewell B nuclear power station clearly visible along the coast to the south.

Southwold's **North Beach** lies beneath the pier with its wooden groynes jutting out to sea. There's sunbathing in deckchairs and sandcastle making aplenty on the sand, while many more visitors are content to stroll the promenade above the beach huts. The town's beaches continue south of the town too – along **The Denes** by the inlet of the River Blyth. Heading inland along the river's northern bank, you'll find a **rowing-boat ferry** across the river that has been operated by the same family since the 1920s and a handful of wooden huts selling very fresh fish at relatively low prices. This part of town, sometimes referred to as **Blackshore**, is my favourite corner of Southwold, atypical though it might be. There's always plenty of activity along here – visitors strolling with children and dogs in tow, sailors pottering with their boats, fishermen unloading their catch. It's picturesquely nautical without a hint of gentrification – a bit more barnacle-rough than the rarefied gentility of the town centre. There's a campsite here too just before the river inlet, and a pub and a café a little further inland before you reach a footbridge across the river to the Walberswick bank.

The **Sailors' Reading Room** above the seaside promenade is a modest building that has photographs, newspaper cuttings and all manner of

---

◀ SOUTHWOLD: **1** The lighthouse stands in the middle of town. **2** An Adnams Brewery tour. **3** Lunch on the pier. **4** The town's iconic beach huts.

maritime memorabilia. Effectively, it serves as an informal museum and, sailor or not, you are free to enter, although photography is not allowed inside the building, presumably because it would interfere with the sailors' reading. The last time I visited, little reading was taking place and the sailors within were, instead, playing a spirited game of pool in the back room. A more formal museum is the **Southwold Museum and Historical Society** (✆ 01502 725600 🖉 southwoldmuseum.org) in a Dutch-gabled cottage on Victoria Street. This covers the whole span of history of the town with a range of interactive displays. The museum, which has equal-access facilities and won the award of Suffolk Museum of the Year in 2016, also organises Tuesday evening lectures throughout August at the Methodist hall on East Green.

Almost as well known as the lighthouse are the town's three hundred or so colourful **beach huts**. Those by the pier below Gun Hill are the most sought after. Other places along the East Anglia coast have similar huts, but none have quite the cachet that goes with owning one on Southwold beach. In truth, the huts are little more than well-appointed garden sheds but this has not prevented them from becoming highly prized *pieds-à-terre* in this neck of the woods. For about the same price as an East Midlands terraced house, you get a single wooden room next to a busy thoroughfare where local bylaws permit you to make tea, snooze in a chair and watch the sea. You are not permitted to sleep overnight in them, however. What can you expect for an asking price that might start around £80,000? Well, not running water and an electricity supply, obviously. Such matters do not deter those with deep pockets and a taste for salt-air real estate. In 2022, one Southwold beach hut, appropriately called 'Here's Hoping', went on the market for around £250,000, about the same price as two two-bedroomed terraced houses in Lowestoft.

> "Almost as well known as the lighthouse are the town's three hundred or so colourful beach huts."

Away from the seafront, the town's high street heads inland past cafés, galleries and old-fashioned shops to **St Edmund's Church**, a towering 15th-century building constructed of imported Caen stone with knapped-flint dressing. Look up as you enter and you will see the forlorn-looking figure of a tied-up Edmund above the door. The church's interior is quite beautiful, with an exquisite angel-bedecked roof and intricate steeple-like font cover that is 24ft high. Look out too for the intricately carved dividers between the misericord seats, where there are all manner of intriguing and bizarre medieval figures including a preaching monkey and a man playing a panpipe. There's also a figure called 'Southwold Jack', a soldier from the War of the Roses, who carries a sword and has an axe that rings a bell when the service is about to commence (there's another Southwold Jack figure on the wall of the

BEER FROM THE COAST: THE ADNAMS STORY

Adnams claim that beer was brewed on the same Southwold site back in the 14th century but the family themselves did not get involved until 1872 when George and Ernest Adnams bought the Sole Bay Brewery with help from their father. George wasn't cut out for the brewery business and soon upped sticks to Africa, where he met an unfortunate fate with a crocodile, but Ernest persisted with the enterprise to establish Adnams & Co Ltd in 1890.

Jack and Pierse Loftus bought themselves a stake in the business in 1902 and the company progressed modestly though the 20th century until 1970 when there was a substantial modernisation of the brewery. The same year also saw, perhaps a little counter-intuitively, the reintroduction of dray horses for deliveries around town. The brewery's 'Beer from the Coast' marketing campaign was launched in 2002, together with a charming set of posters, postcards and coasters which featured many Southwold icons – beach huts, the lighthouse and pebble beaches – all with cleverly disguised Adnams motifs hidden in the scene.

Adnams has strong ties with its Southwold home, most notably through its charitable trust that was set up to provide assistance to organisations within a 25-mile radius

of the town. Adnams was awarded the Queen's Award for Enterprise: Sustainable Development in 2005 and in the following year constructed a new, ultra eco-friendly distribution centre. It was in this same year that the last of the brewery's dray horses were retired, as the road between the brewery and the new distribution centre was too busy and too far for the horses to travel. This was a sad day for Southwold, as the drays had become a familiar sight around town and had played a part in perpetuating the resort's old-fashioned image.

Ever keen to forge ahead on its sustainability route, Adnams went on to reduce the weight of its 500-millilitre bottle by almost half and set about constructing a new, energy-efficient brew house. This opened in 2007 to produce East Green, a new brew that would become the UK's first 'carbon neutral' beer, a feat achieved by using local high-yielding barley, aphid-resistant hops and lightweight beer bottles, and by offsetting the tiny amount of CO_2 left over. It really amounts to something when you can claim that by supping beer you're doing your bit for the environment. The bonus is, East Green tastes good too. It's light, golden, hoppy and bitter – all the familiar characteristics of a traditional Adnams ale.

Adnams Brewery and another in Blythburgh's Holy Trinity Church). The east window, which is by Sir Ninian Comper, has scenes from St Edmund's martyrdom and is a 1954 replacement of an earlier window blown out by a German bomb landing just across the road in 1943.

A little way inland from Southwold is the larger but far more workaday village of **Reydon**, a pleasant enough but unspectacular place where house prices are no doubt considerably cheaper than those of its coastal neighbour. There is an interesting group of almshouses here, dated 1908, that have crow-step gables and an elegant gateway that bears the inscription 'The Rest for the Aged', which pretty much tells it as it is.

Not far from Reydon, at Old Hall Farm on the Halesworth Road, is the **Southwold Maize Maze** (𝒮 01502 723091 𝒮 oldhallsouthwold.co.uk), which provides all sorts of summer fun for families with two maize mazes, a pedal go-kart track and a large play park with giant sandpits. There is also a café and walking trails that lead down to the River Blyth and on to Southwold.

FOOD & DRINK

For food in Southwold, you are fairly spoilt for choice with so many tea rooms and pubs, but there are plenty of places to buy quality do-it-yourself ingredients too. The High Street has the **Black Olive Delicatessen** at 80a/80b (𝒮 01502 722312), which has locally smoked fish and delicious pies, while the **Sole Bay Fish Company** (Shed 22e, Blackshore 𝒮 01502 724241 𝒮 solebayfishco.co.uk) has its own boats with fish for sale at its shed in the harbour and at Southwold's **Monday market**. As well as a fresh fish and deli counter, the shed also has a smokehouse and a restaurant (⊙ lunch only noon–15.00) that gets busy at weekends so booking ahead is a good idea. Blackshore is also home to **Mrs T's Fish and Chips** (𝒮 01502 724709), another local favourite. There is a sister branch of the Sole Bay Fish Company, **The Little Fish & Chip Shop** (𝒮 01502 218120) at 2 East Street in the town, which serves excellent takeaway fish and chips. The greengrocers' shops at the Market Place also have a good range of local seasonal produce.

If it's afternoon tea you're after, Southwold has more tea rooms and cafés than you can shake a buttered scone at. If you're looking for something more substantial and/or a beer then simply choose from any one of a number of Adnams houses in the town. Two other very well-liked pubs in addition to those below are the **Harbour Inn**, right by the boats on Blackshore, and the friendly **Lord Nelson**, centrally placed in East Street.

Buckenham Coffee House 81a High St, Southwold 𝒮 01502 723273. In a basement beneath an art gallery, this place does good coffee cakes, soups and light lunches.

Coasters 12 Queen St, Southwold ✆ 01502 724734 ⌨ coastersofsouthwold.co.uk. A quirky restaurant with beach-hut dining booths that serves meals sourced mostly from locally produced ingredients – meat from Clevely's Moat and Huntsham farms, and locally caught fish. Traditional roasts on Sundays.

The Crown 90 High St, Southwold ✆ 01502 7222275 ⌨ thecrownsouthwold.co.uk. Of all the splendid Adnams establishments in the town, this hotel bar-restaurant is the most sought after and pre-booking is a very good idea, if not essential. The elegantly beamed interior oozes metropolitan sophistication, while the wood-panelled snug to the rear might appeal more to alehouse traditionalists. There's a good range of gutsy world-travelled dishes on offer and an excellent wine list in addition to Adnams ales.

Harbour Inn Blackshore, Southwold ✆ 01502 722381 ⌨ harbourinnsouthwold.co.uk. At the side of the River Blyth, close to Bailey Bridge across to Walberswick, this has excellent credentials as a seafarers' pub and serves up a range of mains dishes that feature mostly locally caught fish, although there are a few meat and vegetarian options too. There is the full range of Adnams ales and a good wine list too. The outside wall has a plaque showing the water level of the 1953 flood and, inside, the bars are full of old photos and seafaring memorabilia.

Randolph Hotel 41 Wangford Rd, Reydon IP18 6PZ ✆ 01502 723603 ⌨ therandolph. co.uk. In a neighbouring village, just inland from Southwold, this late Victorian pub-hotel has a summer garden and modern good looks. There's Adnams beer, and local fish and game.

Sole Bay Inn 7 East Green, Southwold ✆ 01502 723736 ⌨ solebayinn.co.uk. With the lighthouse rising behind it like a minaret, this is another Adnams favourite and about as close as you can get to the brewery. Do they have a direct beer pipe? Good, solid unpretentious food and predictably excellent draught beer.

4 WALBERSWICK

🏠 **The Balancing Barn** (page 276)

Just across the water from Southwold, Walberswick is a former fishing village where the pace of life can make its neighbour seem almost frenetic in comparison. Long adopted by artists, Walberswick has slowly morphed over the years from bohemian to shabby chic. There's still a modicum of fishing taking place but most of the boats sloped in the estuary mud are of the hobby variety these days and, like Southwold, more than half of the properties in the village are holiday homes. Historically, Walberswick took over where Dunwich left off as a trading port. When Dunwich harbour became irretrievably silted in the late 13th century, Walberswick exploited its position at the mouth of the River Blyth to become its replacement.

A stroll from Walberswick

❋ OS Landranger 156 or Explorer map 231; start: the car park at the Flats, ♀ TM501746; 5 miles; moderate

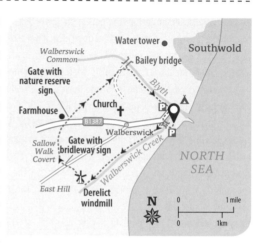

A fine circular walk can be made by following the west bank of the creek past the campsite as far as the derelict windmill, then heading away from the sea towards the trees at East Hill and following the path along the edge of the wood to reach a minor road.

Turn left along the road for a short distance then turn right through a gate with a bridleway sign to head diagonally across a meadow towards a wood – Sallow Walk Covert. Follow the edge of the wood and continue along the bridleway, which follows the route of the Sandlings Walk, beyond the end of the wood. Walberswick church will now be visible ahead to the right, as will the buildings of Southwold beyond.

Approaching the B1387 that lies a little way ahead, take the waymarked footpath to the right across a field towards a farmhouse. Turn right at the road and then left immediately after the farmhouse through a gate that has a **Walberswick National Nature Reserve** sign. Follow the track straight ahead across the common in the direction of Southwold's water tower. Ignore the path on the right that leads to church and continue across the common to reach a tarmac track alongside a large reedbed. To the left, on the other side of the river, is a capped windmill.

Continue to reach the Bailey Bridge that crosses the **River Blyth**. Turn right to return to the village along the river's southern bank. If you are feeling particularly energetic, you could then cross over to Southwold by way of the ferry or the Bailey Bridge a mile inland.

The bridge is all that remains of the old **Southwold to Halesworth Light Railway** that ran its last train in 1929 after 50 years of service and was locally famous because its carriages had originally been intended for the Emperor of China. Reportedly, the forms of Chinese imperial dragons could just about be detected beneath the paintwork. Parts of the old railway route are still walkable, particularly between Blythburgh and Southwold.

Like Dunwich, it declined slowly over the years but managed to survive as a working port until the early years of the 20th century. What remains is the mere shadow of what was once a much larger place. The village has been associated with artists since the late Victorian period: in the 1890s and 1900s, the circle of English Impressionists associated with Philip Wilson Steer came here to paint, and Charles Rennie Mackintosh made it his home in 1914 when, disillusioned with architecture, he came here to paint watercolours (it didn't all go smoothly for him though: he was arrested as a possible spy in 1915). The village remains inordinately popular with media types, with a number of actors and other celebrities maintaining homes here; there's a handful of famous Freuds too. As John Seymour dryly remarked when writing of the village in 1968: 'It is indeed, the haunt of ex-theatrical folk and lady watercolourists, but it is very attractive nevertheless.'

As well as an artistic retreat, Walberswick is popular with walkers, birders and young families who come here to go crabbing. A very popular spot for this activity is the small bridge that crosses the channel by the main car park at the area known as The Flats. My mother once saw *Match of the Day* pundit and former England striker Gary Lineker dangling a line here. The Suffolk Coast Path passes right through the village and it's a lovely walk to Dunwich. It is even possible to walk all the way to Dunwich along the beach, although not really advisable as it is shingle the whole distance and really hard going. Plenty of shorter, circular walks that take in the marshes and bird-filled reedbeds are other options.

⁑ FOOD & DRINK

The Anchor Main St ☎ 01502 722112 ⌖ anchoratwalberswick.com. This Adnams inn housed in an elegant 1920s Arts and Crafts building serves dishes to match the beer and uses produce from local butchers and organic vegetable growers. There's a sun terrace overlooking allotments and beach huts, and occasional summer barbecues out on the lawn.

The Tea Shed The Green ☎ 01502 724468. Located in a wooden building in the middle of the village, this is a good choice for light lunches, coffee and cake or a full afternoon tea.

5 BLYTHBURGH

🏠 **The Gallery** (page 276)

A few miles inland from Southwold at the head of the Blyth estuary, the village of Blythburgh clusters around the busy A12. The estuary itself is quite a sight, especially when the tide is in and its wading birds are squeezed in closer to view, but the major attraction here is undoubtedly the village's remarkable church. Just south of the village, at the junction of the B1387, is the Toby Walk's picnic site, named after the ghost of a dragoon drummer reputed to haunt the area. The footpath that follows the southern shore of the estuary in part traces the route of the former Halesworth to Southwold railway. A lovely linear walk is along the river path from Wenhaston to the church at Blythburgh, before taking the estuary path that leads through woodland to eventually join the Sandlings Walk for the last couple of miles into Southwold.

Holy Trinity Church

Like Cley in north Norfolk, Blythburgh's parish church is a reminder of prosperous times when the village served as an important wool port. The church, towering above reedbeds close to the river, and sometimes referred to locally as 'the Cathedral of the Marshes', is a beacon for miles around and unsurpassed in the area for both its scale and beauty. Like the River Glaven at Cley, the Blyth eventually silted up and Blythburgh's importance waned. The church too fell into decay, but the most devastating occurrence took place in 1577 when lightning struck the tower and it fell into the nave, killing two of the congregation. This, at least, is one explanation. A more fanciful one is that the legendary hellhound Black Shuck ran riot in the church before leaving scorch marks in the north door and scurrying off to Bungay's St Mary's Church to create similar havoc there (page 104). Despite spiteful mid 17th-century defacing by the arch-puritan William 'Smasher' Dowsing (page 184), the church is still a remarkable building, with carved angels flying across its roof space. In his *England's Thousand Best Churches*, Simon Jenkins calls it the 'queen of the Suffolk coast' (although he gives one more star to Southwold's St Edmund's) and it is by far the most evocative of the various settings used for summer concerts in the annual Aldeburgh Festival. Beneath the gaze of the benign angels overhead are poppyhead-carved pews that portray the Seven Deadly Sins. The church also has a wooden bell-striking figure, a brother to

1 Latitude Festival is held in the beautiful grounds of Henham Park. **2** Crabbing in Walberswick. **3** & **4** Carved angels adorn the ceiling of Holy Trinity Church, Blythburgh, which is known as 'the Cathedral of the Marshes'. ▶

SAM MCMAHON

JDW TOG MAN/S

LAURENCE MITCHELL

PETER MARSDEN

'Southwold Jack' at St Edmund's, Southwold (page 35). As well as the angels in the roof of the church there is another to be seen outside on the green. The Blythburgh village sign, renewed as a local Millennium project, features as a remarkable wooden angel with spread wings clutching a shield.

Henham Park

Henham Park, Beccles NR34 8AN henhampark.com during public events only

Just up the road from Blythburgh in the cleft of the A145 and A12 is Henham Park, a glorious estate set in lush parkland landscaped by Sir Humphry Repton in 1791, with ancient oaks, redwoods and even rare service trees and black poplars. Indeed, the oaks seem so old and wide in girth here that you cannot help but wonder how they didn't end up as ships' timbers during the Napoleonic Wars at the start of the 19th century. In 1983 the estate came under the ownership of Keith Rous, the sixth Earl of Stradbroke, known as 'The Aussie Earl' because of his work as a sheep farmer in Australia prior to inheriting the property. His son, Hektor, now manages the estate. Most people come here for the **Latitude Music Festival** at the end of July, a family-friendly rock music festival that also features theatre, comedy, poetry, literature and cabaret. The estate is also used as the location for summer food festivals, steam rallies and game and country fairs. Henham Barns, an oak-beamed Suffolk red brick granary, also hosts events and has a yoga studio. Some of the estate's 50 houses and cottages are available for rent as holiday lets.

¶¶ FOOD & DRINK

White Hart Inn London Rd 01502 478217 blythburgh-whitehart.co.uk. A 17th-century Dutch-gabled coaching inn that once served as the local courthouse and jail but is now an Adnams house with standard gastropub fare. Stirring views of the Blythburgh estuary may be had from the outside tables in the pub garden.

6 DUNWICH

 The Ship (page 276)

A visit to Dunwich is not so much about what there is to see now – a pub, car park, café, a few ruins – but what has disappeared from view. As W A Dutt reports in *Highways and Byways of East Anglia*: 'the story of Dunwich seizes upon the imagination; though when one sees how little remains of what may once have been the chief city of East Anglia it is difficult to believe that Dunwich, too, was not a phantom city of a land of dreams'. That was in 1900 and almost nothing has changed – if anything, the remaining village is even smaller today. Hard to believe, perhaps, but Dunwich was once the capital of East Anglia: a thriving port and shipbuilding centre with several churches, priories and even the seat of the East Anglia bishopric. With the confluence of the Blyth and Dunwich rivers forming a natural harbour, the town grew prosperous as a result of the wool trade in the early medieval period but, as has been the case elsewhere on this coastline, natural harbours are rarely permanent features. Today, the place is reduced to the status of a small village with a large beach car park. It's a popular place for day trippers to take the air, eat fish and chips and stroll along the shingle – all pleasant enough, but the real thrill is to come here and contemplate what existed before.

Given that most of old Dunwich lies buried beneath the waves, it is perhaps inevitable that there's plenty of hyperbole describing the place as some lost Atlantis or Saxon Camelot. Old tales speak of 52 churches that used to exist here, and of tolling church bells heard out to sea during storms. However, Rowland Parker, author of the splendid *Men of Dunwich*, scoffs at such notions, saying that there were never more than six churches standing at any one time in the town, and that he has never heard any local talk of bells tolling out at sea. If you wish to learn more of the history of Dunwich and medieval Suffolk, Parker's book is highly recommended: although it contains a staggering amount of historical detail, it is as gripping as a good detective story.

Dunwich's early history has some grey areas, but what is certain is that, although the place was known to the Romans, it was the Saxons who first developed it as a port. The Christian missionary St Felix of Burgundy founded the East Anglia bishopric here in the mid 7th century when the place was known as Dommoc. The bishopric moved to North Elmham in AD870 before later transferral to Thetford and finally Norwich. Dunewic, a Saxonised version of its original name, is recorded as being a small town in 1060 with a single church. The Norman Conquest brought expansion to the port, and within 20 years of the conquest Dunwich had a population of around 3,000, a considerable number for those days. By the mid 13th century, it had become a vitally important seaport. A conjectural map of the town and harbour of circa 1280 in Parker's book gives an idea of what might have been found here at that time: five churches, two priories, a guildhall, a market place, shipyards, a quay, town gates, a hospital, a leper hospital and even a bit of topography – Cock Hill and Hen Hill.

Dunwich's demise started in the same century. In 1286, a ferocious sea surge swept many of the town's buildings out to sea and the Dunwich River became partly silted up. The next century was no kinder. A storm in 1328 finished off Dunwich's harbour and this was the cue for Walberswick, just to the north, to take over the port trade. This resulted in such hostility between the two towns for the following century or so that confrontations often erupted into violence. That which remained was lost to the sea over the next few hundred years thanks to further coastal erosion.

All that can be seen today are the ruins of Greyfriars, the Franciscan priory, and fragments of a leper hospital (for a leper hospital in fine condition you might want to check out Lazar House along Sprowston Road in Norwich). The sole remaining church, St James, is relatively recent, dating from 1832. Marine archaeologist Stuart Bacon, who has been working here since 1971, has located the remains of two of the town's former churches, All Saints' and St Peter's, out to sea, and recent evidence of the town's shipbuilding industry has also been discovered. All Saints' was the last of Dunwich's medieval churches to be lost. It reached the cliff edge in 1904, although its tower did not collapse until 1922. Old postcards show the ruins of this church, a buttress of which was salvaged and re-erected somewhat incongruously in a corner of the churchyard of St James's Church. You can also see a brass taken from All Saints' inside the modern church. The grounds of St James's Church also contain the Romanesque ruins of the 12th-century chapel of the leper hospital that once stood on the same site.

"In 1286, a ferocious sea surge swept many of the town's buildings out to sea and the Dunwich River became partly silted up."

Dunwich Museum (St James St ☉ Apr–Sep) has some fascinating displays outlining Dunwich's 1,500-year-old history. Even better, it's free to enter, although a small donation is welcomed.

7 DUNWICH HEATH & MINSMERE

North of Dunwich is the dense coniferous plantation of Dunwich Forest and a large marshy area – Dingle Marshes and Westwood Marshes – an

THE DUNWICH DYNAMO

For further information see ⊘ southwarkcyclists.org.uk

For a bicycle ride with a difference, you might want to consider participating in the annual Dunwich Dynamo.

You'll need legs of steel, and night vision would be a distinct advantage too. The ride takes place each year on the Saturday night closest to the full moon in July. The 'Dynamo' leaves Hackney in London on the Saturday night and arrives in Dunwich the following morning – a gruelling 120-mile overnight ride, part of the way marked by decidedly low-tech tea lights in jam jars, and ending up with breakfast on the beach.

This punishing event started back in 1993 when a group of London cycle messengers decided to go on a fun run to the coast. Since then, the route, planned by the London School of Cycling, has been organised on a turn up and go basis, with an increasing number of competitors taking part but less competition between them (if that makes sense). There were 700 participants on the 2006 run, or 'DD' as it is commonly known, while the 2007 event had 450 participants of whom only 400 finished because of problems caused by bad weather. In 2009 an estimated 1,000 riders started out from Hackney, one of whom was riding a penny-farthing bicycle. Even more foolhardy, perhaps, was some brave soul who managed to complete the route on a hired bike from London's bike-share scheme in 2011. A turn-out of around a thousand participants is now pretty much standard – the 2016 run had an estimated 2,000 cyclists, and in 2019 this had increased to about 3,000 before the Covid pandemic put a brake on the event for a couple of years. No doubt in future years participants will continue to find increasingly more challenging ways of completing what is already a demanding overnight ride. This is no race – there's no official start time and no prize for arriving first to the coast. There's no safety car either, so participation is not to be taken lightly. It is certainly no picnic. It is 120 miles at night, and goes all the way through East London, Essex and Suffolk.

uninterrupted squelch as far as Walberswick. A couple of footpaths lead across the marshes – consult OS Landranger map 156 – or alternatively you could trudge north along the shingle beach, but that would be hard work all the way to Walberswick. A more rewarding area for walkers is that to the south of the village – Dunwich Heath, Westleton Walks and the Minsmere RSPB nature reserve.

Dunwich Heath is National Trust-owned and above the cliffs a convenient car park looks down over the Minsmere reserve and on to the giant golf ball of the Sizewell B nuclear power station. The attractive white coastguard cottages next to the car park hold the National Trust visitor centre and a tea room. Dunwich Heath itself is a rare example of typical, unimproved Sandlings habitat, with rare Dartford warblers lurking in the gorse bushes and nightjars at dusk during summer.

Sizewell B nuclear power station

This structure resembling a giant golf ball perched atop a massive concrete block can be seen from much of the Suffolk coast, certainly from as far away as Southwold and Orford Ness.

Contaminated water leaked from Sizewell A in January 2007 as the earlier power station was being decommissioned. Notwithstanding this, most locals are pretty blasé about its presence and some people even prefer to swim on the beach near the water extraction pipes because 'the water's a bit warmer there'. The power station management team has cultivated good relations with the nearby RSPB reserve over the years and has also provided welcome employment for the residents of Leiston. Despite this, many local residents are less sanguine about proposed future developments for the site. A third power station, Sizewell C, is planned, a project that is predicted to provide a massive 7% of the UK's total energy demand when it comes on stream. In spite of considerable local opposition to the project, Sizewell C's construction programme is expected to commence in 2024 and take between nine and 12 years to complete.

The beach here is a favourite place for local dog walkers and the shingle shelters lots of typical heathland plants like harebell, centaury and lady's mantle. The concrete buildings themselves also, surprisingly perhaps, provide a home for wildlife; in this case, birds – black redstart and kittiwakes. The beach also has a café next to the car park that is open more or less year-round.

Minsmere RSPB Nature Reserve

Minsmere, Westleton IP17 3BY ✆ 01728 648281; RSPB

Minsmere is well known, a flagship reserve established in 1948 with year-round interest in its pools and reedbeds. The reserve is a popular place with both twitchers and beginner birders and there's a wealth of information about the place in the visitor centre. Two circular trails around the reserve take you through a variety of habitats, and some of the seven hides are accessible to wheelchairs. Typical reedbed species such as bittern, marsh harrier and bearded tit are all present and it's pretty hard to miss the elegant black-and-white avocets that grace the ponds here.

A heath, marsh & shingle walk around Minsmere

❈ OS Landranger map 156 or Explorer maps 212 and 231; start: Dunwich Heath National Trust car park, 📍 TM477678; 4 miles; easy–moderate .

This excellent walk provides the full Suffolk coast experience, with sea, shingle, reedbeds, grazing marshes, woodland and heath all putting in an appearance along the way. Although the walk does not actually enter the RSPB reserve itself, it overlooks parts of it and catching sight of interesting birdlife is pretty well guaranteed.

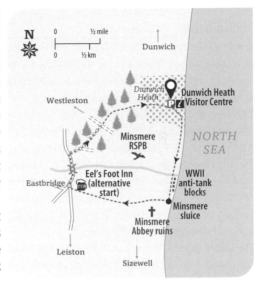

An alternative starting point would be to park at the Eel's Foot Inn in Eastbridge (page 48) and embark upon the walk after eating lunch there.

Start at the National Trust car park and descend the steps down to the shore. Follow the path along the shingle, passing a couple of entrances into the reserve and concrete World War II anti-tank blocks along the way.

At Minsmere Sluice turn right away from the sea and follow the waymarked path inland past a fragment of what was once Minsmere Abbey. This passes grazing marshes and reedbeds, eventually reaching a minor road. Turn right and follow the road past the Eel's Foot Inn and over a bridge at a stream to arrive at an area of dense coppiced woodland to the right. Follow the road to the right that leads to the RSPB visitor centre and veer left when it forks to leave the wooded area.

Continue through an open area with views of the coast and Sizewell B and across a crossroads of tracks through an avenue of oaks to reach a footpath to the right that is waymarked Sandlings Walk. Follow this through more woodland to emerge at a gate and a sign announcing 'NT Dunwich Heath', at the point where it emerges at open heath, a wide expanse of brilliant purple in August. Continue in the same direction across the heath, aiming for the white coastguard cottages and the National Trust car park ahead.

You are far more likely to hear a bittern – a deep 'boom' reminiscent of a distant foghorn – than see one. You might hear nightingales, too, in early summer in the woods close to the visitor centre. The visitor centre has a shop and a tea room, and there are guided walks available as well as plenty of activities for children.

ⴼ FOOD & DRINK

Dingle Hill Tearooms Dingle Hill, Dunwich ✆ 01728 648872 ⌀ dinglehilltearooms.co.uk. Just outside Dunwich village, on a low hill above the marshes, this family-run tea room serves sandwiches and salads, and homemade cakes, quiches and scones. There's limited indoor seating but a much larger outdoor dining area.

Eel's Foot Inn Eastbridge ✆ 01728 830154 ⌀ theeelsfootinn.co.uk. A village pub close to Minsmere RSPB reserve, with good beer and folk music nights. Locally sourced food, but no pre-booking of tables. The inn also offers rooms and a cycle-hire service.

Flora Tea Rooms Beach Car Park, Dunwich ✆ 01728 648433 ⌀ floratearoomsdunwich. co.uk. Famous for its fish and chips as well as for location (you are at the mouth of what was once Dunwich's great harbour), this is a plain no-frills place serving pots of tea and ice-cream sundaes. Outside are trestle tables for dining on fine sunny days, while there's also plenty of seating inside for less inclement weather.

The Ship St James St, Dunwich ✆ 01728 648219 ⌀ shipatdunwich.co.uk. This popular former smugglers' inn, virtually on the beach and well placed for walkers and birdwatchers, has excellent fish and chips and Adnams in the bar, as well as a modern dining room where generous portions of comforting traditional food are served. There's also a conservatory and a large back garden. See also page 276.

8 WESTLETON, MIDDLETON & THEBERTON

🏠 **Argyll House B&B, Westleton** (page 276)

These three villages sit between Dunwich and Yoxford on the A12. Westleton lies on the direct road to Dunwich and Minsmere RSPB reserve, while Middleton is just off it on another minor road. Theberton lies just south of Middleton. All three are inviting, with scattered old houses that seem to determine the route of the road that curves around them rather than the other way around.

Westleton is the largest and most visited of the three, a fairly large attractive village with a green and St Peter's Church, a thatched 14th-century building that was built by monks from Sibton Abbey, close to Peasenhall just across the A12. Legend has it that no grass can grow over the 'witch's stone' near the priest door of the church, and if you put your handkerchief in the grating of the wall and make an anti-clockwise circumambulation of the church you will hear the sound of the Devil clanking his chains beneath the grating. You may notice that this large church is lacking in one department – it has no tower or spire. The original tower collapsed in high winds in 1776. It was rebuilt but its replacement also collapsed during World War II, this time the result of a German bomb. The church stages occasional orchestral concerts as well as hosting Westleton's annual **Wild Flower Festival**.

The village also has two pubs, unusual for a village of this size, and remarkably also possesses two highly idiosyncratic secondhand bookshops. **Chapel Books** (✆ 01728 648616), homed in a former Methodist chapel opposite the post office and village shop, has an emphasis on rare collectables. **Barnabees** (✆ 01728 648848), on the Yoxford Road, is run by Tyona Campbell, a former Chapel Books employee, and is a homely Aladdin's Cave of more affordable literary fare. This is a magical place with comfy chairs and an open fire where, as Tyona says, the books find you rather than you finding them. Not far from Chapel Books, tucked away behind the Crown pub, is the village duck pond where an inscribed bench proclaims: 'Eighteen Lime Trees for Eighteen Men 1914–1918'. The commemorative lime trees line the path behind.

Close to the village on the road to Darsham just east of the A12, you'll find the **Emmerdale Farm Shop** (✆ 01728 668648 ⌂ emmerdalefarmshop.co.uk), which stocks well-matured beef from a local herd of Suffolk Red Poll that are reared in the old-fashioned way, grazing on marshes in spring and summer, as well as locally grown vegetables like potatoes and asparagus and products from other local suppliers; it also has a coffee shop. There's also Reckford Roost (✆ 01728 648936), another farm shop and café on the Leiston Road just south of the village by the Middleton turn-off, which sells its own fruit and vegetables in addition to produce from other local enterprises

Middleton, straddling a road that goes nowhere in particular, has the distinction of being the only village in Suffolk that has its own moor, actually just a big field a mile from the village centre. After following a narrow lane for about a mile from the turn-off, the village comes as surprise when you get there. Middleton is a self-contained little place and its isolation from the main road might help explain its timeless atmosphere. Its church dominates, towering above the village on a rise.

MOLLY DANCING IN EAST ANGLIA

Molly dancing is the East Anglian version of Morris dancing, an earthier tradition that is altogether scarier and might even be described as 'Morris dancing with menace'. Molly involves a type of dance traditionally performed by ploughboys in midwinter. It mostly existed in the Midlands and East Anglia and, before the recent revival, the tradition was last witnessed in Cambridgeshire in the 1930s.

Molly dancing is usually associated with Plough Monday, the first Monday after Epiphany ('Twelfth Night'), a day on which ploughboys would tour their village and offer to dance for money for local landowners, meting out 'trick or treat'-style mischief to those who refused to pay. The commonest penalty would be to plough a furrow across the lawn or garden of the offending party. Anonymity was vital, as it would be these same landowners who would provide employment once the farming season got under way. Consequently, faces would be blackened with soot, Sunday-best clothes modified with coloured scarves and one of the team would cross-dress as a woman.

The revived tradition incorporates all of these elements with a modern twist. East Anglia has several Molly 'teams': Old Glory, who also perform the Cutty Wren Hunt at Middleton (see opposite), Ouse Washes Molly Dancers and Gog Magog Molly.

As well as Plough Monday and the Cutty Wren Hunt, Old Glory Molly can also sometimes be seen dancing at Southwold and Walberswick on Christmas Eve. Whatever the occasion, the proceedings usually have a solemn, dark edge. Old Glory don't smile or talk when they perform, and they don't perform outside winter. They do tend to scare small children though. It's a serious business that seems both primordial and quintessentially English. In fact, one witness is reported to have said that the Molly experience was 'so English, it brought tears to my eyes'.

Below is a tiny green that has benches, a telephone kiosk and a metal sculpture on a plinth at its centre. The faded village sign featuring a cockerel looks more like it belongs outside a pub. But the village pub, a cosy thatched building next to an optimistically large car park, is actually called The Bell and already has its own sign. A path leads up from the green to the churchyard, its gate flanked by tidy cottages with impressive floral displays in pots and hanging baskets – all very attractive and not the slightest bit twee. The village church, Holy Trinity, is welcoming, or at least it seemed that way when I last visited around Harvest Festival time. There were apples in the porch and sweetcorn plants growing in pots in the chancel as well as vases filled with slightly faded bunches of flowers gathered from village gardens. With the pervading scent of ripe apples, sunshine streaming through the stained glass and the sound of children's laughter drifting in from the primary school playground next door, it all seemed delightfully idyllic.

There's an old tradition in the village called the **Cutty Wren Hunt** that is based on an ancient tradition in which a wren is captured on the evening of St Stephen's (Boxing) Day for purposes of divination. The custom finally died out at the beginning of the 20th century, but a modified version of it was resurrected in 1994. Originally, a wren would be captured and killed, and then fastened to a holly and ivy-bedecked broomstick to be taken around the village by boys who would demand gifts from the householders. These days, real live wrens are spared and the ritual consists of a lantern-lit procession bearing a wooden wren that goes from the village hall to the Bell Inn where the Old Glory Molly Dancers (see opposite) perform. The ritual may have prehistoric origins but is a curious one, as it is generally considered unlucky to kill wrens. There may be a connection here with the midwinter tradition of topsy-turvydom in which the usual rules of behaviour are turned upside down, and the wren's perceived association with the underworld is symbolically challenged. Although similar traditions exist in Ireland and Britain's Celtic fringe, the one at Middleton appears to be unique for England. All this bird abuse so close to Minsmere!

Theberton is another village with a thatched church, St Peter's; in this case, a much smaller one than at Westleton but at least complete with tower – a fine round tower no less, topped with an octagonal belfry. A trio of fearsome gargoyles glare down on anyone entering the porch, the Gothic horror effect only marginally diluted by the lengths of modern piping that protrude from their mouths.

"A path leads up from the green to the churchyard, its gate flanked by tidy cottages with impressive floral displays"

A Zeppelin airship was shot down here during World War I and 16 German airmen perished in the crash. There is a memorial in the cemetery across the road from the church, and a piece of the airship itself mounted in a glass case in the porch. The story of the crash in English and German, together with black-and-white photographs from newspaper cuttings, can also be found in the porch, as can a selection of secondhand paperbacks. Fragments of the Zeppelin were repurposed into all sorts of new items such as keepsake brooches made from bits of recycled airship brass,

MARK STAPLES

THESUFFOLKCOAST.CO.UK

ALAN SHEARMAN/S

CHRIS BARBER71/S

SUE CHILLINGWORTH/S

and it's thought that various bits and pieces, handed down through the generations, survive in the area today.

¶¶ FOOD & DRINK

The Bell Inn Middleton ℰ 01728 648286 ⟨⟩ themiddletonbell.co.uk. A cosy thatched Adnams pub with a small dining area and a relaxed bar with sofas; limited choice of food but a welcoming atmosphere.

The Snug Tea Room The Street, Westleton ℰ 01728 648216 ⟨⟩ the-snug-tea-room. business.site. This welcoming, dog-friendly tea room certainly lives up to its name. Serving coffee, cakes, snacks and light meals, with a choice between the cosy interior and a courtyard garden.

Westleton Crown The Street, Westleton ℰ 01728 648777 ⟨⟩ westletoncrown.co.uk. This comfortable former coaching inn claims to have provided 800 years of continuous service to travellers. There's an open fire to warm wind-chilled walkers and a huge map of the locality on the wall. The extensive menu is mostly sourced from local butchers or Lowestoft fishing boats. The food may be a little more pricey than similar places but the quality of the cooking is consistently high. Very popular with dog owners.

White Horse Inn Darsham Rd, Westleton ℰ 01728 648222 ⟨⟩ westleton-whitehorse.co.uk. This has much more of a village local feel to it than the Westleton Crown, with an excellent range of Adnams beers and decent pub meals for sustenance.

9 LEISTON & LEISTON ABBEY

🏠 **Five Acre Barn** Aldringham (page 276)

Leiston used to be a mere village but expanded rapidly in the late 19th century when it became a centre for cast-metal goods and munitions at the factory of Richard Garrett & Sons, better known simply as the 'Leiston Works'. Once a hive of industry, the town is fairly humdrum these days and not as well-to-do in comparison with other towns along this coastal strip like Aldeburgh and Southwold. The close proximity of Sizewell B does not exactly endear Leiston to visitors either, although some townsfolk are grateful for the employment that the nuclear plant provides. Leiston is the home of Summerhill School, founded by A S Neill in 1921, which was the first so-called 'free school', based in the former mansion of Richard Garrett, owner of the Leiston Works. In all honesty though, there's not that much to see in the town itself other

◀ **1** Leiston Abbey. **2** Dunwich Heath. **3** An avocet at RSPB Minsmere. **4** A marsh harrier flies over the Minsmere marshes. **5** The dome of Sizewell B.

than the **Long Shop Museum** (✆ 01728 832189 ⌂ longshopmuseum. co.uk) at the former Leiston Works, which is definitely worth a detour if you have an interest in steam engines or want to get a taste of what Victorian industrial life was like. Another draw for those with an interest in cinema is the **Leiston Film Theatre** (⌂ leistonfilmtheatre. co.uk) at 74 High Street, which despite being the oldest film theatre in Suffolk, dating from 1914, has very up-to-date Dolby surround sound and digital projection technology. If neither of these appeal, it's probably best to make straight for Leiston Abbey, a mile or so north of the town on the Westleton Road.

Leiston Abbey

Free entrance; English Heritage

Set just off the main road, this is a highly impressive set of monastic ruins, the largest of its kind in the county. Most of what you see dates from the 14th century when the abbey, which followed the Premonstratensian rule, was moved here from a less healthy, flood-prone location on swampy ground nearer the coast close to present-day Minsmere (where a fragment of St Mary's Chapel, part of the original abbey, can still be seen close to Minsmere Sluice).

Although Leiston Abbey's buildings date from the second half of the 14th century, the materials used are largely recycled parts of the earlier abbey and 12th-century Norman in style. The new monastery was considerably larger than its predecessor, and several new chapels were added during the extensive rebuild.

What is most impressive, besides the delicate tracery around the windows and perpendicular arches up to 45ft high, is that so much material was reused from the earlier abbey, a remarkable feat of architectural salvage given how difficult it must have been to transport large chunks of wall and archway even the short distance from Minsmere.

The large house that abuts the nave and north transept is a later addition, built after the Dissolution, when the church and other buildings served as farm buildings. The house was extended in the Georgian period and currently it is in the ownership of the Pro Corda music school. Concerts are sometimes staged in the adjoining barn and the site, in the guardianship of English Heritage, is occasionally leased as a venue for weddings and corporate events. The Lady Chapel, the only other complete structure, was restored and furnished in 1918, although when I last visited there was a rather unfriendly 'Keep Out' notice posted on its door.

The ruins ooze atmosphere and make an ideal place to wander around at twilight or when there's a mist over the land. There is a vantage point of the whole complex in the centre of the ruins, where steps lead up to a viewpoint over the refectory. There's a good chance that you may have the place to yourself, although the site is also popular with Leiston dog-walkers as there is a direct footpath from the town.

10 SAXMUNDHAM

⅄ Mill Hill Farm Caravan & Campsite (page 277)

This small market town lies a few miles west of Leiston at the end of a road that passes through some of the less inspiring countryside this coastal strip has to offer – a slightly dreary flat expanse of prairie-type arable fields with few hedgerows, not really typical of the area. This is the exception rather than the rule, and things get much better just a little way south, or indeed north, of here. Saxmundham is not really that close to the coast at all but since it lies just east of the A12, and on the road to Sizewell, Leiston and Aldeburgh, it might be best to include it here. In some ways, the town is a bit like Framlingham but without the castle, the successful independent shops and the gentle buzz. What Saxmundham does have is a functioning station on the East Suffolk coastal railway line, a handy link to Lowestoft and Ipswich. Mostly though, 'Sax' is a quiet, old-fashioned place with ironmongers, bakery and barbers' shops clustered cosily alongside each other in the centre – the classic small market town, although you sense that the high street has seen better days and is slowly dying. It tends to come a little more alive on Wednesday market days but otherwise most of the excitement seems to emanate from the car park of Waitrose down near the church. Sad to say, the two large supermarkets that lie close to each other down here appear to be more of a magnet for local shoppers, and to provide more Sax-appeal, than any number of quality bookshops or organic farm shops. Among other independent businesses, the farm shop, Peakhill Farm Organics, that once also stood on the High Street has been forced to close although you can still buy direct from the farm at nearby Theberton (page 51). Like it or not, the supermarkets are what draw most local people to the town these days, and despite a rather blatant sign that sometimes stands outside Tesco saying 'High Street This Way, Shop Local', many visitors to the town do not bother to venture as far as this.

St John the Baptist Church, just up the hill from Waitrose car park, which has a lovely bright sign at its entrance welcoming visitors, has an intriguing font with a pair of **woodwoses** on opposite sides. The woodwose – a hairy, wild-looking man with a club – is sometimes referred to as 'The Old Man of Suffolk', but for my money, it is really just another expression of what many would call 'the Green Man'. Of the pair here, one has his club raised, the other lowered. The church literature puts it politely: 'clubs raised by the unregenerate, lowered by the regenerate' without venturing red-faced into any explanation as to what the symbolism of the club might actually be. I'll leave you to draw your own conclusions, although it seems a little topsy-turvy to me; as Freud observed, 'sometimes a cigar is just a cigar'. If you are more interested in medieval carpentry than prurient symbolism, look upwards to the fine hammerbeam roof. The graveyard has a highly unusual headstone, that of one John Noller, which takes the form of a sundial.

"'Sax' is a quiet, old-fashioned place with ironmongers, bakery and barbers' shops clustered cosily alongside each other."

The **High Street**, despite being ignored by many supermarket shoppers, has a number of handsome buildings along its length. There's a cluster of one-time pubs – Queen's Head (now a Chinese restaurant and take-away), White Hart (permanently closed) and the Georgian Bell Hotel – with an attractive white market hall next to the latter. Market Place is a little further along, just off to the left, where there is a 16th-century timber-framed building that was once an inn, and an iron hand pump, cast by Garretts of Leiston just down the road.

Returning to the High Street and continuing towards the railway bridge you should be able to spot a crinkle-crankle wall, a Suffolk speciality, fronting one of the gardens (page 188). The **town museum** (⊘ saxmundhammuseum.org.uk ☉ Apr–Sep mornings only Tue, Wed, Fri & Sat), which has displays on local history in a well-preserved 1940s railway booking office, is a little further on, close to the railway bridge at number 49. The museum also has a cinema room where you can see an archive film about East Anglian railways.

Not far from the town, a little way to the east, **Peakhill Farm** (⊘ 01728 602248 ⊘ peakhillfarm.co.uk) is a long-established organic establishment based at Theberton near Leiston. The farm run by Rob and Karen White has a herd of South Devon cattle, some sows and a field of vegetables and salads, all of which are cultivated organically.

¶¶ FOOD & DRINK

There are few choices in the town unless you are fond of supermarket cafeterias. If it's an atmospheric real ale pub with good food you are after then there are several a few miles' drive in any direction – see individual listings elsewhere in this chapter. In the town itself, the places listed below are worth a visit.

The Bell Hotel 31 High St 🕾 01728 602331 ⚓ thebellhotelsaxmundham.co.uk. This old coaching inn has been refurbished and has luxurious themed rooms for guests as well as a restaurant and well-stocked bar. The menu here offers a range of modern British dishes, both simple and sophisticated, that make the most of Suffolk-sourced ingredients like locally grown vegetables, wild game, and lobster s and sea bass from the nearby coast.
Number One Bakery 1 High St 🕾 01728 564211. A family-run bakery and café with good coffee and cakes as well as snacks, sandwiches and soups to eat in or take-away
Trinity's at No. 14 14 Market Pl 🕾 07707 105097. Formerly the Corner House Café, this is a convenient stop near the railway station that is good for cooked breakfasts.

ALDEBURGH, ORFORD & BRITTEN COUNTRY

South of Leiston and Sizewell, the Suffolk coast curves gently south-southwest as the River Alde meanders slowly seawards dividing the mainland of Suffolk from the elongated spit of Orford Ness, the nearest thing to an offshore island in these parts.

11 ALDEBURGH

🏠 **Aldeburgh Cottage** (page 276), **Martello Tower** (page 276)

Aldeburgh is the Suffolk coast's other main contender for the role of favourite seaside resort: a former shipbuilding and fishing town that went into decline when fishing boats became too large to drag up the beach and other, more suitable ports were favoured for the construction of ships. Before this happened though, ships as illustrious as Sir Francis Drake's *Pelican* (famously later renamed as *Golden Hind*) were built here. There's still some fishing done from Aldeburgh's shingle beach and one of the town's great pleasures is to buy ultra-fresh fish from one of the huts on the beach and go off and cook it. Of course, you could have fish from the very same catch cooked for you instead – more on this later.

These days this town is a place of wealth and refinement, with barely a rough edge apart from the workaday fishing huts and 'punts' on the beach. As you might expect, there is a considerable number of incomers and those that live here year-round tend to know that they are on to a good thing, which gives the place just the slightest hint of self-satisfaction. Aldeburgh's connections with the composer **Benjamin Britten** (actually a Lowestoft man) and the annual Aldeburgh Arts Festival bring such kudos to the town that you wonder what a real-life Peter Grimes might make of it – a little highfalutin perhaps?

Despite the widespread fame of its fish and chip shops, it is immediately obvious that Aldeburgh is as much about pan-fried sea bass on a big square plate as it is about fish and chips in paper. It is undeniably lovely though, with bracing sea-scented air, a Blue Flag shingle beach, some interesting buildings and, of course, fantastic fresh fish.

The most striking building is the **Moot Hall**, a Tudor timber-framed building that looks a little odd sitting right next to the beach, and holds a museum of the town's history (✆ 01728 567767 ⌂ aldeburghmuseum. org.uk). Its current location is thanks to longshore drift rather than eccentric town planning as it used to sit smack dab in the town centre. As elsewhere on this coastline, the relentless North Sea has shaved great chunks off what was once the original medieval town.

A better-known landmark these days is *The Scallop*, a large stainless-steel sculpture in the shape of a shell that stands on the northern beach close to the car park. The sculpture, the work of Suffolk artist Maggi Hambling, was unveiled in 2003 to much controversy. It is dedicated to Benjamin Britten and the upright shell bears the words: 'I hear those voices that will not be drowned', taken from Britten's *Peter Grimes*. Some clearly consider *The Scallop* to be an eyesore and a despoilment of a beautiful natural setting. As a result, the work has received a lot of flak since it was first erected, with graffiti, paint splattering and petitions all brought to bear in the case against. It is hard to see why the sculpture has been quite so vilified in some quarters; it is, after all, a natural, seaside

ALDEBURGH: **1** *The Scallop* sculpture. **2** Moot Hall. **3** Prepare for queues at the Aldeburgh Fish and Chip Shop. **4** The town's Food & Drink Festival. ▶

DAVID CALVERT/S

MARK STAPLES

DAVID CALVERT/S

BOKEH PHOTOGRAPHIC

form – a shell. Objectors, some of whom have organised themselves into a campaign group called 'Voices of the People', simply claim that the work ruins an unspoilt bit of coastline, although you cannot help but feel that such antipathy runs deeper and is more to do with lauding the town's Benjamin Britten association rather than with the form of the sculpture itself. Criticism has also come from wider circles: in 2015 *The Guardian* art critic Jonathan Jones listed *The Scallop* as being among 'the worst six works of British public art'. Personally, I like it as I feel it has bedded in to become a vital part of the sometimes bleak Suffolk coastal landscape. For me, the work really comes into its own in the cold dark months when the beach is deserted and the sculpture takes on an almost luminous quality under a pewter winter sky.

Such protest may be nothing new. The poet George Crabbe who was born in the town and in 1810 wrote *The Borough*, the lengthy poem in which the solitary character of Peter Grimes first surfaced, notes a certain philistinism in the local character:

... a wild, amphibious race,
With sullen woe displayed in every face;
Who far from civil arts and social fly,
And scowl at strangers with suspicious eye.

Thankfully, there's not really that much scowling going on these days, nor a lot of flying away from civil arts. It's not always that highbrow either: most who come to see *The Scallop* seem to prefer to have their photographs taken sitting on it rather than contemplating its words.

Time and tide aside, Aldeburgh also has the distinction of having had – in 1908 – the UK's first female mayor. Dr Elizabeth Garrett Anderson (1836–1917), who held the post, was also the first woman in the country to qualify as a physician and surgeon, join the BMA and be elected to the London School Board.

Aldeburgh's 14th-century flint church of **St Peter and St Paul** on a low hill above the town has further local artistic interest. Here, there's a memorial bust of George Crabbe and a gorgeous stained-glass window by John Piper that depicts three Britten parables of the Curlew River. Benjamin Britten and his partner Peter Pears are both buried in the churchyard. For those wishing to uncover more about Britten's time in Aldeburgh there's a **Britten Trail** (⊘ brittenpearsarts.org) to follow, which as well as the church takes in the **Red House**, where the

ALDEBURGH'S ULTIMATE CHIPPIE

Walk one minute inland from the seafront to the High Street and if it's lunchtime or early evening you will almost inevitably come across a lengthy queue. The chances are that this is a hungry crocodile patiently waiting for service at the **Aldeburgh Fish and Chip Shop** at number 226.

The Fish and Chip Shop – yes, that's its name – has been listed as one of the country's top ten by *The Observer* and eulogised by chefs like Rick Stein and Nigel Slater. The secret, according to the owner Margaret Thompson, is that no flour is added to the batter and that vegetable oil, not beef dripping, is used for frying. It has been a family business since 1967. Some even claim it to be the best in the country. A place that can prosaically call itself The Fish and Chip Shop rather than 'The Codfather', 'This is the Plaice' or something similar just has to be good. There's another branch further along the High Street that is run by the same concern but this one is the original. By the time you get your fish supper you'll undoubtedly be very hungry. Walk back to the sea wall to enjoy your food by the sea but beware of local gulls that have become very adept at aerial fish theft.

composer lived with Peter Pears and now the home of the Britten–Pears Foundation, the **Crag House**, where Britten lived for ten years shortly after World War II, and **Aldeburgh Jubilee Hall**, an important music venue in the early years of the Aldeburgh Arts Festival (page 62).

Just south of the town past **Slaughden**, once an important centre for boatbuilding, now a yachting marina, you reach a narrow spit with a **Martello tower**. This is the most northerly of a string of 103 squat defensive towers that stretch from here south as far as Seaford, East Sussex. Twenty-nine of these were built in Suffolk and Essex between 1808 and 1812 as defences against possible invasion by Napoleon, and as well as being the most northerly the one at Slaughden is also the largest, effectively four towers combined into one in a quatrefoil form. The Martello tower belongs to the Landmark Trust (⚓ landmarktrust.org. uk) and may be rented for holiday accommodation. In 2015 an Antony Gormley sculpture called *Land* was installed on the roof of the tower, an enigmatic iron figure that gazed forlornly over the North Sea. Sadly, it was only in place for a year and has since been removed. The spit pushes south with the River Alde on one side and the sea on the other to become Orford Ness – a very long trudge along the shingle and best visited on the National Trust ferry from Orford Quay (page 75) as this route is theoretically closed to the public anyway.

The **Aldeburgh Arts Festival** (⌂ brittenpearsarts.org), an annual June festival of mainly classical music founded by Benjamin Britten in 1948, has become famous over the years. Most of the action takes place along the estuary at the purpose-built concert hall at Snape Maltings (page 65) but some events use other venues like Blythburgh church. The town has also become home to a handful of other festivals: **Poetry in Aldeburgh** (⌂ poetryinaldeburgh.org) in November; the **Aldeburgh Literary Festival**, run by the owners of Aldeburgh Book Shop (⌂ aldeburghbookshop.co.uk) in March; and the **Aldeburgh Food & Drink Festival** (⌂ aldeburghfoodanddrink.co.uk) in September. The last, in part sponsored by Adnams Brewery and several other local businesses, has been running since 2006 and takes place both in the town and at Snape Maltings. The festival's purpose is to celebrate the abundance of local produce, support the regional economy by encouraging sales of local produce, and to help people reconnect with the local countryside and the food it produces – all consistent with the Slow philosophy. There's a different slant to proceedings each year: recent themes have included food security for the nation and for Suffolk, and helping children and their parents reconnect with food, where it comes from and how it is produced.

"These days this town is a place of wealth and refinement, with barely a rough edge."

While Southwold is undoubtedly the beer capital of the Suffolk coast, Aldeburgh has its own speciality product – gin. Located in a modern building overlooking the shingle beach, **Fishers Gin Distillery** (☎ 01728 454201 ⌂ fishersgin.com), which welcomes visitors for tours and tastings, maintains that it is the closest gin distillery to the coast in the UK – a claim that is hard to dispute. The distillery's principle product, Fishers Original, is flavoured using locally sourced botanicals like samphire and myrtle, which impart a distinctively coastal, herbal flavour.

¶¶ FOOD & DRINK

For fresh produce to cook yourself, as well the very obvious fish huts on the beach, there's **Hall Farm Shop & Tea Room** on the Saxmundham road (☎ 01728 453666), which has Aldeburgh saltmarsh beef and lamb and other local foods. **Aldeburgh Market** (☎ 01728 452520 ⌂ thealdeburghmarket.co.uk) at 170–172 High St has a fresh fish and deli counter selling locally sourced products, and a **farmers' market** is held on the morning of the third Saturday of each month at Aldeburgh Church Hall.

Aldeburgh Café 2 Hall Farm Ln ☎ 07927 412346. Located close to town, just off the Saxmundham Road, this relaxed café has a sunny outdoor dining area with views over the Aldeburgh Marshes. Vegan and vegetarian friendly, it's a good choice for breakfasts and lunches.

Aldeburgh Fish & Chip Shop 226 High St ☎ 01728 452250; **The Galleon** 137 High St ☎ 01728 45225); ◊ aldeburghfishandchips.co.uk. Of these two highly rated fish and chip shops, both under the same ownership, the former is considered to just about have the edge – witness the queues – and considered by some to be the best fish and chip shop in Suffolk, some say the world (page 61). If you want to dine on the premises, the Galleon also has The Upper Deck (☎ 01728 452250) fish and chip diner upstairs

Cross Keys Crabbe St ☎ 01728 452637. Sometimes prefixed with 'Ye Olde', right next to the offshore lifeboat station on the seafront, here you can sup a pint of Adnams and eat briny fresh seafood caught by local fishermen. You can drink and dine outside in the garden and courtyard or take refuge inside by a log fire in cold weather. You might even choose to take your drink over the road and sit on the sea wall.

Lighthouse 77 High St ☎ 01728 453377 ◊ lighthouserestaurant.co.uk. With a good wine list and helpful staff, this popular restaurant specialises – surprise, surprise – in fish dishes, making full use of fresh local produce.

Regatta 171–3 High St ☎ 01728 452011 ◊ regattaaldeburgh.com. Another high street restaurant where fish is king, although non-fishy dishes are also available. From April to September the emphasis is on fresh fish landed on Aldeburgh beach with daily specials according to what is available. Vegetarian, meat and poultry dishes are available all year round, which make use of quality seasonal ingredients from other local producers.

Two Magpies Bakery 181–183 High St ☎ 01728 453204 ◊ twomagpiesbakery.co.uk. One of half a dozen branches of this café-bakery in Suffolk (the original is in Darsham), this popular, albeit rather pricey place has good coffee, delicious cakes and a toothsome selection of savoury snacks.

12 THORPENESS

🏠 **The Dune House** (page 276)

Heading north from Aldeburgh along the coast, you soon reach the village of Thorpeness, an odd place created from scratch by a Scottish barrister, Glencairn Stuart Ogilvie, in the Edwardian period. A hamlet had existed before but it was Ogilvie who decided to build a private holiday village here as a place where his friends and family could spend their summers.

ART ON THE COAST

Suffolk's coast has long attracted artists – it may be something to do with the light, or the drama of the crashing waves and shifting shingle of its beaches. The painter J M W Turner, a Londoner, came here many times in the early 19th century to produce several works that depicted the crashing seas of the coast at Lowestoft, Dunwich, Orford Ness and Aldeburgh. Half a century later, Philip Wilson Steer regularly visited this same coastline, specifically Walberswick and neighbouring Southwold, to paint beach scenes.

The early 20th century saw a further influx of artists to the Suffolk coast region. One of these was watercolourist Alfred Heaton Cooper, who came to provide illustrations for a travel guidebook to the county, painting Aldeburgh's Moot Hall and the Walberswick to Southwold Ferry as well as the then still standing ruins of All Saints' Church on the cliffs at Dunwich. A more famous visitor was Charles Rennie Mackintosh, who came to Walberswick in 1914 to paint landscapes and flowers when his architectural career had taken a downturn. Suffering from depression and alcoholism, it wasn't a particularly happy time for him, especially when he was accused of signalling to enemy ships and arrested as a suspected spy when his Glaswegian accent was mistaken for a German one. Nevertheless, it was a highly productive period in artistic terms, and many fine watercolours were painted during Mackintosh's troubled Suffolk sojourn.

Closely associated with the Aldeburgh composer Benjamin Britten – he designed the composer's memorial window at Aldeburgh's church – the artist John Piper was another regular visitor to the Suffolk coast, and it was here that he painted many of the region's churches, including those at Walberswick and Covehithe. Another Britten associate was Mary Potter, who lived in Aldeburgh for 30 years and whose paintings used an unusually restrained palette of pale and subtle colours.

Of contemporary Suffolk coastal artists, it is probably Maggi Hambling who stands out the most. Although best known for her controversial *Scallop* sculpture on Aldeburgh beach (page 58), Hambling has also produced many paintings that have been inspired by the coast near her home. The most striking of these is her series of *North Sea Paintings*, which depict dynamic breaking waves on the beaches of the Suffolk shore.

Work commenced in 1910, with a country club, a golf course and holiday homes in Tudor and Jacobean styles all appearing over the next decade or so. The village remained largely in the ownership of the Ogilvie family until 1972 when much of it was sold off to pay death duties.

The village's iconic landmark – it appears on Suffolk guidebooks as readily as Cley-next-the Sea's windmill does to represent Norfolk – is the **House in the Clouds**, a wooden house on a high, five-storey plinth.

The plinth was originally a disguised water tower but once mains water had been installed in the village it was converted into further living accommodation and a games room. You can rent it – very expensively. The views must be quite something. Thorpeness's other main sight is its artificial boating lake called **The Meare** that was inspired by *Peter Pan*, whose author J M Barrie was an Ogilvie family friend. A regatta takes place here each August in the week after Aldeburgh Carnival.

Whether you like Thorpeness or not tends to depend on your taste for mock Tudor. In some ways, the village has something of Portmeirion in Wales, albeit without the Italianate architecture and the cult appeal of the Portmeirion-set television series *The Prisoner*. Like that place, it feels rather like a film set, although Thorpeness is still waiting for the definitive film.

13 SNAPE, SNAPE MALTINGS & THE ALDE ESTUARY

Snape is a small village a few miles inland from Aldeburgh, close to the Alde estuary, although most people tend to think immediately of Snape Maltings at the head of the estuary itself. Snape village tends to get overlooked in favour of the retail and cultural opportunities on offer just down the road but it's certainly worth a mention in its own right. Surprisingly for a village of just a few hundred, Snape manages to support two dining pubs – The Crown and the Golden Key – although its proximity to the Maltings is a clearly a factor.

The four-panelled **village sign** depicting an Anglo-Saxon ship, a monk, a curlew and a bridge neatly summarises Snape's history. The ship is a reference to the site of an Anglo-Saxon ship burial discovered nearby, while the bridge depicts the old brick bridge that stood here over the River Alde until it was demolished in the 1960s. The praying monk is a reference to the Benedictine order that once had a priory here, and the curlew, a common-enough bird in these parts, is a nod to *Curlew River*, a work by Benjamin Britten, who drew much inspiration from the area.

Snape Maltings

The Maltings (✆ 01728 688303 ⊘ brittenpearsarts.org) are an impressive collection of shops and galleries converted from an assortment of Victorian riverside buildings. Malt production finally ceased here in 1965 and since then a slow restoration and conversion of the buildings has been taking place. A bespoke concert hall was built in 1967 and the slow process of conversion of the existing buildings has been taking place ever since. Currently, its businesses include craft shops, home and garden stores, restaurants, art galleries, jewellery and fashion, and even old-fashioned children's toys. Some buildings have been restored and converted for holiday or residential use. The concert hall, which serves as the centrepiece for the Aldeburgh Arts Festival, finds use all year round as a concert venue. It is a lovely venue, although as something of a cathedral in wood it can be uncomfortable if you are sitting for any length of time. It is probably best to do as Snape regulars do and bring your own cushion. The Maltings are also used as the venue for the annual Aldeburgh Food and Drink Festival. A **farmers' market** is held in the main car park here on the first Saturday of each month.

The Maltings sit in a superb natural environment that is virtually surrounded by reedbeds. The RSPB, which has an information centre here in the small Virginia-creeper-clad building by the quay, provides guided walks on Saturday mornings between May and July and also puts on a range of activities for children and families. Alternatively, you might prefer to strike out along a **riverside footpath**. One of these leads to the village of **Iken** and its isolated church on the south bank (the boat trip sails past here too), while another that links up with the Suffolk coast and Heath Path at Snape village leads north of the estuary along the **Sailors' Path** to Aldeburgh and the coast. **Canoeing** is a possibility too: there is a canoe and kayak hire place, Iken Canoe (✆ 07979 517186 ⌂ ikencanoe.co.uk ☉ Apr–Sep w/ends, Jul & Aug daily), at Iken Cliff close to the car park and picnic site. Walk right from the bottom of the car park and follow the river path to reach a green boatshed.

"It is a lovely venue, although as something of a cathedral in wood it can be uncomfortable."

St Botolph's Church, Iken

East of Snape Maltings, just north of the tiny village of Iken on the southern shore of the estuary stands St Botolph's Church, marked on the OS map as 'The Anchorage'. St Botolph's has an exquisite situation, isolated on a bluff above the water, suggesting that arrival by boat would make far more sense than coming by road. This ancient church, founded AD654, stands on a former site of an island and was likely built on the same site as St Botolph's 7th-century abbey. Inside this small flint, thatched church you can see a large stone Saxon cross, discovered in the wall of the church tower and carved with symbols associated with St Botolph. This dates from the 9th century and probably commemorates the destruction of the original monastery by marauding Vikings around AD870.

An awful lot of marauding went on along this coast in the past and Vikings always seemed to go about their duties with great gusto. Naturally enough, given the church's history as an early flag-bearer for Christianity in the region, this is a place of pilgrimage. Isolated geography has its part to play too and St Botolph's has pilgrimage written all over it (quite literally – even the church sign spells out 'St Botolphs Church Iken Welcomes Pilgrims').

Even without any interest in church architecture or history this is an undeniably magical spot – mysterious and charged by its sense of isolation at the edge of the world . . . or at least Suffolk. With the snaking channel of the River Alde threading through the glistening mudflats of the estuary below and the piping of redshanks and plaintive cry of curlews on the wind, it is a highly atmospheric setting. The gentle and comically hirsute Highland cattle that munch the grass in the field next door might seem a little incongruous elsewhere in Suffolk; here they just add to the tangible sense of otherworldliness.

"Isolated geography has its part to play too and St Botolph's has pilgrimage written all over it."

A couple of miles west of The Maltings lies the village of **Blaxhall**, where George Ewart Evans, author of *Ask the Fellows who Cut the Hay*, used to live; and where he did just that – ask the fellows – in the pursuit of oral history. The **Ship Inn** (✆ 01728 688316 ⬦ blaxhallshipinn. co.uk) has been an important place for local folk song and this tradition is continued to this day, with regular 'sing, say or pay' events and even the odd competition. John Seymour reported that here (in the 1960s) you could hear men sing folk songs like 'The Dark Eyed Sailor' and 'The Larks They Sang Melodious'. You still can, although nowadays you are just as likely to hear a local singer-songwriter airing their compositions.

Two Alde estuary walks

✳ OS Landranger map 156 or Explorer map 212; start: Snape Maltings car park,
♀ TM393574; 4½ miles to Iken church; 6 miles one-way on the Sailors' Path; both moderate

Snape Maltings to St Botolph's Church, Iken

The riverside walk to the church at Iken is about 4½ miles there and back and will take about two hours if you do not stop much. Obviously it is much better to take your time, enjoy the scenery and make enough allowance for a look around the church when you get there. Leave the Maltings' car park at the exit beyond the music-school building. Follow the footpath across farmland and then along a short piece of boardwalk through a reedbed. Continue through an area of saltmarsh that might possibly be flooded during very high tides (if this is the case – unlikely – you will have to wait a short while for the water to subside) then through a little more farmland to reach the Iken picnic site and car park where there's a wooden replica of the stone Saxon cross that you will soon be seeing in St Botolph's Church. Carry on along the riverside path, which might be muddy after wet weather, until you reach a minor road. Turn left and then, soon after, left again to follow the lane to its end at the church. Return the same way.

The Sailors' Path

This is a long walk – six miles one-way, 12 miles there and back – although you can always use the First Eastern Counties 65 bus service for the return leg to return back to Snape or Snape Maltings – it runs pretty much two-hourly throughout the day. The Sailors' Path is supposedly a historic commuting route between coastal Aldeburgh and Snape village. It was apparently also, as so many of these sort of things are claimed to be, a route once used by smugglers. Whatever the historical truth, the path is a lovely bracing walk through a variety of landscapes and in places provides excellent views over the marshes and estuary.

On the way you pass three sculptural installations by local artist Jonathan. These were installed in 2008 and have been left in situ to deteriorate naturally – the striking terracotta

▒ FOOD & DRINK

The Maltings complex has a couple of decent cafés like **Malt** for lunches, snacks, cakes and coffee, and **River View Café & Bar** for brunch, lunch and pre-concert dining, as well as the **Plough & Sail** pub (✆ 01728 688413 🖳 theploughandsailsnape.com), while the nearby village of Snape has two dining pubs both with good food (included here). There's also a food hall at The Maltings selling local produce and luxury food items. Blaxhall, a little west of

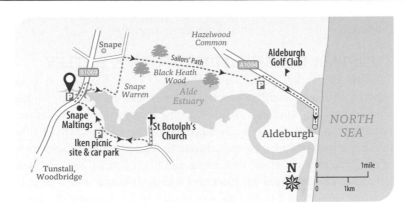

totem in Black Heath Wood that combines the pottery style of the Neolithic, Bronze Age, Iron Age, Roman and Saxon periods actually gets more beautiful with time and will probably last the longest. There are also listening posts installed along the way that give oral accounts of the history of the area.

Leave Snape Maltings by the main entrance and turn right to walk over the bridge. Turn right immediately after the bridge to follow the signed path. The path follows the edge of the estuary next to reedbeds for a while before turning a sharp left away from the water past **Snape Warren**, an expanse of heathland, to the right. This soon reaches a road corner on the edge of Snape village where you turn right and follow the track past cottages and asparagus fields to reach **Black Heath Wood**, an area of mature woodland with oak, Scots pine and birch trees. Leaving the wood behind continue over the boardwalk through a marshy area next to **Hazelwood Common** to reach another area of woodland with a derelict house and a gate and follow the waymarked path gently uphill past another isolated house to eventually reach a car park by a main road. Follow the footpath to the right of the road past Aldeburgh Golf Club on the left to arrive in Aldeburgh.

Snape Maltings has the **Ship Inn** (page 67), which as well as regular live music also has real ales and a restaurant serving good food made using fresh local ingredients.
Crown Inn Bridge Rd, Snape ✆ 01728 689112. This 15th-century Adnams inn is also a smallholding that raises all of its own livestock, so has menus that take advantage of very local meat as well as locally landed fish. There are Adnams ales and wines to choose from, and families and dog-walkers are most welcome.

Golden Key Priory Rd, Snape ✆ 01728 688510 ⌖ goldenkeysnape.co.uk. A 16th-century cottage-style pub in Snape village, close to The Maltings, which is run by the same team as at the Plough & Sail. Adnams ales and daily menus that feature an abundance of locally sourced produce. There is live acoustic music here too on some nights.

14 TUNSTALL FOREST, CHILLESFORD & BUTLEY

Tunstall Forest lies immediately south of Snape Maltings, a large expanse of mostly conifers planted in the 1920s on what previously would have been Sandlings Heath. Like the better-known Rendlesham Forest to the south, it was badly damaged by the Great Storm of 1987 but this at least provided an opportunity to replant with a wider variety of tree species than before. Woodlarks and nightjars can be found here by dedicated keen-eyed birdwatchers although scarce birds such as these are unlikely just to pop up on a branch in front of you. The forest rides are good for walks, although it is easy to get lost as with so many dense stands of conifers it all tends to look a bit the same. The forest is a popular haunt for mountain bikers too.

The village of **Chillesford** sits near the headwaters of the Butley River, a pleasant sleepy place with a church and a pub-restaurant The Froize (page 72) on a rare-for-these-parts bus route. The village lies on a meandering inland section of the Suffolk Coast Path and is also very close to the Sandlings Walk route between Ipswich and Southwold, so there are plenty of walking possibilities in

"The cracks in the wall are evidence of a tank-school accident in the 1940s."

its immediate vicinity. **St Peter's**, the village church, is distinguished by being only one of two churches in the country built from coralline crag, a fossilised shell-rich sandstone quarried in the area that glows a warm apricot in the late afternoon sun. The church also has some delightful modern stained-glass work by Suffolk artist Surinder Warboys. The other coralline crag church is just up the road at St John the Baptist's in the parish of **Wantisden**; this isolated building stands right next to the perimeter fence of the disused airfield at USAF Bentwaters, once home to a huge stockpile of nuclear warheads and one of the busiest military airbases in the world, a strange juxtaposition indeed. The church was enclosed by the military area until the 1950s when a new military fence put it outside the base. The cracks in the wall are evidence of a tank-school accident in the 1940s.

THE BLAXHALL STONE

At Stone Farm close to Blaxhall village stands a large boulder known as the Blaxhall Stone. The stone, a glacial erratic, was discovered in the 19th century when a local farmer struck it while ploughing a field. Like many large stones that have been shifted by ice to end up far from their geological homeland, this five-ton, 6½ft-long lump of sandstone has accrued myth and legend over the years.

The story goes that the Blaxhall Stone has been growing in size since it was first found and brought back to the farm. Legend tells of it starting out the size of a loaf of bread but of continually increasing in girth and weight ever since. Unfortunately, there is no photographic evidence of the stone's growing over the years to support such a belief.

Like any alien stone in a rockless landscape, the stone has long been an enigma, and before geological processes were understood the only explanation for such phenomena was something of supernatural original. George Ewart Evans, writing about the stone in his 1975 book *Ask the Fellows Who Cut the Hay*, suggests how this particular legend came about. 'Knowing nothing of prehistory and the ice sheet there was only one explanation short of the fantastic: the stone grew there.'

Truth be told, the stone's origin is actually in the Lincolnshire Wolds, where it existed perfectly peacefully for many millions of years before it was scooped up by ice and shifted south 150,000 years ago.

For more on Suffolk glacial erratics, see page 270.

Just south of here and a little way west of Chillesford is the small village of **Butley**, which was once home to an Augustinian priory founded in 1171. All that remains of it today is a highly impressive 14th-century gatehouse, which now provides the romantic setting for a wedding and events venue and an unusual and stylish holiday let. The village is also home to Butley Mill, now self-catering holiday apartments, and some converted 19th-century farm buildings that have now found use as artists' studios and workshops. The village also has a traditional pub, the Oyster Inn.

Just west of the village is **Staverton Park**, a hunting park dating from the 13th century that contains a large area of ancient woodland that has more than 4,000 magnificent pollarded oaks and extremely tall holly trees, some of the largest in the country, in a densely wooded area appropriately known as **The Thicks**. Staverton Park is privately owned but there is a footpath leading into The Thicks from the Butley to Woodbridge road.

¶¶ FOOD & DRINK

The Froize The Street, Chillesford ✆ 01394 450282 ⌂ froize.co.uk. En route to Orford, this remote village restaurant set in converted 18th-century keepers' cottages specialises in local game and retro rustic cooking served from an extensive buffet station. Adnams beer and Aspall's cider are on tap and there are excellent desserts too. The restaurant also holds regular Sunday folk music evenings as well as bookable workshops and guided wildlife walks that include breakfast or lunch.

High House Fruit Farm Sudbourne IP12 2BL ✆ 01394 450263 ⌂ high-house.co.uk. Pick your own soft fruit or buy ready-picked at this traditionally managed fruit farm just north of Orford. As well as asparagus and soft fruits, the farm has cherries and plums in summer and several heritage apple varieties in autumn. It also makes its own apple juice and preserves, and a holiday cottage is available to let.

15 ORFORD

⌂ **The Crown and Castle** (page 276)

Arriving at Orford's central square next to the church is a real pleasure, although there is little sense yet of being at the coast. For that, you will need to walk or drive the short distance down to the quay where all will be revealed.

Orford is very much a village of two halves: the village centre is a charming conglomeration of cottages around what was once a market square and hemmed in by the village church to the north and a 12th-century castle keep to the south. **St Bartholomew's Church** dates mostly from the 14th century, although there are traces of a Norman chancel. Of **Orford Castle**, which now belongs to English Heritage, only the keep remains but it is an impressive one and worth paying the entry fee just to climb up the spiral staircase for the view alone. Built by Henry II in 1165, at a time when they tended not to do things by halves, the keep has 10ft-thick walls and is 90ft high – a citadel that would be hard to breach with modern weaponry let alone longbows and maces. This, of course, is only a fraction of the fortifications that once stood here, which does raise the question as to what happened to all the stone that was shipped in to construct the original building.

Market Hill, around which much of the village clusters, is not much of a hill and no longer has a market but it's here you'll find a few shops,

1 Looking across the reeds towards Snape Maltings. **2** The House in the Clouds in Thorpeness. **3** Orford Castle. ▶

THESUFFOLKCOAST.CO.UK

MARK STAPLES

MARK STAPLES

An Orford stroll

✺ OS Landranger map 169 or Explorer map 212; start: Orford Quay, ♀ TM425495; 3 miles; easy

Oford village offers a plethora of walking opportunities. A good, short circular walk is to head south of the quay along the bank of the River Ore. Where the river wall turns sharp left, turn right off the bank, cross a wooden bridge and stile, then turn left through a wooden gate to reach a footpath by a ditch. Follow this through Chantry Marshes, bearing left at the sewage station, then right

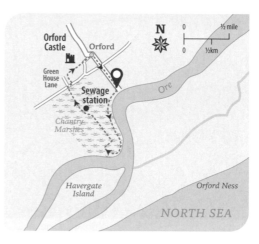

along a wider track. Arriving at a tarmac road turn right and then left along a footpath after passing the entrance to Green House Lane. Continue past Chantry Cottage and turn right to reach Orford Castle and the village centre a little way beyond.

the town hall and the post office. There's a trio of narrow alleyways leading off Market Hill that connect with Broad Street; along the one next to Butley Orford Oysterage (see opposite) you'll find the **Butley Orford Oysterage Shop** (✆ 01394 459183 � pinneysoforford.co.uk) where there is all manner of fresh and smoked fish and naturally, ultra-fresh oysters. The oysterage itself has a sign depicting a merman, which relates to the tale of a wild man-like creature that turned up in someone's fishing nets in the 12th century. In good medieval fashion, the poor creature was tortured but did not, or could not, talk and eventually managed to escape back to sea.

A five-minute stroll along Quay Street brings you to a large car park opposite the **Jolly Sailor** pub and then the **Quay**. Suddenly it becomes maritime, with sailing dinghies bobbing around on the river. The village, like many others on this seaboard, was once a thriving port but the growth of **Orford Ness**, the huge sand spit opposite, eventually denied Orford its ready access to the sea. However, judging by the number of yachts and pleasure boats here, the river seems a perfectly acceptable substitute for most modern-day sailors. There's not much else: a small National Trust shed selling tickets for the ferry across to the Ness, Brinkley's shed selling wet fish and, next door, a tea room. There's no electricity so Mrs Brinkley keeps her fish on ice – she has cod, skate and sea bass, or at least that was what she had on the day when I visited. 'There's just two boats that fish from here these days – us and another boat,' she told me. 'My husband catches the fish and I clean and sell it, so we do alright together.'

⫶ FOOD & DRINK

Orford is very much on the Suffolk gastronomic map these days, having several places where a memorable meal might be had, particularly if seafood is involved.

Butley Orford Oysterage Market Hill ✆ 01394 450277 ⌂ pinneysoforford.co.uk. This long-popular seafood restaurant serves Orford-caught fish landed by its own small fishing fleet and oysters grown at nearby Butley Creek. The restaurant interior is nothing fancy, plain even, but the delicious, unpretentious fish dishes are superb.

Crown and Castle Hotel ✆ 01394450205 ⌂ crownandcastle.co.uk. This stylish 'restaurant with rooms' in the shadow of Orford Castle serves well-cooked locally sourced dishes from an imaginative à la carte menu in its restaurant. See page 276.

Jolly Sailor Inn Quay St ✆ 01394 450243 ⌂ jollysailororford.co.uk. Just before Orford Quay, opposite the town car park, this traditional 17th-century Adnams inn has two cosy nautical-themed bars, good honest home-cooked food (the 'best cod and chips in Suffolk' according to the Ramblers, or so it says on the sign outside the pub) and a beer garden.

Riverside Tearoom Orford Quay ✆ 01394 459797 ⌂ riversidetearoomorford.co.uk. This is a good place for tea and scones while waiting for the ferry to Orford Ness. There's an outside sun terrace overlooking the River Ore.

16 ORFORD NESS

Quay Office, Orford Quay, Orford IP12 2NU ✆ 01728 648024 ☉ Jul–Sep 10.00–17.00 Tue, Thu, Sat & Sun, Apr–Jun & Oct 10.00–17.00 Sat & Sun only; National Trust

If you are not at Orford Quay for the sailing, your eyes will no doubt be drawn across the water to Orford Ness, which exudes an air of mystery typical of places associated with forbidden territory. From 1913 to the mid-1980s, the spit was firmly closed to the public, a top secret, no-go area dedicated to military testing and radar research. The links with its secret past are part of its appeal; otherwise, it's undeniable that Orford Ness is quite a remarkable bit of topography.

Though hardly pretty, this long shingle spit is undoubtedly evocative. Signs warn about unexploded ordnance, and everywhere you'll see tangles of tortured metal and wire netting among the teasels in the shingle. Overall, it's a rather melancholy landscape and you might begin to wonder if Orford Ness should actually be 'orfordness', a state of mind, rather than the name of a wayward landform. Of course, I am not the first to note the singularity of the place, nor will I be the last – in 2012, writer Robert MacFarlane was commissioned to write a libretto for a work titled *Untrue Island*, a performance piece combining sculpture, narration, music and real-time sounds that was performed on location at Orford Ness in July of that year. The Ness also appeared on the television series *Coast* around that time too and so the 'little known' cliché does not apply quite as much as it once did. An impressive number of art projects have taken place on the Ness in recent years, including the play *Anglia Mist* in 2017, a place-specific psychological thriller about hidden secrets, dark conspiracies and spies by the Stuff of Dreams Theatre Company. Despite receiving far more media attention these days than it ever did previously the place retains its magic and still keeps its secrets close to its chest.

To get to Orford Ness, you must take the National Trust boat. The *Octavia* runs across to Orford Ness roughly every 20 minutes between 10.00 and 14.00, with the last boat back around 17.00. 'Please don't miss the last boat back,' the NT boatman will inevitably warn you. 'It gets pretty nippy out there at night and there's only one loo for the whole of the spit.'

Seen from Orford Quay, Orford Ness has the appearance of being an island – it is often referred to as 'The Island' by locals. The ferry trip across the River Ore simply adds to this impression, but it's not an island – it's actually a long sand spit that begins just south of Aldeburgh and gradually widens as it follows the coast south. It is the largest vegetated shingle spit in Europe (nearly ten miles long) and it is only when you disembark at the jetty that you can really appreciate the scale of the place. The National Trust has a number of recommended waymarked

"Everywhere you'll see tangles of tortured metal and wire netting among the teasels in the shingle."

routes to follow but the reality is that you won't see much unless you are prepared to walk some distance. Concrete roads lead around the spit and you have to trudge along these some way before you get to see anything of much interest. Bicycles are not permitted.

The Red Trail leads along the road and across a central dyke to the Bomb Ballistic Building, where you can climb to the roof terrace and survey the surroundings. A track leads across from here to the shoreline, where there are some ruined, boarded-up buildings next to the pile of rubble that once was the lighthouse. From here, you can walk along the shingle as far as the Police Tower, where another track leads to Lab 1, the first of the military 'pagodas' that are clearly visible from the mainland.

If post-apocalyptic landscapes are not your thing then you'd be better off choosing the Green Trail and concentrating on the **wildlife**. You might be lucky enough to see porpoises out to sea from the beach where the lighthouse used to stand (someone had done so the day before my visit) but you are more likely to spot gulls and terns, and nervous rabbits and hares flitting across the shingle. As well as birds galore there are several plant species adapted to this harsh environment that you should look out for, like yellow-horned poppy and sea pea, both shingle specialists. The hares here tend to be larger and chubbier than those on the mainland, although perhaps this may just be a trick of perspective in such an open environment – they really do look big. There are Chinese water deer too, and predatory birds like peregrine and marsh harrier. The Green Trail follows a circuit around King's Marshes on the landward side of the spit, where you should find plenty of waders feeding in the pools and lagoons. You could just about do both Red and Green trails if you came across on an early boat but you would have to get a move on, as that would constitute a total walk of around ten miles.

"You might be lucky enough to see porpoises out to sea from the beach where the lighthouse used to stand."

For me, the appeal of Orford Ness is to experience its otherworldly isolation and imagine (incorrectly) that I have the place to myself, alone at the edge of the world. More gregarious visitors might want to avail themselves of the various **tours** that take place on certain summer weekends – the 'Bombs and Beasties' guided tour is a good one that is quite self-explanatory. For those not able or willing to walk far, occasional tours take visitors across the spit by tractor bus although these do not visit the pagodas. You can take a photography guided tour too – Orford Ness is enormously photogenic. It is just a shame that the iconic red-banded lighthouse no longer stands – the 100-year-old structure was pre-emptively destroyed in 2020 because of sea erosion. All of these tours should be booked in advance; precise dates are given on the NT website or you can phone for bookings (✆ 01394 450900). The 'Island' is also an important place for bird migration and if so inclined you can observe migrants close up on designated 'Bird Ringing Mornings' in autumn.

Havergate Island, Suffolk's only island and an RSPB reserve, lies a little further south between Orford Ness and the mainland. The island can only be accessed by pre-booked boat trips (details from RSPB Minsmere ✆ 01728 648281) from Orford Quay, leaving at 10.00 on the first Saturday of every month except May–July. As well as the breeding avocets for which the island is well known, other birds that are regularly seen here include terns, owls, ducks and a broad range of waders. Seals are also sometimes seen in the River Ore here.

SOUTH OF ORFORD

To reach Shingle Street, the next settlement south along the Suffolk coast, requires a diversion inland from Orford around the River Butley via Chilesford and Butley. A minor road skirts Rendlesham Forest to reach Hollesley, with its HM Young Offenders Institution, before the road peters out completely at Shingle Street. Walkers can take a more direct route by way of **Butley Ferry** (✆ 07913 672499), where a boat will ferry you across the Butley River from where you can follow the Suffolk Coast Path south along the bank of the River Ore. The ferry is reached by following a minor road southwest of Orford past Gedgrave Hall and then following the waymarks to the river. Butley Ferry, which claims to be the smallest licensed ferry in Europe, operates between Easter Saturday and mid October, 11.00–16.00, at weekends and on bank holidays.

17 RENDLESHAM FOREST

Rendlesham Forest is a vast coniferous expanse with a smattering of picnic places and forest walks. Gnarled old Scots pines scratch at the sky but plenty of plantations are relatively new, planted to replace the losses brought about by the October 1987 storm that wreaked havoc across southern England. I visited the area just after the event and I remember being shocked by the extent of the damage: huge shattered trunks, branches split like matchwood – the aftermath of the sort of extreme weather event that we are not supposed to experience in mild, moderate Britain.

The forest has experienced even stranger events than this if you can believe all that you hear. The so-called **Rendlesham Forest Incident** occurred over three successive nights during Christmas 1980, and was probably the most publicised example of a UFO incident ever to have occurred in the UK. It involved a series of unexplained sightings of lights and even the alleged landing of an alien spacecraft in the forest. There were two airbases in the area at the time, RAF Bentwaters and RAF Woodbridge, both of which were being used by the US Air Force. Although witnesses of the event were encouraged to believe that the pulsating lights they witnessed were simply those of Orford Lighthouse, there were those who insisted that they had seen a conical metallic object landing in a forest clearing. As with all events of this sort, the incident provided fertile ground for conspiracy theorists and the Ministry of Defence was accused of engineering

"Gnarled old Scots pines scratch at the sky but plenty of plantations are relatively new."

a news cover-up after the event. The incident did not make national news until three years later when the *News of the World* published the story beneath the headline: 'UFO lands in Suffolk – and that's official'. For those intrigued by these extra-terrestrial claims, the Forestry Commission (∂ forestry.gov.uk) has helpfully marked a three-mile 'UFO Trail' for walkers that begins at the **Rendlesham Forest Centre** and includes the main locations of the incident (two bicycle trails are marked from here too). Inevitably there's plenty more on the internet if you are interested.

A little more prosaically, but only just, Rendlesham has made the news more recently following the discovery of what is believed to be the remains of a 7th-century Anglo-Saxon royal palace in the area. It has been suggested that this may be the palace of King Raedwald, who is believed to have been buried at Sutton Hoo just four miles away.

Rendlesham Forest provides important habitat for woodlarks and nightjars – 20% of the national breeding population of the former and 10% of the latter – and three types of deer, as well as badgers and adders.

18 SHINGLE STREET

This really does feel like the end of the road. On a blustery winter's night, it probably seems like the end of the world. There's really not much to Shingle Street: a row of coastguard cottages and holiday lets, a phone box, a car park and an awful lot of shingle. It does have a certain rather desolate charm; the beach is more or less empty, with wonderful views north towards Orford Ness and the mouth of the River Ore. At the southern end of this short strip of beachside houses stands a Martello tower, and you can see three more of them looking south from here framed by the distant silhouettes of Scots pines. There's virtually nothing else along this coast until you reach the Deben River estuary with Felixstowe sitting on its opposite bank. Standing on the shingle here with the coast curving south to vanishing point it seems hard to believe that Ipswich is only a dozen miles away.

"This really does feel like the end of the road. On a blustery winter's night, it probably seems like the end of the world."

Shingle Street was once a little livelier than it is today: a small fishing village and coastguard station that was home to River Ore river pilots. Unlikely as it may seem, there used to be a pub here too, the Lifeboat Inn, but this met an ignominious end during World War II when it was used for target practice for a newly developed bomb from Porton Down. At least the authorities were decent enough to evacuate the village first. Shingle Street was in fact emptied of its entire population in 1940 and this lasted for the duration of the war. Its fishing boats were destroyed at the same time and the village never recovered as a viable fishing centre, even after its people were allowed back at the end of the war. Many did not bother to return.

Various conspiracies were hatched during the wartime period (perhaps this should be renamed the Conspiracy Coast given how far-fetched tales bordering on the supernatural seem to inhabit the landscape between the Alde and Deben estuaries?). There were lurid accounts of an abortive German landing and of a beach littered with burning bodies, rumours of the testing of experimental chemical bombs and of the sea being set ablaze to repel invaders.

Such rumours, most of them anyway, were later proved to be false but stories like these may well have been encouraged during the war years for purposes of propaganda. The destruction of the pub is certainly true, as is the fact that the bodies of four German airmen were washed up on the beach sometime during World War II.

Leaving Shingle Street, if you want to keep going as far as the River Deben, you'll need to retrace your steps back to Hollesley (pronounced 'Hosely') then head south through Alderton to Bawdsey and then Bawdsey Manor, where there's a passenger ferry across the estuary mouth to Felixstowe. The **Suffolk Coast and Heaths Path** goes this way too, clomping along the shore south from Shingle Street, across the Deben by way of the ferry then past another two Martello towers before reaching the outskirts of the town that is home to Britain's largest container port, **Felixstowe** (page 130).

Nearby **Hollesley** is home to a Category D prison and a Young Offenders Institution. The prison once had the largest prison farm in Britain and was also home to the oldest established stud of Suffolk Punch horses, which were put on display periodically at various county and national shows. The stud has since been sold to the Suffolk Punch Trust (see below), a delightful charity institution that welcomes visitors.

The Suffolk Punch Trust

Sink Farm, St David's Ln, Hollesley IP12 3JR ℰ 01394 411327 ⌂ thesuffolkpunchtrust.org
☉ Apr–Sep Wed–Mon in school holidays inc half term; autumn Fri–Mon; winter w/ends for visitor centre & café only

Although this is a working stud farm, you can visit the stables here and meet the horses as well as get a look at rare breeds of farm animals like black pigs, Red Poll cattle, Suffolk sheep and Ixworth chickens. There's a heritage museum too, where you can find out about the history of the Suffolk Punch breed, and a barn full of various horse-drawn vehicles and cultivating equipment. Three waymarked circular walks around the farm enable you to see the horses and livestock in their 'natural' environment, while a range of hands-on stuff for children includes stable

"Three waymarked circular walks around the farm enable you to see the horses and livestock in their 'natural' environment."

demonstrations, milking a Jersey cow and various horse-related art and craft activities. The licensed café, which serves snacks and light lunches made using Suffolk ingredients wherever possible, has an outdoor terrace and picnic area and makes for a good lunch stop in a corner of Suffolk that offers few alternative refreshment possibilities.

MARK STAPLES

RMC42/S

SIMON COLLINS/S

19 BAWDSEY & BAWDSEY QUAY

🏠 **The Found** (page 276)

The village of **Bawdsey**, a few miles south of Shingle Street and Hollesley, has little to offer other than easy access to the coast – there is a conveniently situated car park immediately east of the village close to a Martello tower. The car park, located next to a World War II gun emplacement and four rectangular ponds filled with wildfowl, is a good setting-off point for walks along the coast, either north to Shingle Street or south to Bawdsey Quay. Looking north, Martello towers dot the coast at regular intervals, the third that you can see marking the location of Shingle Street, just a low line of cottages peering through the haze. This makes for a fine two-mile walk along a raised bank between sea and marshes, with the added interest of the Martello towers as you pass them by. In this minimalist landscape of sea, marsh and sky, you are unlikely to see many people, even in high summer. The fact that the country's largest container port lies a just a few miles south seems highly improbable until you catch a glimpse of a container ship out at sea, Felixstowe-bound. Walking south in the direction of Bawdsey Quay, it is necessary to head inland for a dog-leg around Bawdsey as the original coast path has eroded away in recent years. So, instead of crunching through pebbles on a shingle beach, take the minor road that leads past Bawdsey Hall (follow the Suffolk Coast Path waymark signs as this is now the official route of the long distance path).

"In this minimalist landscape of sea, marsh and sky, you are unlikely to see many people, even in high summer."

A little way short of Bawdsey Quay is **Bawdsey Manor**, a strikingly odd Victorian Gothic building with Tudor-style chimney pots and a dragon weathervane. The eccentricity of the manor's architecture reflects the taste of its first owner, Sir William Cuthbert Quilter MP, a landowner, stockbroker, art collector and member for Sudbury in the late 19th century. Quilter was also a real ale aficionado it would seem, owning several breweries, and he once spoke on the subject of beer purity in Parliament, one of only two occasions on which he stood up to speak during his entire political career.

◀ **1** Bawdsey Manor. **2** A walk in Rendlesham Forest. **3** Ramsholt Church.

The manor came into the ownership of the Ministry of Defence just before World War II when it soon saw new life as a top-secret radar research centre, the first of its kind in the world. The manor came into private ownership once more in 1994 and was sold again in 2017 to become a children's outdoor adventure centre. The Transmitter Block of the former radar station, a concrete bunker tucked secretively away behind Bawdsey Manor, now serves as a museum managed by **Bawdsey Radar** (✆ 07821 162879 ⌂ bawdseyradar.org.uk).

"This was once a much busier place and in the early 20th century a steam-drawn chain ferry used to operate here."

Just beyond Bawdsey Hall, on the north bank of the River Deben where it flows into the sea at Woodbridge Haven, **Bawdsey Quay** really is the end of the road, a long meandering road at that. If you are on foot or bicycle you can cross the river here over to **Felixstowe Ferry**. The ferry (✆ 07709 411511 or 01394 282173 ☉ May–Sep daily; Easter–end Apr & Oct w/ends) is now just a boat and you'll need to attract the attention of the skipper if they are on the opposite bank.

This was once a much busier place and in the early 20th century a steam-drawn chain ferry used to operate here, the brainchild of Sir William Cuthbert Quilter from Bawdsey Manor who was keen to establish a reliable connection with Felixstowe. The chain ferry was replaced by a launch in 1931 but the service was closed to the public during World War II when Bawdsey Manor served as a radar research centre. The ferry was contracted to RAF Bawdsey from the end of the war until 1974, since when it has become a privately operated summer-only service.

¶¶ FOOD & DRINK

Boathouse Café The Quay, Bawdsey ✆ 07900 811826 ⌂ boathousecafebawdsey.co.uk ☉ May–Oct daily, Nov Fri–Sun. Right by the quay, with a veranda overlooking the River Deben, this is ideally situated for a drink or snack before or after taking the ferry. It has soups and sandwiches, cakes and scones baked on the premises, locally caught crabs and smoked prawns from the smokehouse just across the river.

20 RAMSHOLT

On the east shore of the River Deben, halfway between Woodbridge and Bawdsey Quay lies Ramsholt, less a village and more a thin scattering of isolated farmhouses and barns. Other than some gorgeous coastal scenery, there are just two attractions here: a highly unusual church and an idyllically situated riverside pub. The only way to get here, other than by boat, is by way of the road from Shottisham, a village midway between Woodbridge and Bawdsey. The narrow road makes several 90-degree shifts of direction as it zigzags around the field boundaries on its way to the river. Eventually an even narrower road signposted 'church' leads off to the right. This road – grass growing in the middle, sand spilling over it in places – leads up to All Saints' Church. You can either take this and park by the church or continue a little further and take the next right turn to reach the pub and car park, from where you can follow a bridleway from the river across marshes to the church, a distance of about three-quarters of a mile. There again, you could just grab an outside table at the Ramsholt Arms and watch the boats bob up and down on the Deben as you sip your beer. You could, but you'd be missing something.

All Saints' Church is one of 38 round-tower churches in Suffolk – you'll find a lot more in Norfolk – but the thing is it does not really look round-towered on first inspection. This is because the tower has buttresses to shore it up giving it more the oval profile of an old-fashioned medicine bottle. The church is mostly Norman but the base of the tower is probably older and of Saxon origin. The base of the oatmeal-coloured tower is of unusual material too, constructed of septaria, a brown mudstone obtained from the foreshore – one of the materials used to construct Orford Castle further up the coast.

"The churchyard offers a splendid viewpoint over the tops of pines to the River Deben with its hundreds of boats below."

The churchyard offers a splendid viewpoint over the tops of pines to the River Deben with its hundreds of boats below, and across the peninsula to the clustered cranes of Felixstowe Port scratching the sky in the distance. Perhaps it is the presence of these giant tools of modern-day commerce that makes this spot so special – the juxtaposition of a distant view of industry and a tangible sense of the ancient where you stand. Ramsholt was probably a sizeable settlement in medieval times but now, with the exception of the pub and a few cottages and farm buildings, the church is all that remains. The silence here has its role to play too: this is rural tranquillity writ large. Enjoy it while you can as things might not be quite so peaceful down at the shore; it rather depends on how many groups of yachty types have descended on the Ramsholt Arms seeking an outside table and dinners all round.

¶¶ FOOD & DRINK

Ramsholt Arms Dock Rd, Ramsholt ✆ 01394 411209 ⌂ theramsholtarms.com. The only south-facing pub on the river, the terrace here is understandably popular in summer, especially with the sailing set. Offering plenty of locally sourced seafood mains, Sunday roasts and share platters for two, this has what might best be described as posh pub grub.

FIVE ACRE BARN

PHOTOS © BEN MOSTYN

"With adventurous contemporary architecture, cool styling and a warm welcome, this is a chic alternative to Suffolk's many old-fashioned, chintzy B&Bs"

British Boltholes, *The Guardian*

Five Acre Barn
Aldeburgh Road, Leiston,
IP16 4QH

⌂ fiveacrebarn.co.uk
▣ fiveacrebarn
✆ 07595 328529

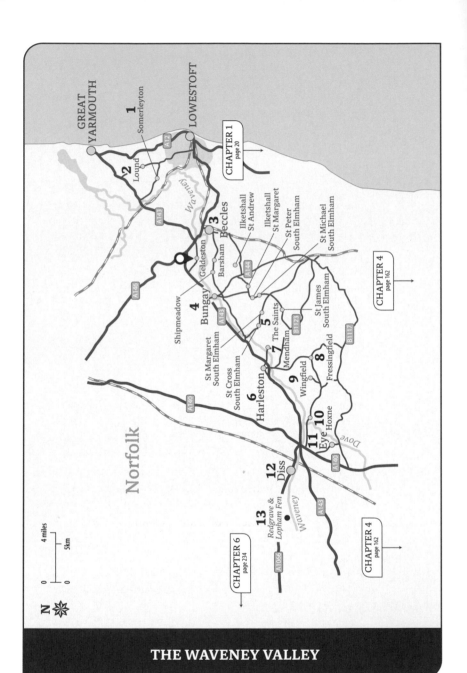

THE WAVENEY VALLEY

2

THE WAVENEY
VALLEY

Two rivers separate Suffolk from Norfolk, its northern neighbour. In the west, the Little Ouse River forms a natural boundary between the two counties, while in the centre and east the River Waveney defines the border. The Waveney's source lies between the villages of Redgrave in Suffolk and South Lopham in Norfolk, close to where the Little Ouse also rises. From its humble origins in Redgrave Fen, the river flows east through the small towns of Diss (Norfolk), Bungay and Beccles (Suffolk) before looping north around Lowestoft to join the River Yare at Breydon Water and eventually go to sea at Great Yarmouth. East of Bungay, the river lies within the boundary of the Broads Authority and is connected to Oulton Broad just west of Lowestoft by an artificial channel, Oulton Dyke. The only deviation that the county boundary makes from the river is between Great Yarmouth and Lowestoft, just north of Somerleyton where, instead of continuing north to reach Breydon Water, it veers east through Fritton Lake to reach the North Sea at Hopton-on–Sea. The reason for this anomalous diversion from the natural river boundary is administrative. It is also a relatively recent departure from topographic common sense – more on this later (page 95).

Not that the Waveney forms an impenetrable barrier: the river is more of a conduit than anything, with plenty of bridges spanning it, especially in its western reaches. The Waveney Valley may not be much of a valley in physical terms but it does have a personality all of its own that is distinct from the rest of the county. I've crossed the county boundary here and there in this chapter, and so both Diss and Harleston are included despite belonging to Norfolk.

A sense of cosy isolation characterises the Waveney Valley, as south Norfolk eases into the clay country of north Suffolk. Here there are fewer big estates, and more commons, ancient hedgerows and moated farmhouses; more meandering tracks that seem to follow every field boundary before ending up nowhere in particular. There has probably been less change over the past 50 years in this region than anywhere else in southern England. Unlike other parts of Suffolk, the area is not a place that tends to lure incomers, downsizers or weekenders. The Waveney Valley has a different kind of draw. Those that have settled here have generally become more integrated into the existing community. It has long attracted artists, writers and craftspeople and there was a noticeable, if small-scale, invasion of folk escaping the city for something simpler and more wholesome back in the 1970s – they, and their children and grandchildren, are mostly still here.

A surprising number of artists work from the towns and villages of the valley. Constable and Gainsborough may have immortalised the Stour Valley further south on the Essex border but that just happened to be where they lived. It might just as easily have been the Waveney Valley. To quote author and pioneer of sustainable living John Seymour: 'If John Constable had been born at Harleston, instead of at East Bergholt, we would have processions of motor coaches along the Waveney instead of along the Stour.' As for more contemporary local artists, perhaps Mary Newcomb (1922–2008) is the most representative for her innocent, yet evocative, vignettes of country life – not exclusively featuring the Waveney Valley but certainly evoking its spirit.

Several well-known writers are or have been based here too. Roger Deakin, who used to live in the village of Mellis just south of Diss, chronicled the changes of the season in *Notes from Walnut Tree Farm* and to a lesser extent in *Wildwood*, while nature writer Richard Mabey moved to the area over a decade ago and his Waveney Valley home features prominently in his book *Nature Cure*. Louis 'Captain Corelli's Mandolin' de Bernières has settled near Bungay, and W G Sebald in *The Rings of Saturn*, his meandering introspective walk through a rather sombre Suffolk, spent enough time in the Waveney Valley to be spectacularly rude about a small hotel in Harleston just over the Norfolk border.

It's easy to get carried away of course. Like everywhere else, there's an element of reactionary nimbyism here on occasion – the greatest fears seemingly being the provision of caravan sites for travellers and windfarms – but overall, it's pretty welcoming and lacking the self-satisfaction sometimes found in higher-profile parts of the county. The keywords here are probably 'self-contained' and 'authentic': real places with real shops serving real people. This chapter begins close to the mouth of the River Waveney at Somerleyton and slowly works its way upstream to end at Diss, just across the border in Norfolk and the urban centre for the west of the valley.

GETTING AROUND

Making your way along the Waveney Valley is easy enough. The main towns and villages are linked by the A143 that runs from Bury St Edmunds to Great Yarmouth. From its Suffolk beginning, the road crosses the county boundary at Diss and continues along the Norfolk side of the river as it heads towards the coast, apart from a brief detour into Bungay on the Suffolk bank. For motorists, it's a convenient way of speeding east or west but the minor roads that thread through the valley are infinitely more enjoyable. Thankfully – and sensibly – the buses that run along the valley avoid the A143 for the most part, preferring to detour through the villages where most of their passengers live.

PUBLIC TRANSPORT

This could be better; there again, it could be worse. Diss has a regular **train** service to Norwich as it lies on the main Norwich–London line. Regular trains also run between Norwich and Lowestoft, from where the East Suffolk Line (⊘ eastsuffolklines.co.uk) to Ipswich passes through Oulton Broad and Beccles. **Bus** transport is somewhat restricted but reasonable enough in daylight hours, with buses running along most of the length of the valley. The Borderbus (⊘ 01502 714565 ⊘ border-bus. co.uk) 524 service runs twice a day between Beccles and Halesworth during working hours, Monday to Friday (excluding bank holidays), and the Borderbus 146 between Norwich, Beccles and Southwold has six services on weekdays and more on a Saturday. Simonds (⊘ 01379 647300 ⊘ simonds.co.uk) bus service 581 runs several times a day between Beccles and Diss via Bungay and Harleston.

Surprisingly, perhaps, the Waveney Valley has better connections to Norwich than it has to Ipswich, the latter always requiring at least one change and usually a considerable detour via Diss or Lowestoft. The Norwich to Lowestoft First Eastern Counties services X2 and X22 connect Norwich to Beccles with at least half-hourly buses through the day Monday to Saturday and hourly on Sundays. The First Eastern Counties 40, 41 and X41 services connect Norwich to Bungay with half-hourly buses during working hours, Monday to Saturday, and the 99A service connects Bungay with Halesworth and Southwold. Simonds bus services 110 and 112 connect Diss with Eye eight times a day on weekdays, connecting with the 113 and 114 services that continues to Ipswich via Debenham at approximately hourly intervals during working hours Monday to Friday. A less frequent service runs on Saturdays.

CYCLING

If you want to use muscle power alone, there is plenty of potential for cycling in the Waveney Valley, although you will want to avoid the A143 wherever possible. Otherwise, there are lots of quiet country roads and tracks to explore. You can **hire** a bike at Hipperson's Boatyard (✆ 01502 712166 ⊘ hippersons.co.uk) in Beccles, at Outney Meadow Caravan Park (✆ 01986 892388 ⊘ outneymeadow.co.uk) near Bungay and at Martha's Cottage Cycle Hire, The Green, Barnby, Beccles (✆ 01502 476789). Visit Waveney Valley (⊘ visitwaveneyvalley.co.uk) has several suggested cycling routes that can be downloaded from the website. These include a 19-mile loop from Beccles that can be extended to Halesworth and Southwold, a 13-mile 'Brewery Tour' that takes in Bungay and Homersfield, and a 16-mile route through 'The Saints', south of Bungay. **Sustrans Regional Route 30**, which begins at Ten Mile Bank in the Fens, runs along the river to Lowestoft by way of Diss, Bungay and Beccles.

BY WATER

Transport by **boat** is an option east of Geldeston, which is the limit of navigation for motorboats a little way upstream from Beccles. Day boats are for hire at Beccles and Oulton Broad and there is scope for **canoeing** too, although the river is noticeably tidal east of Beccles. A canoeing route recommended by the Upper Waveney Valley Project is the 20-mile section of the river between Brockdish, west of Harleston, and Ellingham Weir, east of Bungay. Canoe hire is possible in Bungay at Outney Meadow Caravan Park (✆ 01986 892338 ⊘ outneymeadow. co.uk), and at the Waveney Valley Centre (✆ 01502 677343 ⊘ waveneyrivercentre.co.uk) on the Norfolk bank of the river at Burgh

i **TOURIST INFORMATION**

Beccles Visitor Information Point Beccles Library, 32 Blyburgate ✆ 01502 523442

Broads ⌂ broads-authority.gov.uk

Bungay Visitor Information Point Bungay Library, Wharton St ✆ 01502 523442

Diss Tourist Information Centre 10 St Nicholas St ✆ 01379 652241

Harleston Visitor Information Point 8 Exchange St ✆ 01379 851917

Visit Waveney Valley ⌂ visitwaveneyvalley.co.uk

St Peter. Another place for canoe hire is the The Canoe Man at Beccles Lido (⌂ thecanoeman.co.uk/beccles-hires). Contact the Waveney Valley Canoe Club (⌂ waveneyvalleycanoeclub.org) for further advice. For a less energetic way of viewing the river, short daily tours of the River Waveney aboard the *Waveney Princess* are available in season with Waveney River Tours (✆ 01502 574903 ⌂ waveneyrivertours. com) at Oulton Broad.

WALKING

The Waveney Valley is a fine place for walking and there's a wide choice of lovely walks to be had, particularly alongside the river itself. Most villages lie close enough to one another for decent circular walks to be possible and with such quiet back roads even road walking is a pleasure. The **Angles Way** long-distance route threads its way along the valley between Breckland and Lowestoft; eastwards from Beccles it follows the riverbank – the best option is to walk the nine miles from there to Oulton Broad South station and get the train back to Beccles. Maps for some suggested walks in and around the Waveney Valley can be downloaded from the Visit Waveney Valley website.

LOTHINGLAND: SOMERLEYTON & AROUND

The River Waveney has its confluence with the River Yare at the estuary of Breydon Water at Burgh Castle in Norfolk, from where it flows into the North Sea at Great Yarmouth. This upstream section now belongs to Norfolk but south of St Olaves it is the river that defines the boundary between Norfolk and Suffolk. Somerleyton is a little further south.

1 SOMERLEYTON

🏠 **Fritton Lake Woodland Lodges** (page 277)

Somerleyton lies on the Suffolk side of the river in the far north of the county. The village is home to **Somerleyton Hall** and although relatively remote is blessed with a very convenient stop on the Norwich to Lowestoft Wherry Line railway. Somerleyton is very much an attractive model village with estate houses, railway station, primary school and combined shop and post office all built in the mid 19th century in the same retro-Tudor style by the millionaire eccentric Samuel Morton Peto, the man responsible for rebuilding Somerleyton Hall. It was Peto who brought the railway to the village, a fortunate survivor of the Beeching cuts of the 1960s, and it was he who also rebuilt the village's then derelict church of St Mary's although you would hardly know it from the outside as he was fairly faithful to its original 15th-century style. The hall and gardens are the obvious draw here but there are good walks to be had too – the Angles Way passes close to the hall and through the village.

"The hall and gardens are the obvious draw here but there are good walks to be had too."

Fritton Lake Outdoor Centre (𝄐 01493 484008 ⊘ frittonlake. co.uk) within the grounds of Fritton Lake Retreats Resort, with its lush wooded shoreline, offers open water swimming and bikes and rowing boats for hire. The centre lies just to the north of the estate straddling the county border just off the A143 between Beccles and Great Yarmouth.

Somerleyton Hall & Gardens

Somerleyton Hall, Lovingland NR32 5QF 𝄐 01502 734901 ⊘ somerleyton.co.uk ⊙ house & gardens mid-Apr–late Oct Tue, Thu, Sun & bank holidays, July & Aug also Wed

Owned by the Crossley family who have lived here since the 1860s, this magnificent remodelled Tudor–Jacobean stately home has much to admire – an entrance hall clad in carved oak with marble panels, a ballroom decorated in crimson damask, a large elegant library and a dining room hung with oil paintings. The extensive gardens are equally impressive, and contain a walled garden with an ornate iron and glass greenhouse designed by Joseph Paxton, the architect of the Crystal Palace, and a yew-hedge maze planted in 1846.

¶| FOOD & DRINK

Duke's Head Slug's Ln, Somerleyton ✆ 01502 730281 🖉 dukes-head.co.uk. Popular with boating folk, this red-brick pub five minutes' walk from the river has Suffolk real ales and a menu featuring seasonal fresh ingredients sourced from Somerleyton Estate's own farm and other farms in the locality. The beer garden overlooks the Waveney River.

2 LOUND

East of Somerleyton is Lound, a small village with a duck pond, a church and the Mardle Café, an ideal place to stop if walking in the area. Lound has the interesting Anglo-Catholic **round tower church** of St John the Baptist. There seems to be a concentration of round tower churches on both sides of the Norfolk–Suffolk border in this neck of the woods. Others may be found nearby at Blundeston (fictional birthplace of Charles Dickens's *David Copperfield*), Herringfleet, Belton, Burgh Castle and Fritton, the last three now in Norfolk but formerly in Suffolk (see box, below). Best of all for location and atmosphere is the isolated thatched **church of St Mary's** at the hamlet of Ashby a little way east of Lound, which stands alone among fields on the route of the Angles Way. Close to the churchyard gate is a memorial to the crew of a bomber that crashed near here in 1944. The sundial on the church tower sports the legend 'Aim Higher than the Mark', the meaning of which you can contemplate while taking a breather on one of the churchyard's benches.

THE ISLAND OF LOTHINGLAND

The Lothingland region north of Lowestoft is an island in the sense of being surrounded by water on four sides: the North Sea to the east, the River Waveney to the west, Breydon Water to the north and Oulton Broad and Lowestoft's Lake Lothing at its southern limit. Historically, Lothingland was a Half Hundred of the Suffolk Archdeaconry that was incorporated with the neighbouring Mutford division to the south to become the Mutford and Lothingland Hundred in 1763. All of this 'island' used to be part of the county of Suffolk, which extended north as far as Breydon Water; however, a redrawing of the county boundary in 1974 resulted in the most northerly settlements of the peninsula – Belton, Burgh Castle, Fritton and Hopton – being transferred from Suffolk to Norfolk. The logic behind this boundary change was to streamline administration in the wake of the Local Government Act of 1972 which aimed to allow all of Great Yarmouth's suburbs and outlying villages to be taken into Norfolk control.

¶¶ FOOD & DRINK

The Mardle Café and Bakery 51 The Street ℰ 01502 730820. On Lound's main street, this popular café has a real community feel to it. There's a good range of coffees, teas and snacks on offer, as well as breakfasts and excellent home-baked bread and bakery goods.

BECCLES & THE LOWER WAVENEY VALLEY

Heading upstream along the Waveney, the river changes direction near Lowestoft to lead west through a largely uninhabited marshy area to reach Beccles. These days the river is wide enough for navigation as far as Geldeston Locks, a little way beyond the town but in the not too distant past boats would have been able to travel as far as Bungay considerably further upstream. This, of course, has considerable effect on the river's character, which morphs from busy thoroughfare to a relatively sleepy backwater within a matter of miles.

3 BECCLES

🏠 **Waveney House Hotel** (page 277)

The largest town in the valley, Beccles is a place that most tend to pass through rather than stay in but there is plenty to see here and it is certainly worth lingering a while to explore and soak up the town's easy-going, unhurried atmosphere. As with any market town, market day is a good time to visit if you can manage it – here it's on Friday. The town is solidly Georgian as, like elsewhere, its timbered Tudor core was destroyed by a succession of ravaging fires. The river used to have far more significance to town life than it does now, and Beccles was once a flourishing port with many wherries passing by. Herrings from the coast used to be an important commodity here and, in the medieval period, Beccles annually provided tens of thousands of the fish to the monks at Bury St Edmunds.

Boats still have a part to play, as Beccles is the most southerly point on the Broads system. The river here is not quite as hectic in summer as the Bure and Thurne are in Norfolk to the north but it's busy enough. There's some good walking on the Beccles Marshes close to the town and also along the north bank of the River Waveney to Geldeston Locks where

1 Canoeing on the River Waveney. 2 Somerleyton Hall. 3 Beccles Quay, on the Broads. ▶

MIKE J ROBERTS/S

KINGTA/S

MARK STAPLES

there is a community-owned pub (page 100). There is also a regular **boat service** to Geldeston Locks, the Big Dog Ferry ($\mathscr{O}$ 07561 607263 $\mathscr{O}$ bigdogferry.co.uk), which runs three times a day from Beccles Lido between Easter and October – it is best to book beforehand.

Although there are a few specific sights worth investigating, the best way to experience Beccles is to simply wander through its attractive Georgian streets and see what you come across – you are certainly not in any danger of getting lost. Stick to the 'gates' – Saltgate, Northgate, Ballygate – and you won't go far wrong.

With luck, you'll find some crinkle-crankle walls and a handful of older medieval buildings scattered here and there. Sometimes you'll get more than you anticipated. On one occasion, visiting the town with my wife, we were admiring the town's octagonal town hall on The Walk when we were approached by an elderly man. 'Are you tourists here, then?' he enquired in a friendly tone. 'Well, sort of, we live in Norwich.' 'In that case you want to take a look at that', he responded, pointing across the road. 'See that chimney pot up there, what do you think that is next to it?' It looked like a small gravestone and this is what we said. 'Yes, that's exactly what it is, although most people round here don't pay much attention to it. It's where a young boy got stuck up a chimney and died in the Victorian time. They say that he were up there for years before they found him.' This last bit didn't quite ring true but we didn't say anything as he went on tell us that there were more rooftop graves like this one in the town. After a full 15 minutes of hearing his life story, an interesting one peppered with remote Scottish and Cornish connections – his wife's family were tin miners – we made our excuses and bade him goodbye. We didn't see any more chimney-pot gravestones though, despite scouring the town's rooftops.

For the best view in town you should climb the hundred or so steps that lead up from Puddingmoor to **St Michael's Church**. Horatio Nelson's parents, Edmund Nelson and Catherine Suckling, were married here in 1749. The churchyard looks out west across the river to the marshes that lie beyond on the Norfolk bank. There are some benches here but they may well be already occupied by Beccles folk eating their sandwiches or snatching a bit of quiet time. This close to the church you cannot fail to notice that its bell tower is detached from the body of the church. It is also at the wrong end of the church, to the east rather than the west. There's a simple answer to this conundrum as if the tower had

A walk to Geldeston Locks & back

❄ OS Landranger map 134 or Explorer map 231; start: Beccles town centre ♀ TM422912; 7 miles; moderate.

The beauty of this walk is that there are several permutations. You can walk to Geldeston along the Norfolk bank of the Waveney, cross the footbridge and return along the Angles Way to Beccles, or alternatively you could return the same way. Another possibility is to take the Big Dog Ferry to the pub from Beccles Lido and return to Beccles on foot using either bank . . . or vice versa. I'll just deal with the first option here. The full walk is around seven miles in all but it is good sense to break it midway with a picnic or a meal at either of Geldeston's pubs.

From Beccles town centre, go along Northgate to reach Bridge Street then turn left and follow this to cross the bridge. Turn left immediately after the bridge and follow the riverside footpath for a mile and a half before the path turns inland towards a house set among trees. Turn right at the junction and go uphill along the footpath to reach a road. Follow this quiet lane through Geldeston village and just after passing the Wherry Inn turn left at the T-junction down Station Road. After crossing the course of the old railway line take the track to the left signposted Locks Inn. Continue to the inn and go over two footbridges to cross the River Waveney then head across a marshy field towards a wooden bridge. Carry on to reach a gate and stile (warning – there may be inquisitive cattle here). Go through the gate and follow the footpath left through more gates and over more stiles along the signed route of the Angles Way. This eventually reaches the main Beccles to Bungay road near Roos Hall. Turn left and walk on the grass verge until reaching Puddingmoor Lane, where you turn left and follow it back into town.

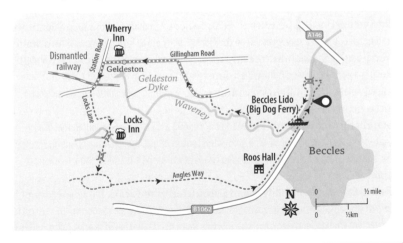

been erected where it ought to be it would be virtually on the edge of a cliff so its incorrect location makes good architectural sense. Why the bell tower only has a clock face on three of its sides is a matter of speculation. Local lore suggests that there is no clock on the western side because Beccles townsfolk do not wish to give the time of day to their Norfolk neighbours.

Close to St Michael's Church, just off Puddingmoor down by the river, is **Beccles Lido** (✐ 01502 713297 ♂ beccleslido.com). The Lido represents a real local success story in terms of community action. This outdoor pool was purchased by a community-run charity from the local council and since reopening in 2010 has been comprehensively refurbished, with leaks repaired and a solar power system installed to heat the water. Clean, warm, good value and fun for families, the lido is open from Easter to September and gets very busy in hot weather and during school holidays. With good views and nice places to sit around the pool area, it's a popular picnic spot; refreshments are available at the cafeteria.

¶¶ FOOD & DRINK

As well as Beccles itself, which has several decent pubs and cafés, the nearby village of Geldeston just to the west on the Norfolk bank of the river has a couple of good pubs.

Beccles Farmers' Market at Beccles Heliport (✐ 01502 476240 ♂ becclesfarmersmarket. co.uk ☉ 1st & 3rd Sat of month 09.00–13.00) has around 30 stalls.

The Locks Inn Locks Ln, Geldeston ✐ 01508 830033 ♂ thelocksinn.com. An isolated, traditional pub with a sunny garden on the Norfolk bank of the River Waveney three miles west of Beccles. The pub, which became a community owned enterprise in 2020, has almost 1,600 shareholders, giving it the widest ownership of any pub in the country. Pub grub, and a good variety of local real ales including Green Jack ales from Lowestoft, regular musical events and a beer festival in September.

Graze at the White Horse 29 New Market ✐ 01502 715974 ♂ grazewhitehorse.co.uk. Graze serves reasonably priced, well-presented food in bright, convivial surroundings. There are a couple of local real ales like Lacons to choose from at the bar and an attractive terrace garden for outdoor dining.

Station Café and Community Rooms Station Rd ✐ 07544 038313. This social enterprise café closes early afternoon but opens around 07.00. Handy for trains, of course, but convenient enough for the town centre too, this has a good selection of snacks, cakes, coffees and teas.

Waveney House Hotel Puddingmoor ✆ 01502 712270 ⏠ waveneyhousehotel.co.uk. With a pleasant terrace right next to the river, the Riverside Bar offers a good menu for lunch and dinner that makes use of local fish and meat. See page 277.

Wherry Inn 7 The Street, Geldeston ✆ 01508 518371 ⏠ wherryinn.co.uk. Geldeston's other place to eat – a traditional pub with Adnams ales and a seasonal menu.

BUNGAY & THE CENTRAL WAVENEY VALLEY

It's just a few miles from Beccles to Bungay along the B1062, although it is considerably further by river as the Waveney meanders lazily through the Geldeston and Barsham Marshes. Following the road, you'll pass the hamlet of Shipmeadow with its large former workhouse now converted for domestic use. If you look at the village sign you'll see that the 'ship' in Shipmeadow actually refers to sheep rather than boats. Next comes Barsham, with yet another round tower church. This one, Holy Trinity, whose churchyard is entered through a charming thatched lych gate, is particularly noteworthy for its unique east gable. Here, the pattern of criss-cross tracery on the window extends into the flint flushwork across the entire face of the wall; the overall effect is rather like that of a fancy pastry lattice topping a fruit tart. The gable flushwork probably dates from the 15th century, although the core of the church is much older – 12th century or earlier. Back in the 1970s the paddock next to the church used to be the location for the Barsham Faire, one of several Albion Fairs in the region at that time. The last was held in 1976 and I recall an event that successfully if haphazardly blended the carefree atmosphere of a medieval fair with that of a mini Glastonbury festival.

4 BUNGAY

Å **Outney Meadow Touring and Camping Park** (page 277)

> Were I in my castle
> Upon the River Waveney I wouldne give a button For the King
> of Cockney.
> Hugh 'the Bold' Bigod, 1173

The ideal defensive site for a fortified town is either at the top of a hill or in the meander of a river. The second of these conditions is provided for perfectly at Bungay where the River Waveney coils like a flexing eel.

ST PETER'S BREWERY

GREG BALFOUR EVANS/A

PATRICK GOSLING/DT

SIMON BUCK

BUTTER CROSS
REBUILT
AFTER THE FIRE
IN THE YEAR
1690

DINAMICA

The town has a hill of sorts too, and this is the site Hugh Bigod, the first Earl of Norfolk, chose for his castle in 1173, on high ground overlooking a meander. Hugh 'the Bold' Bigod was a fierce rival of Henry II (who had made his castle at Orford; page 72) but was forced to surrender his Bungay fortress to the king as a penalty for aligning himself with an insurrection led by Henry's rebellious sons. If it had succeeded he would have gained custody of Norwich Castle; the words quoted above record his regrets.

Bungay is a self-contained, likeable place that, with a castle, an independent theatre and a distinctive eccentric character, seems to punch well above its weight for somewhere so small. Over the years, it's been a centre for leatherworking, boatbuilding and more recently printing, but it has always also been an important market town for the region.

As with most small towns in East Anglia, Bungay's heart is its marketplace. Central to this is the octagonal **Butter Cross** (sometimes written as 'Buttercross') that has a lead figure of Justice with her scales on top of its cupola. Like many other settlements where medieval wood and thatch predominated, a serious fire spread through the old town in the late 17th century and Bungay's plentiful Georgian buildings reflect a post-1688 rebuild. There's a pleasing mix of architecture spread throughout the centre but **Bridge Street**, with its colourfully painted houses sloping steeply down towards the river, is particularly attractive. This is a street that seems to happily harbour some of Bungay's undeniable eccentricities too: take a look at the anarchic bric-a-brac shop with its backyard chicken coops opposite The Chequers pub for a taste of what indifference to convention can do.

Most of what you see now of **Bungay Castle** was actually constructed by Hugh's descendent Roger Bigod at the end of the 13th century. With 16ft-thick walls and standing 108ft tall, the castle was considered to be impregnable in its heyday. Neglected after Bigod died in the Crusades, it fell into ruin and in 1483 passed into the hands of the Howards, Dukes of Norfolk, who continued to own it almost without break until the end of the 20th century. Today, there are two crumbling towers of the original gatehouse and some outer walls that you can visit and with a bit of luck

◀ **1** St Peter's Hall, home to St Peter's Brewery. **2** & **3** Bungay's Butter Cross sign and St Mary's Church. **4** Inspecting the harvest at Flint Vineyard.

they will have removed the scaffolding by the time you get here. There's a café, Bigod's Kitchen, at the entrance, which has an interpretive model of the castle in its courtyard. To get a good view across to Earsham on the other side of the Waveney Valley you can climb up **Castle Hills** from the visitor centre. In celebration of its founder, the **Bigod Way** is a ten-mile loop around the town that starts and ends at the castle. It's a lengthy walk that takes four or five hours but there's plenty of historical and wildlife interest along the way.

Although there were said to be five churches in the town in the 11th century, just three of these survive today: **Holy Trinity** with its Saxon round tower, the oldest complete building in town, the Victorian Catholic church of St Edmunds, built on the site of an earlier church and **St Mary's**. St Mary's, now deconsecrated, is famous in these parts for its role in the **Black Shuck legend**, when the legendary black dog with fiery eyes ran amuck in the church and killed two worshippers having already caused untold damage at far-off Blythburgh church that same morning of 4 August 1577. This fanciful tale has long passed into local folklore, although versions of it differ quite widely. According to one account, a woman who went to school in Bungay in the late 19th century remembers Black Shuck as being a cat and recalls children singing the song:

Scratch cat of Bungay
Hanging on the door
Take a stick and knock it down
And it won't come anymore.

Whatever his form, puss or pooch, Black Shuck did not leave any evidence of his visit at St Mary's (there are at least putative 'scorch marks' at Blythburgh), although he does put in an appearance on the town's coat of arms. There's also an attractive tapestry of Bungay's history hanging in the church with a panel detailing the rampaging dog with the legend, '1577: Black Dog entered during a fearful storm and two men died.'

For more background on the town's past, it is worth paying a visit to the recently refurbished **Bungay Museum** ($\lozenge$ bungaymuseum.co.uk $\odot$ end May–early Nov Sat & Sun), which is located on the ground floor of the Town Hall on Broad Street. This has displays of prehistoric, Roman and Saxon artefacts from the area as well as information on the history of the town's printing industry (the long-established Clay's Ltd

THE CHICKEN OF THE EAST

Like Black Shuck (see opposite), the tale of Bungay's 'chicken roundabout' has now become part of local folklore. But what came first, the chickens or the roundabout? The chickens did, in fact. It is thought that the colony of chickens that used to live in the middle of a roundabout on the A143 just outside Bungay were originally allotment escapees that managed to survive on grain from the nearby maltings. The chickens survived the building of a bypass in 1983 thanks to this grain, but when the maltings went up in flames in 1999 their free food supply vanished. Thankfully, this was when a local character known as the 'chicken man' appeared on the scene and began to make a two-mile round trip with his wheelbarrow most days just to feed them.

There was always considerable pressure to remove them as these very free-range chickens had been branded a potential danger to traffic by local authorities. Bungay citizens strongly resisted their removal however, and signed petitions and even dressed up in chicken costumes to promote their cause. It seemed that the chickens were safe until a sharp decline in their numbers was reported in 2009 and, following incidents of animal abuse, the remaining few birds were removed by animal welfare groups.

The chickens may now have gone but they still seem to have a place in the hearts of most local people. A campaign was launched in 2012 to install a commemorative statue to them in the middle of the roundabout. As one campaigner stated, 'They have the Angel of the North, why can't we have the Chicken of the East?'

Predictably perhaps, spoilsport planners have deemed such a monument a 'safety hazard' to motorists but it seems likely that even without such a memorial the chickens will live on in local folklore for many years to come. The chicken man, Gordon Knowles, who fed the birds daily for nearly 20 years and died in 2020, is commemorated with a plaque on Bungay's Falcon Bridge close to the roundabout.

printing works, which stands at the edge of town, continues to be the town's biggest employer). Across the road from the town hall is the tiny **Fisher Theatre** (∂ fishertheatre.org), which has been entertaining local people for the best part of 200 years and still punches above its weight in terms of the variety of music, film and theatre it stages.

Bungay is not all about castles and churches, or even printing. With the River Waveney just a shadow of what it used to be, it is easy to overlook the importance that the river once held for the town. Once the lock at Geldeston was established in the late 17th century, and the river canalised, wherries were able to ship goods up here from the coast. Upper Olland Street in the town centre probably gets its name from a derivation of 'oak lands' and locally plentiful oak would have been used to build wherries in the Staithe area of the town. Indeed, William Brighton, builder of the *Albion*, one of the few wherries that survive today, used to work here, while the boat itself used to ply its trade between Bungay Staithe and the coast at Lowestoft. These days, Geldeston is as far as navigation goes for anything larger than a canoe.

All this serious talk of history and tradition is well and good but if you ask a local for an instant word association with Bungay you'll probably end up with 'chicken roundabout'. Although now just a memory, Bungay's so-called **Chicken Roundabout** (page 105) was the sort of small town silliness that local newspapers and regional television networks delight in.

The roundabout in question is just across the river where the roads to Norwich, Ditchingham and Beccles spin off and, yes, it really did once have chickens living on it. Sadly, this is no longer the case as the chickens were finally removed by animal welfare groups after becoming the target for persistent animal abuse.

For cycling, the **Godric Way** is a 24-mile route around Bungay that starts and ends at Butter Cross and passes through Ellingham, Broome, Ditchingham, Earsham, Denton, Alburgh, Homersfield, Mettingham and The Saints – all places in which a slow cycle through is worth a dozen drive-bys.

"Ask a local for an instant word association with Bungay, you'll probably end up with 'chicken roundabout.'"

Close to Earsham Hall, which lies just across the River Waveney on the Norfolk side of the border, is **Flint Vineyard** (✆ 01986 893942 ⊘ flintvineyard.com), which was established in 2015 with 26,000 vines over six hectares. Flint produces a range of wines – Bacchus, Silex Blanc and Pinot Noir – and offers tours, tastings and tours with an optional '15 mile lunch', which includes a selection of local produce sourced within a 15-mile radius of the vineyard. There is also a barn shop and tasting garden.

🍴 FOOD & DRINK

Several cafés and tea rooms are dotted around the town centre, along with a handful of pubs.

Bigod's Kitchen 7 Castle Orchard ✆ 01986 896567. At the entrance to the castle grounds and a convenient place to stop for a drink or a bite, this is good for cakes, snacks and lunches.

Buttercross Tea Rooms 6 Cross St ℰ 01986 893002 ⌖ thebuttercrossteararooms.com. Just down from the Butter Cross, this is an unfussy but perfectly pleasant place for a snack, coffee or all-day breakfast. There is also a hidden garden with a pond.

Castle Inn 35 Earsham St ℰ 01986 892283 ⌖ thecastleinn.net. With an imaginative menu that does its level best to utilise locally sourced food, this is probably Bungay's nicest place to eat. There's also an elegant but cosy bar that serves local cider and ales and a good selection of wines.

Earsham Street Café 11–13 Earsham St ℰ 01986 893103 ⌖ earshamstreetcafe.co.uk. Located in an attractive 17th-century building, this is a little more upmarket than the Buttercross Tea Rooms and has a more adventurous menu. At the back is a courtyard garden where a cockfighting pit once stood. Good for cakes, light meals and weekend brunches.

The Old Bank Tea Room & Bistro 8 Market Pl ℰ 01986 894050 ⌖ theoldbanktearoom. co.uk. As its name suggests, this is a retro-style, 1920s-themed tea room with a good choice of coffees, loose teas, cakes and sandwiches.

Queen's Head Station Rd, Earsham ℰ 01986 892623. Just west of Bungay in the Norfolk village of Earsham, this pub has its own real ale brewery, the Waveney Brewing Company.

5 THE SAINTS

South of Bungay on the Suffolk side of the river is a handful of small villages known locally as 'The Saints'. They are St Mary South Elmham, St Cross South Elmham, St Margaret South Elmham, St Nicholas South Elmham, St James South Elmham, St Michael South Elmham, St Peter South Elmham, All Saints South Elmham, Ilketshall St Margaret, Ilketshall St John, Ilketshall St Andrew, Ilketshall St Lawrence and All Saints Mettingham. I suppose you might also call them 'The South Elmhams and Ilketshalls', but that does not quite have the same ring to it.

These are medieval parishes that never coalesced to form a city as they did in Norwich. It has been remarked that if one of these villages had been a port, a defensive fortress or important market place, then the history of the area might have been quite different and, instead of a clump of tiny villages, we might find a city. But it can seem as if the medieval period has not yet completely passed by in this corner of Suffolk where even Harleston and Bungay can feel a long way off.

There are no specific sights here, apart perhaps from South Elmham Minster – the charm of 'The Saints' is subtle – but it's an area that rewards relaxed wanderings. It is worth noting that one of the villages, St Michael South Elmham, is one of only two 'thankful villages' in Suffolk (there are none at all in Norfolk). It is, in other words, a rare village in which all soldiers returned from World War I and has no need of a war memorial.

'The Saints' is definitely an area for cycling. It's the sort of terrain where satnavs tend to have nervous breakdowns. Driving around it in a car, you will inevitably get lost – cars are just too fast for this maze of narrow lanes and confusing signposts. South of the curiously named St Cross South Elmham stands **South Elmham Hall**, a 16th-century farmhouse that these days functions as a swanky rural wedding venue with rooms (𝒮 01986 782526 𝄞 batemansbarnweddings.co.uk). Just south of the hall, standing alone in a field surrounded by trees, is the evocative ruin of **South Elmham Minster**. The minster was an Episcopal chapel built for Herbert de Losinga, Bishop of Norwich, who also founded a monastery at North Elmham (in Norfolk) and a smaller one at Hoxne. It has been dated as 11th century, although a Saxon 10th-century tomb slab has been found on the same site and so some place of worship must have existed previously. It's a mysterious place and the hornbeams that surround the ruin provide a wonderful haven for birds.

The land beside The Beck, the stream that runs through it, which has buttercup meadows, coppiced elm hedges (kept like this to prevent a return of Dutch elm disease) and ancient hornbeam pollards, was once a medieval deer park. Now it provides grazing for rare breed British White cattle. The permissive paths that used to provide walks on the farm are no longer here but it is still possible to access South Elmham Minster using public footpaths. Park at the layby a little way west of South Elmham Hall (♥ TM306835), walk down the green lane away from the road and at the bottom turn left to follow the footpath that runs through fields next to The Beck. After about half a mile you will see a woodland copse on slightly higher ground to the right – the minster stands here hidden among the trees. Just north of St Peter South Elmham is **St Peter's Hall**, a 13th-century moated hall that was extended in the 15th century using what is euphemistically known as 'architectural salvage' from nearby Flixton Priory, hence its fine Norman stone. The hall itself is a restaurant today but St Peter's Hall is probably best known for its **St Peter's Brewery** (𝒮 01986 782322 𝄞 stpetersbrewery.co.uk), established in 1996, which produces tasty, traditionally brewed beers in distinctive oval bottles.

> "It's a mysterious place and the hornbeams that surround the ruin provide a wonderful haven for birds."

The range of beers includes organic and gluten-free varieties, along with traditional bitters, pilsner, Indian pale ale, stout and porter. Local malts are used for brewing and the water used is drawn from a deep chalk aquifer beneath the ground. The rather medicinal bottle design, which dates back to 1770, helps to create the impression that what you are drinking is actually doing you good – it works for me. Brewery tours had been put temporarily on hold at the time of writing while building work was being completed but in their place 'Talk & Taste' sessions are offered on Saturdays at 11.00 and 13.00 from 1 April to the end of December (check the brewery website for information on when tours recommence). The visitors' shop opposite the hall is open every day of the week but closes at 15.00 at weekends.

If cider is your thing then you might wish to pay a visit to the **Cider Place** (✆ 01986 781353) at Cherry Tree Farm, Ilketshall St Lawrence, which has a wide range of ciders, country wines and meads, and has tastings most days of the week. The **Metfield Stores** (✆ 01379 586204 ⬧ metfieldsuffolk.com ☉ daily), a community shop in Metfield village, just west of St James South Elmham, specialises in local produce and the volunteer-staffed shop, which is, in fact, the only shop in the village, is very active in promoting the produce of local suppliers and sells a wide variety of bread, including organic and sourdough, local meat and cheeses such as Baron Bigod.

¶¶ FOOD & DRINK

Trio's Restaurant at St Peter's Hall St Peter South Elmham ✆ 01986 782288
⬧ trioscatering.co.uk/trios-restaurant ☉ noon–16.00 Fri–Sun. Dine in the slightly eccentric surroundings of a wood-panelled Tudor great hall. The focus is very much on seasonal local produce, with Sunday roasts very popular.

HARLESTON & AROUND

Heading west along the Waveney Valley, Harleston is the next place of any size. It lies just across the Norfolk bank of the river, the nearest market town for a sizeable chunk of north Suffolk and south Norfolk.

6 HARLESTON (NORFOLK)

A little way north of the Waveney on the Norfolk bank of the river, Harleston is the urban magnet for this stretch of the valley, although

THE ANGLES WAY IN WINTER

I did this long-distance walk in midwinter, over eight days of the coldest weather to hit East Anglia so far this millennium. I started each stage from my home in Norwich, using public transport to reach the day's trail head. Some of the bus and train connections were tight but it was all just about feasible – on weekdays at least. The first section involved a lengthy stretch along the south bank of Breydon Water, always at its best on bright, frosty days when the water sparkles and migrant waders work the mud. The waymarked footpath left the estuary at Burgh Castle to dawdle through the dormitory village of Belton, probably the dullest stretch along the entire route. After skirting a golf course, the way led across fields to pass the Redwings Animal Sanctuary where I was delighted to see a large number of the eponymous winter thrushes congregating in the paddocks. After passing two charming churches –

first, thatched and round-towered Fritton St Edmund's, then Ashby St Mary's, isolated among fields – I arrived at the slightly eccentric estate village of Somerleyton. Next day, I followed the railway line east along the marsh edge to wind up at Oulton village.

The stretch from Oulton Broad to Beccles followed the bank of the Waveney for much of the way – an elemental landscape of water and grazing marsh. Beccles to Earsham came next: hard work on my chosen day because the ground was frozen solid. I slithered my way out of the town, past Roos Hall then through fields that looked down upon the Waveney and picturesquely frozen marshes that, with only the distant thrum of traffic to remind one of the 21st century, resembled a scene from a Constable painting.

Emerging at the hamlet of Shipmeadow, I crossed the A143 to head across fields next to a converted workhouse that was now a

'urban' is probably too big a word for a pleasant little market town. As with many places of this size, medieval fires saw to it that most of the town's earlier thatch and timber frames went up in flames so what remains today is mostly solid Georgian red brick with the odd Tudor survivor. Market day, still important to the town, is on Wednesdays.

Harleston's most conspicuous landmark is the almost minaret-like **clock tower** on the market place that used to belong to St John's Chapel of Ease. The chapel was founded in the 14th century but was in a ruinous state by the 18th. A new church was built on Broad Street to replace it and the old chapel was demolished and replaced with a grocer's shop, which remains there today. As with many agricultural towns in the region, there's a conspicuous Victorian **corn exchange**: a stark white Neoclassical building that was opened for commerce in 1849 but served

desirable residence but which must once have been a miserable place to live. Close to the ruins of Mettingham Castle, I followed a timeless green lane lined with coppiced hazel and, before I knew it, found myself gazing down on Wainford Mill just outside Bungay.

Rather than diverting into Bungay, the Angles Way crosses back into Norfolk here to follow the meander of the river. I took the track through woodland above Ditchingham Lodge and, arriving at Earsham Mill, crossed into Suffolk once more to traverse lush riverside meadows as far as the village of Mendham. After a gentle climb up the north side of the valley I arrived in Harleston. The next leg followed the south bank of the river as far as Brockdish, where the way crossed a bridge back into Norfolk and, after climbing and skirting the village churchyard, I followed another lengthy stretch of green lane and farm tracks across beet fields to end up in Scole. Arriving at Diss Mere the following day, I found the resident ducks looked rather confused by the frozen state of things. I headed west out of town alongside Roydon Fen to reach the gorse-covered heath of Wortham Lings and eventually arrived at the source of the Waveney (and the Ouse) near Redgrave after a splendid leafy section through the woodland area of the nature reserve.

A final day's walk brought me to Knettishall Heath in Breckland where future options awaited me: the Peddars Way north to Holme-next-the-Sea or the Iceni Way to Thetford and Hunstanton. I had walked around 80 miles in total – perhaps more like 90 – and had encountered virtually no-one along the way give, or take the odd dog-walker. For those in search of tranquility and midwinter exercise, walks like this certainly have plenty to recommend them, although this same walk would be equally enjoyable in any season.

as a local court in later years. Since its early days, when its walls must have resounded to the bargaining cries of Norfolk farmers, the building has seen use as a skating rink, furniture market, dance hall and even a delicatessen. In more recent times it has seen service as an antique centre with a 1940s-style tea room and a museum.

The market place, which tends to be on the sleepy side apart from on Wednesday mornings, has another town landmark: the J D Young Hotel, originally known as the **Magpie Inn** – the original distinctive sign can still be seen – which has served as a coaching inn for centuries. Churchill and Eisenhower are reputed to have met here during World War II, presumably not over a pint. Just across from the hotel is a large Georgian house with two enormous sequoias that look as if they will burst out of the garden in the next century or two like slow-growing triffids. The town's other coaching inn is **The Swan** in The Thoroughfare, which was built by Robert Green, a conspirator in Norwich's Kett's Rebellion in the summer of 1549, who may have been rewarded with this property for snitching on his colleague – hardly the noblest of ways to get a start in the pub trade.

The Old Market Place, which no longer has a market, has Harleston's oldest building at number 18, an Elizabethan hall house that originally would have been jettied. There is no medieval parish church to be found in Harleston because the town shares the same parish as **Redenhall**, a neighbouring village, which has the magnificent 14th-century church of St Mary's with its inordinately tall tower of finely worked flint.

¶¶ FOOD & DRINK

The Hungry Cat 25 The Thoroughfare ✎ 01379 308971. A vegan café and deli on the high street that serves good coffee, a great choice of cakes and Mediterranean-influenced snacks and light meals.

7 MENDHAM

Just across the Waveney from Harleston in Suffolk is the small village of Mendham. This was the birthplace of **Sir Alfred Munnings**, the East Anglian painter of horses and rural scenes and one-time president of the Royal Academy, whose father owned the mill just outside the village. If you approach the village from the south via the Witherdale road, Mendham seems remote despite its proximity to Harleston. The village is set in the river's flood valley amid lush water meadows and lines of poplars. It's a quiet, dreamy place, with a church and a single pub that is called, appropriately, the Sir Alfred Munnings. The car park opposite the pub has a noticeboard with a suggested five-mile circular walk – along Sconch Beck to St Cross South Elmham. The Angles Way passes through the village as it crosses into Norfolk and there's a footpath that leads across Mendham Marshes past the ruins of a Cluniac priory.

Alternatively, you could just saunter past the pub down to the river. This is classic Waveney Valley scenery – the sort of thing Munnings might have painted if he had not concentrated on horse fairs or attacking modernism quite so much. It's the kind of landscape that brings reverie.

---

1 A wintry scene along the River Waveney near Mendham. **2** The market town of Harleston.
3 Fressingfield's sign reflects its history on a pilgrimage route. ▶

KATHY WRIGHT/A

IAN CARSTAIRS

The iron bridge crossing the Waveney seems like a giant staple attaching Norfolk to the Suffolk mainland. Brown cows wandering the meadows contentedly graze and flick flies away, keeping their eyes on a pair of locals fishing beneath the trees and catching nothing. As poplars rustle in the breeze, the very English sound of an accordion drifts down from the Munnings pub. It could almost be the 18th century, if it wasn't for the fishermen's car parked by the road. As I am taking all this in, a man who is clearly the worse for drink ambles down the road towards the bridge. He stumbles exactly halfway across, pauses for a moment, then goes back the way he has come. It is as if he is fearful to place his feet on Norfolk soil, or there is some sort of invisible barrier. Two minutes later, a sleek Jaguar arrives from the north to pick the man up. Then it turns around and ferries him back across the bridge… into Norfolk.

8 FRESSINGFIELD

South of Harleston on the B1116 Framlingham road, a knot of houses cluster around a church at Fressingfield. The village has a tidy, prosperous air and two thriving pubs to bear this out – unusual in a place of this size. In warmer weather, there's inevitably a handful of people enjoying a drink at an outside table of the Swan Inn, and a nearly full car park at the rather grander **Fox and Goose Inn** (just up the hill behind the church of St Peter and St Paul), built in 1509 and formerly serving as the village's guildhall. This Tudor building operates as a popular gastropub these days and it was famous for its food even in the late 1960s according to the author John Seymour, who suggested that people came from as far away as Yorkshire 'just for the eating' and recommended booking a day or two ahead. Back in those days, most pubs served just crisps and pickled eggs along with very unreal ale – or scampi and chips if you were lucky – so you have to admire the continuity of tradition here. Rumour has it that Hollywood actor Johnny Depp and party once turned up here but could not get a table because they hadn't pre-booked.

The **church of St Peter and St Paul** is a veritable cathedral to the use of unstained oak, with some marvellous 15th-century bench ends in the form of saints and a hammerbeam roof. There's a fine example of medieval graffiti here too, with the initials 'A P' incised into a bench. This is considered to be the handiwork of Alice de la Pole, granddaughter of the poet Chaucer, who was perhaps the medieval equivalent of a graffiti tagger. All that wood ripe for carving must have been just too much of a temptation and as Duchess of Norfolk she would hardly expect to be punished for her petty act of vandalism.

The **village sign** at the junction at the top of the hill depicts a pilgrim with a pack mule in tow. This represents the village's place on a late Saxon pilgrimage route to Bury St Edmunds. There are even older roads in the vicinity. Just east of the village there's a very obvious Roman road that links Pulham with Peasenham, following the route of the B1116 for some of the way through Weybread. There's a Saxon diversion around Fressingfield, but it re-emerges at Little Whittingham Green where it continues to Chippenhall Green, the sole survivor of the parish's common land that had been mostly enclosed by the end of the 18th century. If you take this same old Roman Road north from Fressingfield towards Harleston, you'll pass through **Weybread**, a linear sprawl of houses with a seemingly endless stretch of 30mph speed limit – imposed perhaps because of the irresistible temptation that dead-straight pieces of road like this offer to speed merchants.

"The village has a tidy, prosperous air and two thriving pubs to bear this out – unusual in a place of this size."

Suffolk is yet to earn the reputation of Bordeaux or the Napa Valley but it does have a few vineyards where brave English wine growers do their best to conjure the spirit of Bacchus from the heavy clay soil. **Oak Hill Vineyard** (✆ 07710 249001) in the centre of the village, behind the church, produces its own Oak Hill Wines, named after an 800-year-old oak tree that overlooks the vines, the last vestige of an ancient wood. Four hundred vines of the Bacchus variety were planted here back in 1987 and the three-acre vineyard produces three types of white wine – dry, sweet and oaked. Wine sales are by appointment only.

¶¶ FOOD & DRINK

Fox & Goose ✆ 01379 586247 ⌘ foxandgoose.net. In a Tudor building that was the former guildhall. With AA and Michelin credentials for fine dining – 'Modern European cooking in the heart of Suffolk' – this is a highly regarded and very popular place so booking is almost essential. Most produce is sourced within a six-mile radius. The extensive wine list features wines from Flint Vineyard (page 106).

Swan Inn ✆ 01379 586280 ⌘ fressingfieldswan.co.uk. With outdoor tables overlooking the road and the beck, this has straightforward bar food made using local produce and a decent selection of real ales. There's also a popular, good-value Sunday carvery.

9 WINGFIELD

**Wynkefelde the Saxon held Honour and Fee
Ere William the Norman came over the sea.**

West of Fressingfield is the village of Wingfield. The Wingfields were an old Saxon family who gave their name to the village. Sir John de Wingfield, chief of staff of the Black Prince, founded both Wingfield College and St Andrew's Church in the mid 14th century. Wingfield Castle, which was the seat of the Wingfields and their successors the de la Poles, Earls and Dukes of Suffolk, is now just a ruin next to a farm. **Wingfield College** was partly demolished before being remodelled in a Palladian style in the 18th century. The college's farm buildings now incorporate **Wingfield Barns** (℘ 01379 384505 ◈ wingfieldbarns.com), hosting arts, drama and theatrical events as well as weddings and civil ceremonies. Wingfield College itself is a private residence and is no longer open for guided tours. The collegiate church of **St Andrew** in the village has the stone tomb of Sir John de Wingfield alongside the wood and alabaster tombs of Michael and John de la Pole and their wives. The church also contains a curious 18th-century wooden sentry box called 'The Hud', which was used outside by priests performing funeral services in inclement weather.

¶¶ FOOD & DRINK

De la Pole Arms Church Rd ℘ 01379 384983 ◈ thedelapole.co.uk. This free house has Adnams, Earl Soham and St Peter's ales although it sadly no longer serves food. There's an outdoor patio for sunny weather and a log fire inside during the winter months.

HOXNE TO DISS

10 HOXNE

Hoxne (pronounced 'hoxen') is a pretty village just south of 'The Crotch', the confluence of the Waveney and the Dove. As well as some elegant cottages and a historic pub, one of the village's several claims to fame is for traditionally being the place where **St Edmund** was killed by marauding Danes. This may not be true of course – it may well have been elsewhere; another strong contender is Bradfield St Clare near Bury St Edmunds (page 268) – but Hoxne has claimed the legend for its own and it has the monument to prove it, so there you are. The legend dictates that St Edmund was taken prisoner here and tied to a nearby oak tree before being shot dead with arrows. A stone monument to him stands at the spot where an old oak was brought down by lightning in the 19th century. When it was subsequently broken up for timber, the tree apparently revealed a piece of iron, which some have interpreted as belonging to a Viking arrowhead. Such history may be rather tangential but it is captivating all the same. Naturally, the tree in question would have to have been at least a thousand years old, which, of course, is highly unlikely.

If you walk south along the village's main street past The Swan, you'll soon come to a minor road off to the left. Turn down here and you'll see the stone **Goldbrook Bridge**, under which, according to legend, Edmund was supposedly discovered hiding, his glinting spurs spotted by a young, newly-wed couple who snitched to the Danes. St Edmund is said to have put a curse on all newly-weds crossing the bridge so Hoxne is probably not the ideal place for a honeymoon. The bridge makes no claims to be the original: one side bears the legend, 'KING EDMUND TAKEN PRISONER HERE – AD870' and the other, 'GOLDBROOK BRIDGE – AD1878'. Just over the bridge stands the village hall in brick and flint, appropriately called St Edmund's Hall, which was built at the same time as the bridge and is a rather impressive building as village halls go. The gable wall has a plaque beneath the window that tells of King Edmund being taken prisoner and slain, while the apex has a relief carving that shows Edmund lurking beneath the bridge with sword in hand as Danes cross above him. The car park has an information board with details of a five-mile circular walk that snakes into Norfolk to take in Billingford windmill. Thoughtfully, perhaps because this is still a pilgrimage site of sorts, there is also a picnic table for weary walkers. If you wish to see the St Edmund monument where the oak tree used to stand, then continue south a little way past some very smart thatched cottages and you'll soon see a sign pointing towards the monument, which at the time of writing stands amid a building site although a path between the houses is planned for the future.

Further references to St Edmund can be found in Hoxne's **St Peter and St Paul Church**, as you might expect. A bench-end shows the saint's head between the paws of a wolf, and an oak screen depicting events from his life is reputedly made from the tree that was destroyed by

MARK STAPLES

DISS MUSEUM

BEN GOULDING'S

RICHARD GIFFIN

lightning where his monument stands. Hoxne's history clearly stretches back further than the Saxon time of St Edmund: in 1992, a local man looking for a lost hammer in a nearby field found instead an enormous hoard of 15,000 Roman gold and silver coins, jewellery and tableware, probably hidden in the turbulent 5th century when Roman rule was breaking down. The Hoxne hoard, the largest ever found of its type in the United Kingdom, is now in safe keeping in the British Museum.

History at Hoxne actually stretches back further still – much further, into prehistory and the misty realms of deep time. In 1797, a Lower Palaeolithic hand axe was discovered in the village by the antiquarian John Frere, a sharp-pointed butchery tool that dates to approximately 400,000 years ago. In the 1970s, an extensive flint-working area was discovered close to the village on the edge of a long-vanished, ancient lake. Pollen and animal bone analysis of the site has shown that elephant, rhinoceros and lion once occupied the area, alongside early man, during a warm, interglacial period that has become known as the 'Hoxnian interglacial' after the site.

¶¶ FOOD & DRINK

Swan Inn Low St ☎ 01379 668275 ⌨ theswaninnofhoxne.co.uk. Built in 1480 by the Bishop of Norwich as a lodge, this atmospheric listed building is all bare sloping floors, oak beams and open fires, with a 10ft-wide inglenook in the main bar. Food is seasonal and locally sourced where possible. It is very popular at weekends, so it's best to book ahead.

11 EYE

🏠 **Cowpasture Barn**, Mellis (page 277)

West of Hoxne, Eye is a quiet, self-contained little market town just south of the River Waveney. It actually lies on the west bank of the River Dove, a tributary of the Waveney, and is home to a church tower that the architectural writer Nikolaus Pevsner deemed 'one of the wonders of Suffolk'. The church in question is that of **St Peter and St Paul** and its 101ft-high tower is remarkable for the flint flushwork on its west side. The church stands beneath a Norman **castle mound**, which is now all mound and no castle but gives quite a view of the town nevertheless. The town clings tightly to the base of this: a small maze of streets and

◀ **1** The picturesque town of Eye. **2** Dancers in Diss town centre. **3** An icon of St Edmund in Hoxne's church. **4** A wild Konik pony on Lopham Fen.

ancient houses dominated by the brick-and-flint panel Victorian **town hall** with its ornate clock tower. The town's guildhall stands beside the church, an impressive Tudor building.

The town gets its curious name from an Old English word for 'island', and when it was first settled it probably was almost entirely surrounded by water and marshland associated with the River Dove: the surrounding area still sometimes floods.

Eye Castle was constructed in the years that immediately followed the Norman Conquest and a Benedictine Priory was founded shortly after in the town in 1086–87. Hugh Bigod, the first Earl of Norfolk, attacked the castle in 1173 during the rebellion against Henry II and it never really recovered, although its prison continued in use as late as the 17th century. You can climb up to the castle mound by following the signs from the car park at Buckshorn Lane. The path takes you through a small estate of modern wedge-shaped Toblerone-like houses, across a meadow and up some steps to the top. At the top, there used to stand a building known as **Kerrison's Folly**, constructed in the mid 19th century by General Sir Edward Kerrison, reputedly as a home for the batman who had served him at the Battle of Waterloo. Part of the folly was used as a museum in the early years of the 20th century but there are just remnants of walls left now – it collapsed in the 1960s. If the story is true, then Kerrison's batman must have enjoyed waking up to a bird's-eye view of the town in his later years. You can enjoy the same perspective by climbing up the enclosed wooden staircase. The interpretive board here has a drawing of what the castle might have looked like in the 16th century when a windmill stood on the top – quite a sight in this land without hills.

Once down from the castle, the town's **Guildhall** is worth a look too: a timbered Tudor building that has the archangel Gabriel carved into one of its corner posts. There's another impressive Tudor building on the corner of Church Street and Buckshorn Lane, close to the town hall; it's currently a pharmacy. There's also a fine example of a crinkle-crankle wall (see box, page 188) beside the road that leads into the town from the direction of Diss.

¶¶ FOOD & DRINK

Caféye 14 Broad St ✆ 01379 873000. A conveniently placed café for coffee, cakes, all day breakfasts and lunches, with a good choice of vegetarian and vegan options on offer.

Queens Head 7 Cross St ☎ 01379 870153 ⌂ queensheadeye.co.uk. This 16th-century inn has good traditional pub food and daily specials and is the only survivor of around 15 pubs that served the town a few decades ago.

DISS & AROUND

In this upstream part of the Waveney Valley the river is little more than a stream by the time it reaches Diss in south Norfolk. A little way beyond the market town the source of the river lies in marshes close to the source of the River Little Ouse that flows westwards and delineates the Suffolk/Norfolk border in the west of the county.

12 DISS (NORFOLK)

Diss is a town of two halves. The modern part of the town, east of the centre close to the A140, is pretty undistinguished and could be almost anywhere but do not judge the town on the basis of this, as the old part of Diss is far more appealing.

Old Diss centres around a body of water, **The Mere**, a six-acre, spring-fed lake that gives the town its name, as dice in Anglo-Saxon means 'standing water' or words to that effect. Diss folk claim that this glacial remnant is at least 60ft deep, with about 20ft of water and 40ft of mud. The common theory is that it was formed when the underlying chalk bedrock collapsed, an altogether more plausible theory than it being the mouth of an extinct volcano, as a few Diss residents still believe. The Mere was badly polluted in the 19th century, with high mercury levels brought about by local hatters and dyers making use of its water. Bizarrely, it was also around this time that The Mere was stocked with eels, which, according to some accounts, threw themselves from the water at every opportunity such was the level of pollution. Thankfully, it's clean enough to swim in these days, although this is expressly forbidden. Global warming being what it is, it is unlikely that there will ever be a repeat of the winter cricket matches and ice carnivals that were held on its frozen waters in the early 19th century.

"Thankfully, it's clean enough to swim in these days, although this is expressly forbidden."

A waterside path leads from the southern shore to what is usually referred to as the **Mere's Mouth**, where there is an information centre and the Diss Publishers Bookshop and Café, which as well as a selection of local books has café tables by the water. It's a place to feed the ducks, lick an ice cream and have a 'mardle' (local-speak for leisurely chat) on market days. These days, there's an electric fountain in the middle of The Mere that spouts like a mini Jet d'Eau on Lake Geneva.

Mere Street leads north from the Mere's Mouth up towards the **market place** past a few pubs, cafés and independent shops. There's a good showing of Tudor timber-framed buildings in addition to some fine red-brick Georgian and Victorian houses. Friday – market day – is definitely the day to be here as, unlike in much of clone-town Britain, it's still an important weekly event. there's also a **farmers' market** held here on the second Saturday of each month.

Diss Museum (✆ 01379 673613 ∂ dissmuseum.co.uk ⊙ Mon–Sat), located in a small building right at the top of the market place, is a community museum run by enthusiastic volunteers. **St Mary's Church**, just beyond, dominates the market place, a fine 13th-century building in the Decorated style. The church's most famous rector was John Skelton, who was rector here from 1504 until his death in 1529. Skelton, who had earlier served as tutor to the young Henry VIII and had been Poet Laureate of both Oxford and Cambridge universities, remains firmly in the number one place of the town's most illustrious citizens. A later Poet Laureate, John Betjeman, was another admirer of the town.

Opposite the church stands the 16th-century **Dolphin House**, a striking black-and-white timbered building that has seen life as a wool merchant's house and a pub in the past. These days it houses various small businesses. Further north along Mount Street from St Mary's you'll find more handsome Georgian houses lining a quiet street. If, instead, you head west along St Nicholas Street you'll come to the **Corn Hall**, which like most such buildings in these parts is in the mid-19th-century Neoclassical style. The days of cereal wheeling and dealing may be past but it is still an active place, with regular concerts and plays.

"The days of cereal wheeling and dealing may be past but it is still an active place, with regular concerts and plays."

Fair Green is set apart from the rest of the old town but worth a detour. You can reach it by walking west along Park Road from the bus station and turning left at the roundabout. Once you round the corner, the contrast is extreme. Gone are the noisy lorries thundering along

Park Road; you suddenly find yourself next to an idyllic village green with a café, a pub and a restaurant clustered around its eastern end. The green, which is surrounded by highly attractive 16th- and 17th-century houses, was granted a charter for a fair in 1185 and must have presented quite a sight back in the days when bear-baiting and cockfighting were regarded as quite ordinary pursuits. The Cock Inn no doubt gets its name from such activities, as do many other 'Cock' pubs in the region. The fair was finally closed by Parliament in 1872, ostensibly because of its reputation for 'disorderly behaviour'.

¶¶ FOOD & DRINK

If you are just looking for a coffee and a snack, there are several options along Mere Road. **Diss Publishers Bookshop and Café** (✆ 01379 644612 ⊘ disspublishing.co.uk) at number 41 has some tables outside overlooking The Mere, as does **Café Culture** (✆ 07552 330340) at number 11, by the Market Place further up. **The Saracens Head** (75 Mount St ✆ 01379 652853 ⊘ saracensheaddiss.co.uk), just behind the church, has standard pub grub and steaks. The options listed below are at Fair Green, a little further away from the centre but really not that far.

Angel Café 1 Fair Green ✆ 01379 641163 ⊘ angelcafediss.co.uk. Rustic, friendly and low-key, the Angel Café serves up organic meals and snacks, with plenty of vegetarian options. It's also good for espresso coffee, homemade cakes and desserts.
Cock Inn Lower Denmark St, Fair Green ✆ 01379 643633 ⊘ cockinndiss.co.uk. With a decent selection of real ales and a great view over the green, this is a sound choice. Live music events on some Saturday nights.

13 REDGRAVE & LOPHAM FEN

West of Diss, the Waveney begins as a tiny trickle at Redgrave and Lopham Fen, very close to where the Little Ouse also rises. The Fen, which covers 300 acres and is the largest surviving area of river valley fen in England, has been managed by the Suffolk Wildlife Trust (⊘ suffolkwildlifetrust.org/redgrave) for the past 50 years (although the reserve straddles both counties and the visitor centre is actually in Norfolk) and has an impressive cluster of designations as a wetland of national and international importance. It is also one of only two sites in the country that has native **fen raft spiders**, as well as being a prime habitat for dragonflies and butterflies, mammals like otters and pipistrelle bats, and a recorded 96 bird species.

Like the Norfolk Broads, the fen was traditionally used for reed and sedge cutting for thatching, as well as cattle grazing at its drier margins. Part of the Suffolk Wildlife Trust's management strategy is to use Hebridean sheep and Polish Konik ponies to control the vegetation. The black Hebridean sheep look strangely at home grazing here, as do the small grey ponies that thrive in the wet conditions. These all add to its atmosphere as quite a primeval place and the presence of the semi-aquatic raft spiders certainly fits in with this image. Arachnophobes should probably be aware that the fen raft spider is one of Britain's largest, although even here they are pretty scarce. I once spent a long time looking for them to no avail at one of the designated viewing pits but you may be luckier. There's a **visitor centre** (Low Common Rd, South Lopham ✆ 01379 687618) run by the Suffolk Wildlife Trust, and three dedicated nature trails. Be warned, the mosquitoes can be vicious here in summer, especially in the woodland areas – either lather up with Jungle Formula or similar, or wear long sleeves and trousers.

If you visit here, then you might also take a look at nearby **Redgrave** village, a pleasant place that has all the essentials of village life: a pub, a green, a church and a community shop (✆ 01379 898848) in the premises of the original village shop.

The award-winning Slow Travel series from Bradt Guides

Over 20 regional guides across Britain.
See the full list at bradtguides.com/slowtravel.

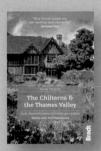

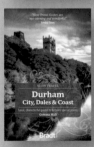

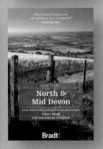

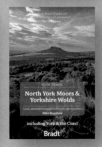

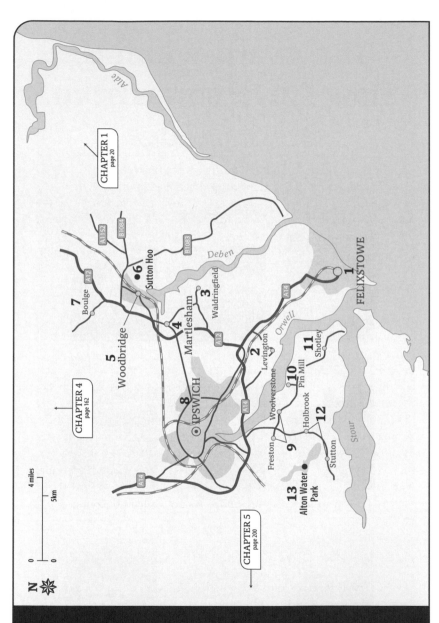

SOUTHEAST SUFFOLK

CHAPTER 1
page 20

CHAPTER 4
page 162

CHAPTER 5
page 200

Alde

Deben

Orwell

Stour

FELIXSTOWE

Sutton Hoo

Boulge

Woodbridge

Martlesham

Waldringfield

Levington

Woolverstone

Freston

Holbrook

Pin Mill

Shotley

Stutton

Alton Water
Park

IPSWICH

A1152
B1084
B1083
A12
A12
A14
A14
A14

N

4 miles
5km
0
0

1
2
3
4
5
6
7
8
9
10
11
12
13

3
SOUTHEAST SUFFOLK

This chapter continues from where the first left off, dealing with the southern part of the Suffolk coast – Felixstowe and its peninsula, the county town Ipswich and its surrounding area, Woodbridge at the head of the Deben estuary and the Shotley Peninsula that extends between the ports of Felixstowe and Harwich south of Ipswich. It's a mixed bag that deals with some of the largest places in the county as well as tiny estuary villages. The various inlets and estuaries that punctuate the coastline further north continue to do so in this part of the county, although they tend to be much larger and wider. The Rivers Deben, Orwell and Stour all flow into the North Sea along this stretch and the sea trade that dwindled centuries ago in the silted-up ports of the northern part of the coast still thrives here. The Port of Felixstowe is currently the largest container port in the country, which might not suggest very much in the way of Slow credentials but the port is just one aspect of Felixstowe and the town itself has many redeeming features. Ipswich, too, might seem on first inspection to be brash and traffic-blighted, but the town has far more going for it than might immediately be apparent. Woodbridge, on the other hand, has abundant Slow appeal. As for the Shotley Peninsula, if anywhere were to be awarded the clichéd epithet of 'best kept secret' then this might be a worthy contender. It's not a secret of course, just a little unsung.

GETTING AROUND

The A12 connects Ipswich with Woodbridge and Lowestoft to the north. Felixstowe is connected to Ipswich and the rest of the country by the A14, a very busy road that carries a great deal of container traffic to and from the Port of Felixstowe over the Orwell Bridge and continues west to Stowmarket, Bury St Edmunds and the Midlands. The Shotley

Peninsula has just one main road running its length to reach Shotley at the end, the B1456, while the A137 runs south of Ipswich across the western end of the peninsula to reach Cattawade at the mouth of the estuary of the River Stour and the eastern extremity of the Stour Valley.

PUBLIC TRANSPORT

Ipswich, at the centre of this region, has excellent rail connections with London, Norwich and Stowmarket, although reaching the rest of the country directly without a connection in the capital tends to be less straightforward. There are, however, regular train services from Ipswich to Cambridge, Ely and Peterborough. Felixstowe, although somewhat out on a limb, has regular trains to Ipswich. The East Suffolk Line, run by Greater Anglia, connects Lowestoft with Ipswich at roughly hourly intervals, stopping at Beccles, Halesworth, Darsham, Saxmundham, Wickham Market, Melton and Woodbridge along the way. Local **bus services** from Ipswich connect some of the smaller villages of the Felixstowe and Shotley peninsulas with the county town and, although the service is far from perfect, even the smallest villages here seems to have a bus going somewhere near them at sometime in the day. The First Eastern Counties 75, 76, 77 and X7 services all connect Ipswich with Felixstowe via Trimley, the 64, 65, 70, 70A and 79 services connect Ipswich with Woodbridge, while the 97 and 98 services run more or less hourly between Ipswich and Shotley Gate at the end of the Shotley Peninsula via Holbrook and Chelmondiston respectively. First Eastern Counties bus 78 runs between Ipswich and to Levington on the Felixstowe Peninsula and the same company's 73 service connect Felixstowe with Woodbridge.

𝑖 TOURIST INFORMATION

All About Ipswich ⮐ allaboutipswich.com

Choose Woodbridge ⮐ choosewoodbridge.co.uk

Felixstowe Felixstowe Library, Crescent Rd; also Visit Felixstowe Tourist Information Centre beach hut on promenade, opposite Town Hall ✆ 03330 162000 ⮐ visitfelixstowe.org.uk

Suffolk Coast & Heaths AONB ⮐ suffolkcoastandheaths.org

The Suffolk Coast ⮐ thesuffolkcoast.co.uk

Woodbridge Woodbridge Library, New St ✆ 01394 446510

A couple of **ferries** are useful too. Bawdsey Ferry (✆ 07709 411511), a foot-passenger service between Bawdsey Quay and Felixstowe Ferry, operates from May to the end of September and also at weekends during Easter. This is a useful lifeline for venturing north along the coast from Felixstowe Ferry to avoid a very long detour by road. The other service worth considering is the Harwich Harbour Foot & Cycle Ferry (✆ 01728 666329 ⬦ harwichharbourferry.com) that runs between Landguard Fort and Shotley Gate, calling in at Harwich in Essex along the way. This operates about eight times daily between early April and the end of October, and weekends only in November and December. First Eastern Counties bus 77 operates hourly through the day between Landguard Fort and Ipswich via Felixstowe and Trimley.

CYCLING

Away from the main trunk roads – the A12, A14 and A137 – cycling is generally enjoyable in this part of the county, especially on some of the quieter roads on the Felixstowe and Shotley peninsulas. The OS Landranger 169 covers most of the area in this chapter and is useful for planning quiet, virtually traffic-free cycling routes and avoiding pitfalls.

WALKING

Surprising though it might seem given the number of largish towns, the walking in this part of the county can be extremely good. Two long-distance walking routes pass through it: the Stour and Orwell Walk, and the Sandlings Walk. Both offer potential for day walks between points along the route or for circular walks that incorporate just part of them.

The **Stour and Orwell Walk** does pretty much exactly what its name suggests. Starting at Landguard Point in Felixstowe, where the Suffolk Coast Path terminates, it follows the southern edge of the Felixstowe Peninsula, close to the shore for much of the way, then goes in and out of Ipswich before following the entire shoreline of the Shotley Peninsula, first along the southern shore of the Orwell estuary and then along the northern shore of the River Stour. It ends at Cattawade close to the Essex border, where the Stour Valley Path begins along Dedham Vale.

The **Sandlings Walk** offers an alternative route to the Suffolk Coast Path between Ipswich and Southwold, via Woodbridge, Snape and Dunwich. Rather than following the coast, the route passes through the Sandlings heaths a little way inland. Really keen walkers could join all three routes together with the Suffolk Coast Path to make a continuous circuit of around 160 miles.

Far more modest undertakings are, of course, possible. **Day walks** of both of the routes already mentioned are worth doing if transport connections are not a problem. For example, the first section of the Sandlings Walk between Ipswich and Woodbridge, which is much better than it might seem, or the section of the Stour and Orwell Walk on the Shotley Peninsula that stretches between Pin Mill and Shotley Gate. The peaceful Shotley Peninsula is also excellent territory for short circular walks; some suggestions will be indicated in the text. Fearless urban warriors might want to go for the ultimate road walk challenge and cross the Orwell Bridge south of Ipswich. There's a pavement beside the road here and it's perfectly possible to cross the bridge using this although this is probably the antitheses of a Slow experience and will not be to everyone's taste.

THE FELIXSTOWE PENINSULA

This large tract of land south of Ipswich and Woodbridge is sandwiched between two of Suffolk's principal rivers – the Deben and Orwell. At the end lies Felixstowe, a popular resort and also the location for Britain's largest container port, tucked away behind Landguard Point in Harwich harbour, at the mouth of the River Orwell. Away from the frantically busy A14 dual carriageway, which shuttles lorry traffic to and from the port, this is mostly an area of mixed farmland like much of the rest of the county. The Deben shore is largely undeveloped, a land of marshes and muddy creeks, while the east bank of the River Orwell on the western side of the peninsula is a little more populated, with small villages like Nacton and Levington that have a country park and marina respectively.

1 FELIXSTOWE

🏠 **Grafton Guesthouse** (page 277)

Mention Felixstowe to anyone from outside Suffolk and the thing most think of is the Port of Felixstowe, hardly classic Slow territory. The port, though, is actually quite separate from the main part of the town that has long been a popular seaside resort and continues to be so despite a slight economic downturn of late. The fact that Felixstowe's role as a resort has been overshadowed in recent years is actually welcomed by many Suffolk natives, especially those of the Ipswich area, who quite like to have the place to themselves. It's all pretty much traditional seaside and gentrification is yet to happen here, as are sky-high property prices and a deluge of well-heeled incomers. For the time being, Felixstowe does not quite have the 'Let's Move to...' kudos celebrated in the resorts further north along this coastline. This is not such a bad thing. Certainly, the town is nowhere near as smart or refined as Southwold or Aldeburgh but it does not make any claim to be so. It's an old-fashioned seaside resort

"Certainly, the town is nowhere near as smart or refined as Southwold or Aldeburgh but it does not make any claim to be so."

pure and simple: gastropubs, posh delis and art galleries may be a bit thin on the ground but what you do have is a pier, albeit somewhat truncated these days, a long pleasant promenade and more beach huts than you shake a stick of seaside rock at.

In some ways Felixstowe is actually several towns in one. There's the seaside resort that flanks the promenade and beach, there's the port of course, all swivelling cranes and multicoloured mounds of stacked containers, and there's Old Felixstowe, an area of town that stood long before there were any notions of a holiday resort or container port. Finally, there is Felixstowe Ferry, a place apart, barely a village, where people mess about in boats, fish are landed by a handful of fishermen and not much ever happens. Most of the action takes place at the other end of the town in the vicinity of the port. It did in the past too, at nearby Landguard Fort, a redoubtable defensive structure that continues to keep watch over Harwich harbour with a steely military gaze.

Felixstowe's life as a resort began like so many similar places when the railway arrived at the end of the 19th century. A relative of Queen Victoria, Princess Augusta Victoria of Schleswig-Holstein, wife of Kaiser Wilhelm II, visited Felixstowe for an extended holiday in 1891; this put the town on the must-go-to map for London's wealthier citizens. Felixstowe water was considered to have curative properties and the town was granted 'spa' status in 1902, following which paddle steamers started to come direct from London, dropping off passengers on the pier that in those days was more than half a mile long, much longer then than it is today. Another famous visitor to the town – not quite royal in this case but very nearly – was Mrs Wallis Simpson who resided in the town at Beach House on Undercliff Road East for six weeks in 1936 in order to achieve resident status necessary to divorce her American husband and marry Edward VIII. She was clearly used to better things, though, and recorded in her diary that 'the little house in Felixstowe was dismaying. It was tiny, there was barely room for the three of us [two friends and herself], plus a cook and a maid, to squeeze into it.' The house was demolished in 1994 and so you can no longer go there yourself to check whether the wannabe queen was being a little too picky. There is a tea room named after her on Undercliff Road East now, which she probably would have hated too, although she obviously had some sort of interest in the catering trade as it was while staying in Felixstowe that she is said to have invented the club sandwich. Of other celebrity figures associated with the town, T E Lawrence ('of Arabia') is probably the best known. The author and World War I hero was based here incognito for two years in the 1930s while serving as an aircraftsman at RAF Felixstowe.

Felixstowe: the resort

A good way to see the best that Felixstowe has to offer is to the start at **Felixstowe Quay** north of the town. There's a car park here and a foot ferry across to Bawdsey Quay on the other side of the River Deben, where the ornate chimney pots of Bawdsey Manor can be seen to good advantage across the water. There's not that much here besides a waterfront, quay, a few huts selling fish, a café and a pub but it's a good place to watch the world go by and imbibe some briny sea air. A Martello tower stands a little way south of the quay and there's another to be seen a little further on towards the town, situated a little incongruously on the edge

"The original pier that stood here was dramatically shortened during World War II to ward against enemy landings."

of a golf course. There are beach huts too, the first of what must be hundreds lining the seafront on the way into town. These eventually peter out around the point where the coast bends eastwards at Cobbold's Point and a procession of groynes runs out to sea.

The sea-wall promenade begins a little further on, the cranes of the port clearly visible ahead. The promenade runs parallel to Undercliff Road East beneath a very large, imposing building on top of Bath Hill that was once a hospital but has now been redeveloped into apartment units. Until recently this functioned as a convalescent care centre and before the building's construction in 1926 was the site of another

Martello tower and also the Bath Hotel, burned down by suffragettes in 1914, their last major outrage before receiving the vote in 1918.

The promenade continues along Undercliff Road West past more beach huts and seafront gardens to reach the **Spa Pavilion Theatre** (⌀ spapavilion.uk), the original building of which was also bombed and burned to the ground, this time by bombs during World War II (Felixstowe was one of the few places in the United Kingdom to be attacked by Italian planes during the Blitz). The current building dates from the 1950s and is host to a wide variety of live music shows and family entertainment. It also boasts two sea-view restaurants. Further ahead is the **pier**. The original pier that stood here was dramatically shortened during World War II to ward against enemy landings. Constructed in 1905, it once stood over half a mile long and had its own electric tramway to bring *Belle* paddle steamer passengers from London into town. The original pier head building was demolished in 2016 and a brand new £3 million building, larger than its predecessor, with a café-bar, fish and chip shop and boardwalk, opened in summer 2017. Unfortunately the part of the original jetty that remains is closed to the public.

Beyond the pier, where the cranes of the port loom ever larger as you continue south, are all the things that you might expect of a seaside resort of the old school – amusement arcades, bingo halls, ice-cream parlours and fast-food places. Continuing south, you come to the third of the town's Martello towers, which now finds useful service as a coastguard lookout station. There's a caravan and campsite just beyond here and then a track across a common that leads to Landguard Fort.

Landguard Fort

Landguard Fort View Point Rd IP11 3TW ✆ 01394 675900 ⌀ landguard.com ◷ Apr–Oct & Feb half-term week Thu–Sun, daily during school holidays; English Heritage; **Felixstowe Museum** ✆ 01394 674355 ⌀ felixstowemuseum.org

At the peninsula's southernmost tip is this large pentagonal fort protecting Harwich harbour. It was built in 1744 to replace an earlier structure that in turn had replaced an older building that had originally been commissioned by Henry VIII. The fort stands on the site of the last invasion of England in July 1667 when Dutch soldiers landed nearby but failed to capture it, as they were repulsed by the Admiral's Regiment, the forerunners of today's Royal Marines. The fort remained in military

ARCHER PHOTO/S

1

CHRIS LAWRENCE TRAVEL/S

2

LANDGUARD FORT

3

RONALD ROBERTS/DT

4

hands until as recently as 1971, mostly as barracks in its later years. English Heritage took the fort over in 1997 and carried out structural repair work before opening it to the public. Although the fort now lies firmly in the county of Suffolk, this territory was once considered to be part of Essex. Daniel Defoe mentions this in his account of his early 18th-century tour of East Anglia in which he observes that 'The fort is on the *Suffolk* side of the bay or entrance; but . . . our surveyors of the county affirm it to be in the county of *Essex*.' Whichever side of the county line, there's certainly plenty to see here – soldiers' quarters, magazine tunnels, ammunition chambers and so on – and the entrance fee includes a good free audio tour that describes the everyday lives of the men who were posted here. Guided tours are available too for those who prefer a live human to an anonymous voice in the ear. Tours of the outer batteries take place on Sunday afternoons, as do ghost tours.

The fort is home to **Felixstowe Museum**, housed in the neighbouring Ravelin Block, a former mine storage depot, which has various exhibits on local history as well as details of the history of the fort itself. South of the fort at the very end of Suffolk is a small nature reserve where migrating birds are kept under close observation, up-to-date details of which are usually chalked up on a blackboard outside the entrance.

The Port of Felixstowe & Old Felixstowe

You can follow the road around the back of the fort to a car park where there's an excellent view across the mouth of Harwich harbour and a very welcome caravan snack bar too. This is also the departure point for the foot ferry that crosses from here to Harwich and Shotley Gate. To the right lies the **Port of Felixstowe**, with its clattering lorries, swirling cranes and four-high stacks of containers; more than likely there'll be a massive cargo ship in dock too. If you really want a closer look at this, make for the quite surreal viewpoint, where there's a bench, directly above the dockyard a couple of miles west along the route of the Stour and Orwell Walk as it heads out of Felixstowe. A little further on, out of town but still within

"South of the fort at the very end of Suffolk is a small nature reserve where migrating birds are kept under close observation."

1 The River Deben near Waldringfield. 2 Felixstowe's pier. 3 A barracks room in Landguard Fort. 4 Levington Creek.

the acoustic shadow of all the metallic activity in the port, are **Trimley Marshes**, a nature reserve with pools full of wading birds.

Felixstowe is more than a mere appendage to a massive container port, and more than just a holiday resort too. North of the centre, **Old Felixstowe**, with its leafy streets and elegant three-storey Victorian and Edwardian houses, is well worth a wander. Fans of unusual buildings might want to check out St Andrew's Church in the town centre, which has the distinction of being England's first reinforced concrete church. Don't expect a squat bunker-like structure though – it's quite elegant, a mock-Perpendicular edifice rising among mock-Tudor semi-detacheds.

¶¶ FOOD & DRINK

The Alex 123 Undercliff Rd West ☏ 01394 282958 ⌖ alexcafebar.co.uk. Very convenient for the seafront, this busy café-bar with a first-floor brasserie is just across from the prom. The downstairs café-bar offers grill and seafood dishes as well as a good choice of plant-based options, plus all-day breakfasts, brunches, snacks, light meals and good cakes and coffee. There are also Adnams ales to be had and quite extensive wine, gin and cocktail menus to ponder over.

Ferry Boat Inn Felixstowe Ferry ☏ 01394 284203 ⌖ ferryboatinn.org.uk. Nicely situated down by the quay at Felixstowe Ferry, a great base for a seaside stroll, this has real ale, decent fish dishes as you might expect, and a good choice of gluten-free options too.

Greenhouse Café 5 Orwell Rd ☏ 01394 279311 ⌖ felixstowegreenhouse.com. A vegan café with a green-thinking ethos that uses local produce for its dishes. Also dairy-free cakes and savouries, plus coffee served with a variety of plant milks.

The Little Ice Cream Company 59–61 Undercliff Rd West ☏ 01394 670500 ⌖ littleicecreamcompany.co.uk. This is the place in Felixstowe to come for a seaside ice cream, much of which is made on the premises from local produce. There's also light lunches and artisan coffee on offer too.

Regal Fish Bar Sea Rd ☏ 01394 273977. This fish bar on the front is highly rated by locals for its consistent high quality and large portions.

View Point Café View Point Rd ☏ 01394 675892 ⌖ viewpointcafe.co.uk. It's hardly surprising that, given the name of both the road and the café, this commands fantastic views across the port and mouth of the River Orwell. This no-nonsense café on the Landguard Peninsula is the perfect place for a mug of tea and a bacon sandwich while watching the ships come in.

The White Horse 33 Church Rd ☏ 01394 277496. This traditional pub in Old Felixstowe serves locally sourced home-cooked food and a good selection of real ales. There's also a beer garden for fine weather.

2 LEVINGTON

There is not a huge amount between Felixstowe and Ipswich to detain most visitors but the area around Levington on the south side of the peninsula is not without interest. The village, which these days is a peaceful little place with a thatched pub and a church overlooking the River Orwell and across to Pin Mill on the other side, was a centre for digging coprolite back in the 18th and early 19th century. Coprolite – fossilised dung from prehistoric animals – was highly regarded as a fertiliser and dug by hand from just beneath the surface in the area. The industry has long since declined and is now just a memory, but the name lives on in Ipswich where there is still a Coprolite Street, which sounds considerably better than Fossilised Dung Street (or worse).

Levington Creek just below the village has long been connected with the sea and was once a working harbour. Coal was landed by barge here up until World War I, and long before this Viking boats would have made landfall here, as evidenced by the discovery of remains of what was probably one of the Danish fleet that raided Ipswich in AD991. Smugglers, too, used to take advantage of the creek's inconspicuous situation and in 1817 a boat named *Daisy* was apprehended carrying 48 tubs of spirits that it shouldn't have had. Although the creek hasn't seen any barge trade since the 1920s you can still make out some of the harbour furniture, with some old mooring posts and fragments of wooden jetties still visible.

Just east of Levington Creek is the Suffolk Yacht Harbour at Levington Marina, constructed in 1967 on reclaimed land. West of the village is **Broke Hall**, surrounded by parkland landscaped by Humphry Repton in 1794. He was obliged to incorporate specific design specifications in his plan to obscure the view of neighbouring Orwell Park and also hide views of the estuary's mudflats yet keep views of the river channel itself. Repton's near 300-year-old avenue of lime trees can still be seen leading down to the hall.

3 WALDRINGFIELD

Across the peninsula on the Deben shore, Waldringfield, like Levington, was another centre for coprolite mining. Now, like its counterpart on the other side of the peninsula, it is a quiet village with a yacht club. Unlike Levington, there's also a river beach here, and a golf course too on what used to be Waldringfield Heath. Behind the beach is a sandy cliff of the same red crag that used to yield copious quantities of coprolite that brought wealth to the village. Waldringfield village makes a decent enough base for walks along the marshes of the Deben River – The Maybush pub down at the water's edge is a good place to start and finish. There's also an enjoyable short walk from here up to the village's hilltop church, All Saints', with its Tudor red-brick tower.

Southwest of the village, just outside Newbourne you'll find **Newbourne Springs nature reserve**, a Site of Special Scientific Interest (SSSI) managed by the Suffolk Wildlife Trust that has an impressive array of wildlife from willow tits, siskins and orchids in its swampy woodland to butterflies and nightingales on the heath. The various springs here provided the water supply for Felixstowe until the 1980s and what was once the pumping station is now the visitor centre. There's also a disused crag pit, once a source of coprolite, across the road from the car park, which now has sand martins nesting in its steep, red crag slopes. A circular walk can be made around the reserve starting at the visitors' car park.

¶¶ FOOD & DRINK

The Maybush Cliff Rd ✆ 01473 736215 ⌖ debeninns.co.uk/maybush. Beautifully situated on the west bank of the Deben River, this former 15th-century farmhouse has excellent views of the waterfront, Adnams beer and a decent menu that features local game and fresh seafood.

4 MARTLESHAM

Martlesham sits at the head of the peninsula, west of Waldringfield, close to and more or less midway between Ipswich and Woodbridge. The village is probably best known for being the Suffolk Constabulary headquarters and also for its aviation museum in the former control tower of what used to be RAF Martlesham Heath. Hopefully you will not require the services of the former but might want to investigate the latter. **Martlesham Heath Control Tower Museum** (✆ 017707 711104 ⌖ mhas.org.uk ☉ Apr–Oct Sun afternoons only; free) has interesting displays about the aerodrome's history. Both Peter Townsend and Douglas Bader once flew missions from here. Truth be told, these days Martlesham Heath receives the majority of its visitors because it is the home of Martlesham Heath Retail Park, an out-of-town shopping centre with ample parking and all the big-name stores that is a magnet for folk from this part of Suffolk in need of a little retail therapy.

That said, Martlesham also looks set to become an important place for wildlife in the near future. In 2023 Suffolk Wildlife Trust announced that a 286-acre organic arable farm was to be transformed into a new wetland nature reserve. The plan is for the farm on the banks of the River Deben to be left fallow so that it will encourage the return of wildlife as diverse as slow worms and turtle doves as well as providing habitat for declining redshank and lapwing populations.

Martlesham Creek, an inlet where the River Fynn forms a confluence with the River Deben, is a little way northeast of the village. Once a centre for contraband smuggling, now a haunt for wading birds and boat enthusiasts, it is a strangely quiet place given the proximity of Woodbridge just to the north and Ipswich to the west. A riverside footpath here follows the route of the Sandlings Walk along the west bank of the River Deben all the way into Woodbridge, an excellent way to approach the town.

IPSWICH & WOODBRIDGE

Suffolk's county town, its largest by far, sits on the River Orwell straddling the head of two peninsulas, Shotley and Felixstowe. Far smaller Woodbridge lies a little way northeast on the bank of the River Deben. In many ways, the two towns are like chalk and cheese: one brash, noisy and traffic-addled, the other traditional, refined and relatively peaceful. An over-simplification perhaps, but while Woodbridge seems a natural contender for honorary Slow status almost any way you look, in Ipswich it is necessary to be rather more selective.

5 WOODBRIDGE

🏠 **The Crown** (page 277), **Station Guesthouse** (page 277) 🏡 **Jasmine Cottage** (page 277), **Teachers House** (page 277) ⛺ **Secret Meadows** (page 277), **Suffolk Yurt Holidays** (page 277)

William A Dutt in his turn-of-the-century *Highways and Byways* referred to Woodbridge as 'a delightful little town – one of the prettiest little country market towns in England'. Dutt was quite right: it is. This is not one of those cases where you lament how things have changed since imagined halcyon days. No, it's a fact: take away the cars and the town really hasn't changed that much since Dutt wrote his account. The urban blight that has despoiled parts of neighbouring Ipswich seems to have kept well clear of Woodbridge. It is a living, breathing market town, well-to-do, certainly, but it still belongs in the real world rather than just the lifestyle pages of the Sunday supplements.

The town stands at the head of the River Deben estuary, where you'll find yourself if you arrive by train – and perhaps by car too, as there's a big car park down here by the railway lines. From here it's just a short walk uphill to The Thoroughfare, the commercial heart of the town. There's also a footbridge across the railway and a riverside path that leads south along the estuary past reedbeds and rowing clubs. If you head in the opposite direction and walk around the back of the riverside theatre you'll soon reach a quay that has one of the town's most distinctive buildings, the **Tide Mill** (✆ 01394 388202 ⊘ woodbridgetidemill.org.uk ☉ Easter–Sep daily, Oct w/ends). This elegant, white-planked 18th-century building operated until the 1950s, harvesting the power of the incoming tide to turn a waterwheel. If you want to see the mill working, it is best to plan ahead using a local tide table: the mill's website lists the best times to see the wheel turning and the old wooden machinery in operation, although nothing can be guaranteed as it is all slightly unpredictable. This is largely because the pond that used to store the tidal water has now been replaced by a much smaller one, while the original has morphed into a kidney-shaped **yacht harbour** that is closed to the general public unless you are wearing the right kind of sailor's hat. Much less fancy but, I think, more characterful boats are moored at the quay beside the tide mill. You can detect a real sense of community in the slightly battered craft with pot plants and bicycles on their decks moored in the boatyard beyond the yacht harbour.

Nearby is the newly located **Woodbridge Museum** (✆ 01394 380502 ⊘ woodbridgemuseum.com), just off Tide Mill Way. This has a range of exhibits detailing the history of the town and its people, especially local luminaries Thomas Seckford and Edward FitzGerald. Next door to the museum is **The Longshed** (✆ 01394 610983 ⊘ woodbridgeriversidetrust.org/the-longshed), a warehouse-like building on the site of a former boatyard that is used as a community space for exhibitions, talks and events. Among several projects based here, one is the building of a replica of the Sutton Hoo burial ship, an ongoing project that began in 2019. Also on Tide Mill Way is **Woodbridge Art Club** (⊘ woodbridgeartclub.org.uk), which has regular exhibitions by local artists. the **Riverside Restaurant** and Theatre (𝒜 01394 382174 ⊗ theriverside.co.uk), which offers occasional tempting deals that combine a three-course dinner at its A-listers restaurant with a film in its retro-style cinema.

Away from the riverside, central Woodbridge is delightfully traffic-free, with the pedestrianised streets of Quay Street, Church Street, New Street and The Thoroughfare combining to provide a compact shopping and strolling area. One of its glories is that there are so many small retailers and so few chain stores: the Woodbridge Town Centre Management Group has come up with the slogan, 'Choose Woodbridge for real shopping'. Choose Woodbridge is also the name of the town's business and tourism association (⊗ choosewoodbridge.co.uk), which encourages visitors and residents alike to 'Stay Local, Choose Woodbridge'. **The Thoroughfare**, in particular, has several independent bookshops and tea rooms. In fact, the town has so many coffee houses and tea rooms you suspect that the town council may have shares in Twinings.

Woodbridge's **historic core** lies a little further uphill. Woodbridge is surprisingly hilly and slopes sharply away from the river. Melton Hill, which has St John's Church, is claimed by some to be the inspiration for the 'Grand Old Duke of York' nursery rhyme, although there is no historical evidence of 10,000 soldiers marching up and down this particular hill. Other Woodbridge hills have been suggested, as has Ipswich, which has an actual Grand Old Duke of York pub (Woodbridge only has a 'Duke of York' pub to its name). The Duke of York in question, Frederick Augustus, the second son of George III, actually had far more than 10,000 men under his command in his Napoleonic campaign, and he wasn't old either – just 31 at the time. The song more than likely came about following an unsuccessful campaign in Flanders, and that is probably where the hill in question is.

Returning to terra firma in Woodbridge, Church Street and New Street merge at Market Hill where the imposing Dutch-gabled **Shire Hall** has pride of place. Built by Thomas Seckford in 1575, the ground floor of this building once served as the town's corn exchange while the upper level was used for judicial purposes. In front of the shire hall on Market Square stands an elegant stone pump built in 1876. You can get a great view of the rooftops of the town by climbing up the steps to the small balcony on the southern side of the Shire Hall. North of the Shire Hall, on Market Hill, there's a pleasant shady square, a surprisingly tranquil spot to find right in the centre of town. Here you'll find the King's Head pub and Wild Strawberry Café, with outside tables in summer beneath the trees in front of the Shire Hall. Keep going along Theatre Street and you reach **Buttrum's Mill** ($\mathscr{D}$ 01473 264755 ☉ summer w/ends & bank holidays), a nicely restored six-storey tower mill dating from 1836.

ⵂ FOOD & DRINK

You have a wealth of cafés and pubs to choose from in Woodbridge – below is just a small selection. Among the food shops are a couple of excellent delis and bakeries in town. The **Woodbridge Deli** ($\mathscr{D}$ 01394 610000) home of the Woodbridge Fine Food Company at 2a New Street has fresh shellfish, wines, picnic foods and its 'world famous pies'. There is a branch of **The Two Magpies Bakery** ($\mathscr{D}$ 01394 383085 ⊘ twomagpiesbakery.co.uk/woodbridge) at 60 Thoroughfare, which has an excellent range of cakes and pastries as well as numerous options for brunch or lunch. Another fine bakery is **The Bakehouse** (21 New St $\mathscr{D}$ 01394 384398 ⊘ thebakehousebakery.co.uk), which has all manner of breads, savouries and fancy cakes.

Cherry Tree Inn 73 Cumberland St $\mathscr{D}$ 01394 384627 ⊘ thecherrytreepub.co.uk. A traditional inn with home-cooked food and a good selection of cask ales and wines.
King's Head 17 Market Hill $\mathscr{D}$ 01394 387750. Located in one of the oldest buildings in town, this has decent ales, a decent pub menu with meats from Five Winds Farm in nearby Melton, and a roaring fire in winter.
Spice Bar @The Table 3 Quay St $\mathscr{D}$ 01394 382007 ⊘ thetablewoodbridge.co.uk. This brasserie-restaurant offers an interesting fusion menu that puts a modern twist on classic Asian food and makes use of local seasonal produce. It offers a number of appealing vegetarian options and there's an attractive courtyard.
Whistlestop Café Station Rd $\mathscr{D}$ 01394 384831. A conveniently situated, good-value and friendly café right next to the station. A top choice for breakfast or all-day brunches.
Wild Strawberry Café 19a Market Hill $\mathscr{D}$ 01394 388881 ⊘ wildstrawberrycafe.co.uk. Well located overlooking Market Hill, with shady outside seating in summer, this has a seasonal menu that utilises local produce wherever possible. Everything here from cakes to sausage rolls is homemade on the premises.

6 SUTTON HOO

Trammer House, Sutton Hoo, near Woodbridge IP12 3DJ $\mathscr{D}$ 01394 389700 ☉ Apr–Oct daily, Nov–Mar w/ends; National Trust

---

1 Woodbridge by the River Deben. **2** A millstone in the 18th-century Tide Mill. **3** A life-size sculpture of the Sutton Hoo ship. **4** The grave of Edward FitzGerald in Boulge. ▶

SIMON COLLINS/S

SIMON BALLARD

JOHN WORRALL/A

WIRESTOCK CREATORS/S

Just across the Deben estuary from Woodbridge is the **Sutton Hoo Burial Site**, unearthed in 1939 to reveal a large Anglo-Saxon ship. This had been buried stuffed with treasure which included magnificent garnet-set gold jewellery, silver, drinking horns and armour: Anglo-Saxon notables tended to leave this world in great style. Ship burials seem to have been a Suffolk speciality: there were others here, and one in nearby Snape, but treasure-hunters raided the Sutton Hoo mounds in the 16th century and only missed finding this one by a few inches. The notable in question here is most probably Raedwald, who was King of East Anglia in the early 7th century. As famous as the ship burial is the beautiful silver and gold ceremonial helmet found at the site.

The discovery is a saga in itself: the landowner, Mrs Edith Pretty, a widowed spiritualist, commissioned a self-taught local archaeologist, Basil Brown, to excavate some grassy mounds that she somehow sensed had some significance. To his everlasting credit, rather than simply digging down for treasure, Brown recognised that the lines of metal rivets in the sandy soil represented all that was left of a ship's hull, still in position, and excavated with great skill. But once the discovery became national news, he was sadly sidelined by the 'professionals' directed by the British Museum. At least Brown gets to tell the tale: it is his voice that does the narration on the audio guide. Reasonably enough, it is Brown, sensitively played by Ralph Fiennes, who is depicted as the hero in the 2021 Netflix film *The Dig*, a fictionalised account of the ship's discovery in the months leading up to the outbreak of World War II.

You might want to join one of the tours led by local volunteers to get the best sense of what happened here. Run by the National Trust, the site is set in a 245-acre estate with attractive woodland and estuary walks. An easy half-hour circular walk can be done round the perimeter of the mounds, which passes a 56ft-high viewing tower and has good views across to Woodbridge and the Deben estuary along the way. There's also an excellent view of the estuary to be had from the terrace of King's River Café, which does decent snacks and lunches. The exhibition at High Hall has a full-size reconstruction of the burial chamber and displays that tell the story, including a replica of the iconic Anglo-Saxon helmet found with the ship burial. Tranmer House, built in 1910 and the former residence of Edith Pretty, has displays of the archaeological work that was carried out on the site. There is another place for take-away drinks and snacks – Keeper's Café – located next to the house.

7 BOULGE

You may struggle to find tiny Boulge on the map. The village – more just a collection of lanes – does have an interesting story to tell though. Across the A12 from Woodbridge and a little further north, a minor road leads west to the village of Bredfield. After less than a mile it comes to a junction with a water pump and some fancy wrought ironwork that has finger signs pointing in every direction. Take the one that says 'Debach and Clopton' and just after Partridge Farm you should notice a crude hand-painted sign pointing along a rough track to Boulge church. Take this and you'll soon come to **St Michael's Church**, hidden away on the edge of a small wood, a delightfully peaceful spot that seems much further from the A12 than it really is.

The graveyard here is the resting place of Edward FitzGerald, a slightly oddball Victorian polymath who was responsible for translating Omar Khayyám's *Rubáiyát* poems from the Persian. FitzGerald's family owned the Boulge Estate to which the church belongs – the hall was destroyed in the 1950s – and he lies buried in the graveyard here under a simple carved granite slab. Some straggly rose bushes around the grave are rather more special than they might first appear, having been planted by admirers from the Omar Khayyám Club in 1893, ten years after FitzGerald's death. The original rose was raised from seed brought from

WHO'S (OR WHAT'S) HOO?

East Suffolk has a number of places that describe themselves as 'Hoo'. There's Sutton Hoo, of course, the site of the Anglo-Saxon ship burial close to Woodbridge, but take the back road from here towards Framlingham and you will find a few more. There's Dallinghoo village, a little way north of Bredfield, and there's another – more a parish and cluster of houses than a village – simply called 'Hoo', whose church of St Andrew and St Eustachius was used in the 1974 film version of *Akenfield*. There's also a Hoo Hall, a Hoo Lodge and a Hoo House Farm. There's even a Hoo Ho marked on the OS map, but sadly without a sign on the road to match.

So what does 'hoo' mean? There's a clue on the Hoo village sign, which depicts a plough team ascending a steep (for Suffolk) incline. Sharing the same name as the Hoo Peninsula that separates the estuaries of the Thames and Medway rivers in Kent, it is an Old English word for 'spur of land'. This same word might even have an etymological connection with the Suffolk (and Norfolk) colloquial term 'on the huh', which is best translated as 'on the wonk' or more correctly as 'on the slope'.

the grave of Omar Khayyám in Nishapur, Persia, and more have been planted since, although none of them appeared to be doing very well the last time I came here. Nevertheless, their oriental origin provides an exotic touch to what might seem a perfectly ordinary, half-forgotten Suffolk graveyard.

Edward FitzGerald lived a life somewhat at odds with the rest of his family, and that his grave lies separate from the large family tomb is probably indicative of the alienation he felt. FitzGerald disliked the stuffy life of the estate and spent much of his adult life at Woodbridge where he dressed in odd clothes and befriended herring fishermen at the quay. One in particular, Joseph 'Posh' Fletcher, had a long-term relationship with FitzGerald that was most probably not entirely platonic – quite scandalous at the time. Ironically, FitzGerald's Woodbridge boat was named *Scandal* too. If you think Edward FitzGerald sounds like a typical W G Sebald character, then you are right. Sebald passed this way in *The Rings of Saturn* and wrote movingly of FitzGerald's predicament.

> *"Their oriental origin provides an exotic touch to what might seem a perfectly ordinary, half-forgotten Suffolk graveyard."*

8 IPSWICH

🏠 **Freston Tower** (page 277), **Kesgrave Hall** (page 277)

Ipswich, Suffolk's largest town by far, may not seem to readily fit with the notion of Slow. For a start, although the Suffolk county town has 'town' status, it is the size of a city, with a population comparable to that of its rival Norwich across the county border to the north. It is perhaps a little unfair to compare Ipswich to Norwich – I will confess to a personal bias here as I live in the latter – but while planning mistakes have certainly been made in the Norfolk cathedral city these are as nothing compared with the way that Ipswich has been shoddily redeveloped in places and carved up by a traffic system that does no favours for its historic core.

Ipswich has plenty of fine sights and much of historical interest; the trouble is the sights seem to sit in isolated pockets. Here you'll find half-timbered Tudor houses juxtaposed next to concrete car parks and slapdash 1960s development. There are exceptions though, most notably the pedestrianised zone in the town centre. The regenerated waterfront area also holds plenty of appeal. The problem is that at present these two areas are not very well linked together, especially for walkers.

The town centre

Quite a few specific things are worth seeking out in the town centre, parts of which still retain a medieval character. For pargeting aficionados, the town has what is perhaps the very best example in the county at the 15th-century **Ancient House** on the corner of St Stephen's Lane and Buttermarket. This was once a merchant's house, known as Sparrowe's House after its one-time owner, Robert Sparrowe, who added the Royal Arms of Charles II in the 1660s. The building is now owned by Ipswich Town Council and, having served as a bookshop and a branch of a kitchen-utility chain in the past, there are now plans afoot to use the Ancient House as a combined information hub, restaurant and department store filled with independent traders and local artisans. Here, four pargeted panels represent the continents of Europe, Asia, Africa and America as seen through Tudor eyes (Antarctica and Australasia are both missing, unknown at the time). Some of the imagery, as you might expect, reflects the perceived stereotypes of the period, with Africa represented by a naked man with a spear. Just around the corner from here, an interesting story concerns the bells at **St Lawrence's Church** on Dial Lane, currently used as a café and community centre. In 2009, the church's five bells were returned to their place in the tower after a 25-year absence. Cast in the mid 15th century, the bells, known as the Wolsey Bells after the town's famous cardinal, are the oldest circle of bells in the world. They were removed in 1985, but have now been overhauled and reinstalled, complete with their original clappers. Their sound is reckoned to be unique and beautifully mellow by those able to judge these things. Whatever the quality of this genuinely medieval sound, it is humbling to think that when these bells first chimed in the streets of Ipswich, Columbus had not yet 'discovered' America. Although you are unlikely to hear its ancient bells peal during your visit, it is worth stopping for a drink and a look at the church's cavernous, heavily Victorianised interior. As you sip your mug of tea you can admire the wooden pulpit and the stained glass above the kitchen area, and heed the instructions of the frieze that circuits the wall: 'Blessed are the pure in heart for they shall see God... Blessed are the...' and so on. St Lawrence's is just one of many, mostly disused, medieval churches in Ipswich, enough indeed to give even famously church-rich Norwich a run for its money. Bells aside, it also has a rather lovely 15th-century tower with a wealth of fine flushwork detail. South of Buttermarket another redundant church, **St Stephen's**, which ceased to be used as a church in 1978, was used as the town's tourist information centre until its closure in 2020. Following considerable investment, the church reopened as a music venue and creative meeting space in 2023.

Central to the whole of this pedestrian zone at Cornhill is **Ipswich Town Hall**, an impressive Victorian edifice that looks as if it should belong in a middle-sized city rather than a county town. There is a market in front of the town hall four days a week and just around the corner on Queen Street you'll find a bronze statue of Grandma, the character created by *Daily Express* cartoonist Giles who used to work in the offices opposite. More controversially, a large modern sculpture consisting of four reconstituted stone plinths was erected on Cornhill in 2018. Dubbed 'Cornhenge' by locals, the plinths were meant to document Ipswich's history but were widely unpopular and soon showed signs of rusting. Despite briefly held plans to replace them with plinths of 'more polished stone' the ill-fated sculpture was laboriously removed from the site in September 2019.

West of Cornhill, on Elm Lane, is the **Church of St Mary at Elms**, a redbrick-towered Anglo-Catholic church set among the drab surroundings of tower blocks and offices. This houses the statue of **Our Lady of Ipswich**, which once belonged to a nearby Marian shrine that in the medieval period was second only to Walsingham in Norfolk in terms of its importance as a centre for pilgrimage. The statue on show is a modern replica of the original, which was taken away to be burnt during the English Reformation, although it is strongly believed that it was rescued and taken overseas by English sailors, ending up at the Italian seaside town of Nettuno.

For more timber-framed buildings you should head to St Nicholas Street and Northgate Street, where Oak House dates from the 15th century, as does nearby Pykeham Gatehouse. A little way west of Cattle Market bus station on Silent Street is a modern **statue of Cardinal Wolsey** with a cat at his side, opposite his childhood home. The cardinal, Henry VIII's chancellor, wanted to build a college in the town that would act as a feeder school for Cardinal (now Christ Church) College, Oxford, which he had also founded. But thanks to the Reformation and

IPSWICH: **1** The waterfront. **2** The tower of St Lawrence's Church. **3** Pargeting on Ancient House. **4** The market outside the Town Hall. ▶

CKTRAVELS.COM/S

RICHARD MACRAE

TIM LEGGETT

TIM LEGGETT

PARGETING

Pargeting is the traditional art of decorative plastering on the walls of houses. The technique involves moulding wet lime plaster to create a form of bas-relief. Pargeting is most commonly seen in Suffolk although there are examples in other parts of East Anglia like Norfolk, Cambridgeshire and Essex. There would have been plenty of pargeting on show in London too before the Great Fire of 1666 destroyed it all. It is most commonly seen on buildings that date from the 16th or 17th century when the art reached its zenith, although there was also a revival of interest during the Arts and Crafts Movement of the late 19th century. There are also a few contemporary examples. The art probably began in the time of Henry VIII but no pre-Elizabethan examples survive. The best examples in the county are The Ancient House in Ipswich (page 147) and on the County Museum (also known as 'The Ancient House' in Clare; page 230).

Wolsey's fall from power the college was closed and demolished within a year of opening. All that remains now is Wolsey's Gate on College Street and the nearby church of **St Peter's by the Waterfront**, which was commandeered by Wolsey to become the college chapel. The church, probably on the site of Ipswich's very first church, is now a heritage centre and music venue (⊘ stpetersbythewaterfront.com). It is just south of the town centre close to the waterfront as the name suggests, but the river probably once ran even closer to the church than it does today (to reach the waterfront proper from here, turn right down Foundry Lane then left along the quayside to arrive at the new Neptune Marina development). St Peter's is home to the **Ipswich Charter Hangings** – eight tapestries commissioned to celebrate the millennium and depict the 800 years since the town received its charter from King John. The tapestries, which took over three years for a team of 30 to complete, have the River Orwell as a constant theme on each of them along with a collage of buildings, coats of arms, ships, town life and prominent figures in Ipswich history from the Viking period through to the present day.

Ipswich Waterfront

The Waterfront has been Ipswich's biggest project in recent years – a large-scale regeneration begun in 1999 that has entailed the building of a large number of new apartments, a hotel, several restaurants, university buildings and a marina. At the centre of all this is the **Old Customs House** (⊘ 01473 231000), a Victorian Neoclassical building that now serves as the offices of the Ipswich Port Authority. Nearby is the Waterfront union building of the University of Suffolk, which has its campus near here. Across the water on the other side, just west of the customs house, stands the Jerwood Dancehouse, the permanent home of Dance East, built on the site of a former mill. Although not really old enough to have fully developed much real character, the Waterfront is an enjoyable place to visit, especially on a sunny day; a place to drink, eat, stroll and watch the boats come and go.

This being the Waterfront, naturally enough there are boats here aplenty. One permanently moored here sees service as Mariners, a smart floating restaurant (page 153), while another, *Orwell Lady*, moored at Orwell Quay, runs regular **cruises** along the River Orwell between Easter and early October (✆ 07736 299653 ♂ orwellrivercruises.com), from a short one-hour trip passing underneath the Orwell Bridge to various theme-night trips and what it calls 'English Afternoon Tea Cruises', which involve either a 2½ hour trip to Pin Mill and back or a 3½ hour exploration of Harwich harbour. A wind-powered trip can be had on the old Thames sailing barge *Victor* (♂ sbvictor.co.uk), which sails from the Old Customs House on a variety of cream tea, supper and do-it-yourself picnic cruises along the River Orwell in late spring and summer.

Christchurch Park

Ipswich has several pleasant parks but Christchurch Park, formerly the grounds of an Augustinian priory, is by far the most special. Sloping down to the town centre from the north, this large leafy space is a great place to come for leisurely walks and picnics, and on sunny Sundays that is exactly what many Ipswich folk do – it's deservedly popular with locals.

A BOAT OF MANY FLAGS

The boat that currently serves as Mariners floating restaurant at Neptune Quay down at Ipswich's Waterfront began life as the SS *Argus* in Bruges in 1889. Requisitioned for the Belgian Navy and sunk by the Germans in 1940, it was raised and repaired by them before becoming a Dutch Red Cross hospital ship renamed the *Florence Nightingale* in the 1950s.

Following this, it became a party boat for a while before being brought to Ipswich to be opened as an Italian restaurant in 1990. Nowadays, it is a French brasserie – truly an international vessel.

There's plenty for children, with duck ponds, ice-cream kiosks and a dedicated play area. The park also has two arboretums and free tennis courts. At its centre stands a red granite **monument** to the nine Ipswich martyrs executed during the reign of (Bloody) Queen Mary.

The **Christchurch Mansion** (✆ 01473 433554 ⊘ ipswich.cimuseums. org.uk), a handsome Tudor building at the bottom end of the park, was presented to the town by Felix Thornley Cobbold, a philanthropic brewer, in 1892 and now serves as a museum. The mansion has a collection of Victorian toys and games and an interesting Tudor kitchen as well as an art gallery that includes works by notable Suffolk artists like Alfred Munnings and a good collection of paintings by John Constable and Thomas Gainsborough. At the rear of the building you'll find a tea room.

¶¶ FOOD & DRINK

Ipswich has a wide choice of cafés, restaurants and pubs – a small selection is given below. Probably the most atmospheric place to eat and drink, certainly the most up-and-coming, is at one of the restaurants that line the quay at the newly developed Waterfront area.

For food shopping there are a couple of places for quality Suffolk produce close to the town. Just south of Ipswich, close to the west side of the Orwell Bridge, is the **Suffolk Food Hall** (✆ 01473 786610 ⊘ suffolkfoodhall.co.uk), probably the largest and best-known farm shop in the county. This is open seven days a week and stocks a huge array of local produce – bread, cheese, meat and fish – as well a bistro restaurant, café, a cookery school and activities for children. Nearby at Wherstead is **Jimmy's Farm & Wildlife Park** (Pannington Hall Lane, Wherstead IP9 2AR ✆ 01473 604206 ⊘ jimmysfarm.com; see opposite), a rare-breed farm with a shop, restaurant, woodland trail, events and courses, a butterfly house, a vegetable garden, petting farm, and special activities for children.

Bistro on the Quay 3 Wherry Quay ✆ 01473 286677 ⊘ bistroonthequay.co.uk. Overlooking Ipswich Marina, this is now managed by the same team who run Mariners. The menu here features local produce like Orford fish and Suffolk cheeses, and there's an extensive wine list.
Dove Street Inn 76 St Helens St ✆ 01473 211270 ⊘ dovestreetinn.co.uk. With an excellent range of real ales and other drinks, including beers from its own brewery next door, this friendly pub is close to the city centre and university campus. Good homemade pub grub and a choice of different rooms to sit in, as well as an outdoor beer garden.
Fat Cat 288 Spring Rd ✆ 01473 728524 ⊘ fatcatipswich.co.uk. Sister pub to Norwich's famous Fat Cat, itself something of a legend in the real ale movement, this lies east of the

BACK FROM THE BRINK: JIMMY'S FARM SAVES THE ESSEX PIG

Jimmy Doherty's farm is one of the best known in the country thanks to a BBC2 television series that documented the trials of raising rare-breed pigs. Although Jimmy's Farm now trades under the broader banner of Jimmy's Farm & Wildlife Park, part of Jimmy's business still goes under the name of the Essex Pig Company and you might be fooled into thinking that the farm stands on the wrong side of the River Stour. It doesn't – it's in Suffolk, just south of the A14 near a village called Wherstead. The pigs, however, have an impeccable Essex pedigree.

The Essex Pig is a direct descendant of the breed that once foraged East Anglia's wildwood. Modernisation brought about a dramatic decline in their numbers following World War II, and by 1967 the breed was considered extinct. Luckily, one farmer, John Crowshaw, managed to keep his pedigree Essex bloodline pure. Although the Essex Pig remains officially extinct, Jimmy Doherty is currently hard at work building up the numbers of this rare animal. Jimmy's Essex porkers are in suitably aristocratic company, having both Saddlebacks and hefty Gloucestershire Old Spots as farmyard neighbours. In acknowledgement of his conservation work with rare breeds, Jimmy became President of the Rare Breeds Survival Trust in 2016, the youngest president to date.

city centre between the university campus and hospital. Like its sister, this has an enormous choice of real ales – more than a dozen on tap. Inexpensive snacks are available too like pasties, pork pies and Scotch eggs, and there's all the (lack of) amenities you'd expect in a traditional pub – no fruit machines, and no jukebox or TV.

Mariners Neptune Quay ✆ 01473 289748 ⬦ marinersipswich.co.uk. Down at the Waterfront, this floating brasserie is located in an 1899 Belgian gunboat. This is one of the smartest places to eat in Ipswich and so quite formal and expensive, although the set meals are reasonably priced. Although the food might be described as French with a modern twist, almost all ingredients are locally sourced.

St Lawrence Centre Café Dial Lane ✆ 01473 225267. Decent, inexpensive food and snacks in the lovely stained-glass setting of a deconsecrated church right in the heart of town. This is a social enterprise business that provides work for adults with disabilities.

The Grazing Sheep 15a Regatta Quay ✆ 01473 216832 ⬦ thegrazingsheep.com. A good place on the quay for coffee and pastries, as well as breakfasts and brunches made with locally sourced ingredients.

Waterfront Bar Bistro 15 Regatta Quay ✆ 01473 226082 ⬦ waterfrontbistroipswich. co.uk. A French-influenced place on the waterfront with an outside terrace and a fair few vegetarian and vegan choices.

THE SHOTLEY PENINSULA

South of Ipswich, a finger of land extends southeast, delineated by the River Orwell to the north and the River Stour to the south. At the tip of the finger is Shotley Gate, once a naval training base, isolated from the rest of Suffolk by land yet close to both Felixstowe and Harwich in Essex by sea, both of which lie just a mile or two away across the water of Harwich harbour. In sharp contrast to the busy urban centre of Ipswich to the west, the peninsula has an essentially rural character – a place apart that is a gently rolling terrain of arable farms and pockets of woodland with lonely marshes and creeks close to the shoreline. The Stour and Orwell Walk long-distance path follows both shores of the peninsula before ending at Cattawade, close to Manningtree in Essex.

9 FRESTON & WOOLVERSTONE

Freston, a little way along the northern side of the peninsula, is sufficiently close to Ipswich to still have the imposing bulk of the Orwell Bridge in its sights and the distant thrum of the A14 in its ears. Nevertheless, this already feels very rural and slow-paced. There's a church here, St Peter's, which has an unusual war memorial in its churchyard, a life-sized *Peace* in the form of a young woman holding a laurel wreath aloft. The figure is made out of wood, sculpted from oak in 1921 and restored on Armistice Day 2006. The churchyard stands at the south side of

"If you come here in spring you'll be greeted by the delicious garlicky aroma and pretty white flowers of ramsons."

Freston Wood, an atmospheric ancient wood with gnarled pollarded oaks and many species of bird, flower and butterfly. If you come here in spring you'll be greeted by the delicious garlicky aroma and pretty white flowers of ramsons that cloak the bottom part of the wood. Walk a little higher, towards the church, and the aroma morphs to the sweet hyacinth smell of bluebells that festoon the wood in late April and May.

Across the road that leads to the church, opposite The Boot pub, a footpath leads through woodland to Freston Park where **Freston Tower**, a six-storey, red-brick Tudor folly stands. It was built in 1578–9 by Thomas Gooding, an Ipswich merchant who bought Freston Manor in 1553 and clearly liked to show off a bit. He also must have enjoyed having an unimpeded view of Ipswich and the River Orwell from his very own lookout tower – no Orwell Bridge in those days, of course. The tower is now owned by the Landmark Trust (⟨⌂⟩ landmarktrust.org. uk) who rent it out for accommodation, a single room for each storey.

Woolverstone, the next village reached heading out along the peninsula, is home to Ipswich Girls' School which moved to its current premises at Woolverstone Hall in 1992. This is very much an estate village with no pub, shop or post office, but it does have a church, St Michael's, fronted by an avenue of neatly clipped yews, and down at the river there is a marina that has been the base for the Royal Harwich Yacht Club since World War II.

10 PIN MILL

A little way east of Woolverstone and close to the village of Chelmondiston, Pin Mill is probably the place on the peninsula that most know about. The waterfront pub here, the Butt and Oyster, is rightly very popular with sailors and Sunday-lunchers from Ipswich and beyond. Pub or not, though, the waterside hamlet here is an enticing spot. Pin Mill has always been very much centred on sailing and this was once the place where Thames barges came for repair and barges used to be unloaded here in the 19th century. The hamlet was also a centre for sailmaking and there used to be a maltings and a brickyard here too. Naturally enough given its waterside credentials, it is also one of those places deemed to be a former smugglers' haven. There is still an active boatyard here, Harry King and Sons Ltd, and these days there is also a gallery and art studio, Pin Mill Studio (⟨✆⟩ 01473 780130), which runs workshops for adults and children in addition to watercolour painting days and photography courses – Pin Mill is nothing if not photogenic.

The hamlet also provided inspiration for the children's author Arthur Ransome, who kept his yacht *Selina King* anchored here in the late 1930s. The seafaring action in *We Didn't Mean to Go to Sea*, Ransome's tale of hapless child adventurers inadvertently sailing across to the Netherlands, begins here at Pin Mill at Alma Cottage close to the Butt and Oyster.

"Naturally enough given its waterside credentials, it is also one of those places deemed to be a former smugglers' haven."

The cottage also features in his following book, *Secret Water*.

Beyond the pub, heading east along the footpath through Pin Mill Plantation, a tract of woodland owned by the National Trust, you'll see

RICHARD BOWDEN/S

MARK STAPLES

JONATHAN WILLIAM PROSSER/S

KIRSTYL1990/S

lots of moored houseboats through the trees below, some in poor repair and apparently abandoned, others that look quite enticing. Many of these are converted Thames barges that have not seen the eponymous river for many a year. Continuing along here eventually brings you to Clamp House at Butterman's Bay, which takes its name from the schooners that used to transport dairy produce from the Channel Islands. A barge race, organised by the Pin Mill Sailing Club, has been held here every summer since 1961. From here you can retrace your steps or follow the path around the wood back in the direction of Pin Mill.

If you have plenty of time and energy you could continue all the way to Shotley Gate, a wonderful walk alongside marshes full of ducks and wading birds. The contrast between the near-silent saltmarsh on the Shotley side and the frenzied commercial business of the container port on the other side of the Orwell is really quite remarkable. From Shotley Gate, there should be a more or less hourly 97 or 98 bus back to Ipswich railway station via Chelmondiston, just half a mile from Pin Mill, but be sure to check first.

¶¶ FOOD & DRINK

Butt and Oyster Pin Mill Rd, Pin Mill IP9 1JW ✆ 01473 780764 ⬡ debeninns.co.uk/buttandoyster. A very popular waterside pub on the south bank of the River Orwell that is nearly always busy. The wonderful location counts for a lot and is the reason why people come here. The Adnams beer is fine, while the food offered is a decent choice of pretty standard pub grub fare.

11 SHOTLEY

Shotley, a mile short of Shotley Gate on the B1456, does not have much to recommend it other than one of the peninsula's few pubs, The Rose, but Church End just to the north of the village has the parish **church of St Mary's**, itself unremarkable but with a fascinating churchyard. Here you'll find the graves of sailors who served in two World Wars, hundreds of them, many of them just young lads, as well as the tombstones of German sailors from World War I. There is also a memorial to the victims of a collision between two submarines. It's a sad and haunting spot, with the feeling of melancholia perhaps heightened further by

◀ **1** Wooden boats at Pin Mill. **2** Red campion growing on Shotley Peninsula.
3 Freston Tower. **4** Alton Water reservoir.

hilltop views across to the lines of cranes of the Port of Felixstowe in one direction and Harwich docks in the other.

West of Shotley, **Erwarton Hall** has a particularly striking gatehouse, a splendid 16th-century Gothic edifice with six brick pinnacles like rockets ready for the launch and with something of the look of an oriental tomb. Sir Philip Parker of Erwarton Hall was Anne Boleyn's uncle and she is said to have often stayed at the hall. It is rumoured that after her beheading her heart was buried at Erwarton's St Mary's Church according to her wishes. This might appear an unlikely story but a small heart-shaped cask was discovered in an alcove of the church during restoration in 1838. On opening it contained a small quantity of black dust and it was subsequently reburied beneath the organ. There is a plaque in the church giving details of the story. Whatever the truth of the Anne Boleyn connection, there are obvious signs that link her name with the Erwarton area. The village's Queen's Head pub, closed since 2009 and most probably destined to be converted into a private home despite local efforts to keep it, used to display a portrait of Anne Boleyn as its pub sign while not very far away, close to Beaumont Hall Farm, is a small wood called Boleyn's Covert.

Shotley Gate lies at the very end of the peninsula. Not an alluring place in itself, it was the home of HMS *Ganges*, a large training base for Royal Navy cadets, it is now more just a spot to watch ships come and go across the waters of Harwich harbour. HMS *Ganges*, which was originally a training ship in Harwich harbour but moved to a purpose-built onshore facility in 1905, finally closed in 1976 although it was used as a police training centre for some years afterwards. A small museum (✆ 01473 788723 ⌂ hmsgangesmuseum.org.uk) dedicated to the ship stands next to the marina entrance. The Harwich–Felixstowe Ferry also departs from near here. Shotley Gate has a pub should you need it, the Bristol Arms, and a reasonable bus service to and from Ipswich, but the best thing about the place really is its location and you are better off getting your boots on and heading away from the village. **Shotley Marshes**, immediately north of the village and reached by a footpath, is an expanse of low-lying farmland behind the river wall that is an important breeding site for wading birds like snipe and redshank as well as a wintering ground for flocks of Brent geese.

"Erwarton Hall has a particularly striking gatehouse, a splendid 16th-century Gothic edifice with six brick pinnacles like rockets ready for the launch."

¶¶ FOOD & DRINK

Bristol Arms Bristol Hill, Shotley ✆ 01473 787200 ⏚ bristolarms.com. With real ale, decent food made with ingredients from mostly local suppliers and good views over Harwich harbour, this is a convenient port of call in the Shotley area.

12 HOLBROOK & STUTTON

Holbrook, on the south side of the peninsula roughly halfway along, is best known for its Royal Hospital School, the enormously tall tower of which can be seen for miles around. The school, which is in Neoclassical style and the largest boarding school in East Anglia, was constructed here in 1933 as a school for Royal Navy children when the school was moved from its original base at Greenwich Hospital. Its 200ft campanile tower can be seen from as far away as Ipswich.

The spread-out village of **Stutton** lies just west of Holbrook, and has fine pargeting on some of the cottages. Crowe Hall, one of six manor houses listed in the Domesday Book, lies just south of the main street, surrounded by a long ornate wall. The parish church, St Peter's, lies to the east. Once the houses would have clustered around the church but they were burned down in medieval times in an attempt to thwart the spread of plague. Whether this worked or not is uncertain as Pin Mill on the other side of the peninsula was one of the last places in Britain to have an outbreak of plague recorded. The village has its own volunteer-run community shop (✆ 01473 328133), which sells a selection of local produce and has its own café.

A road leads south of the village past Crepping Hall to Stutton Ness and the path that leads west along the river beach here to Stutton Mill is particularly lovely, passing fragments of woodland and sculptural dead trees. **Stutton Mill** at Newmill Creek is appealingly situated too, an isolated group of buildings shaded by willows next to an inlet. From here, the Stour and Orwell Walk continues west for its final leg to **Cattawade**, an unremarkable village at the head of the estuary.

13 ALTON WATER

Alton Water Park ✆ 01473 328268 ⏚ anglianwaterparks.co.uk/alton-water
Alton Water, close to both Stutton and Holbrook, is a reservoir popular with both windsurfers and sailors. This, the largest body of inland water in the county, is a good place for walks too, with footpaths around most of its eight-mile shoreline and a nature trail with bird hides. Kingfishers,

nightingales and grass snakes are all regularly seen here. Cycling is also a good option, especially along the southern shore where there is a surfaced cycle track. **Cycle hire** is available ($\mathscr{D}$ 01473 328408) at the visitor centre on the south side of the water between Stutton and Holbrook, where you'll also find a tea room. There is also a camping and caravanning site, should you wish to stay here.

Tattingstone on the west side of Alton Water might be said to be where the Shotley Peninsula begins – west of this everything starts to feel rather more suburban as you get drawn into Ipswich's gravitational field. The village was split into two in the 1970s when the area was flooded to create Alton Water. A road bridge connects the two halves – plain old Tattington south of the water and Tattington White Horse (after the pub) on the northern side. Alton Hall, which used to stand in the village, was one of many properties to vanish beneath the water – a necessary sacrificial lamb to ensure Ipswich's future drinking water supply. Another building in the flood zone, Alton Mill, was dismantled completely and re-erected at the Museum of East Anglian Life in Stowmarket (page 194). Tattingstone is home to the so-called **Tattingstone Wonder**, a folly dating from 1790 that is made up of a group of cottages with an added square tower and a Gothic flint façade. The story goes that Edward White, the incumbent squire, wanted to improve the view from his library window and so went about creating this architectural trompe l'œil in order to achieve the desired effect. From the front it really does look like a small parish church; from the rear it looks much more like three small cottages with a fake three-sided tower.

¶¶ FOOD & DRINK

White Horse White Horse Hill, Tattingstone $\mathscr{D}$ 01473 328060 $\mathring{\diamond}$ whitehorsetattingstone. co.uk. This nice country pub in a village just north of Alton Water has a good selection of cask ales and wines, and traditional pub food including some vegetarian and gluten-free options. There is a small campsite at the rear of the building.

Adventures in Britain

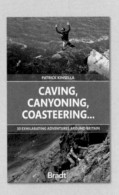

Bradt GUIDES

TRAVEL TAKEN SERIOUSLY

bradtguides.com/shop

 BradtGuides  @BradtGuides @bradtguides

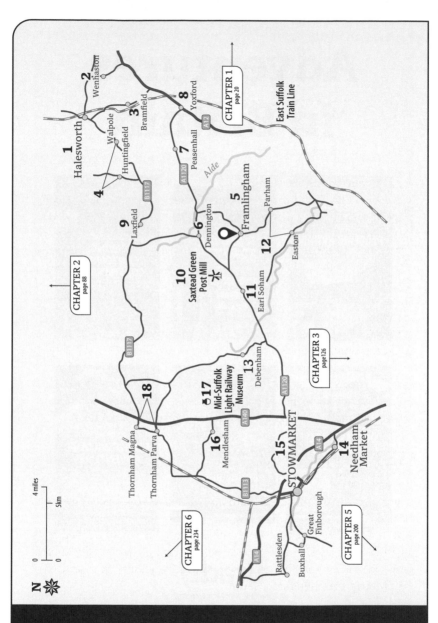

N

CENTRAL & EAST SUFFOLK

4
CENTRAL &
EAST SUFFOLK

This chapter covers the 'High Suffolk' plateau that rises south of the Waveney Valley. Let's not get too carried away with the words 'high' or 'plateau' though – as you might expect for East Anglia, it's pretty modest stuff. 'High Suffolk' may be overstating it a bit but compared with the rest of the county it is just that: a rolling plateau of arable farmland interspersed with villages and small market towns. A hundred years ago, this area was almost entirely devoted to agriculture and most of the land is still used for arable crops, although these days most local inhabitants are involved in pursuits other than farming. Despite the vast seas of golden wheat that turn some of these settlements into virtual islands in August, farming involves a very small workforce these days: agriculture may well be big business, but is no longer a big employer. Nevertheless, the towns and villages of this area retain plenty of connections with the soil, as do the people, and although daily village life may no longer revolve around the changing seasons, it still takes notice of them.

GETTING AROUND

It's easy enough in a car. The main roads are the A12 and A14, both of which lead roughly north to south on either side of Ipswich. The A140 runs south from Norwich to Ipswich, dividing this area laterally. The A1120 is the major east-to-west route through central Suffolk and road signs identify this as a tourist route as it passes close to bona fide tourist draws like the Suffolk Owl Sanctuary at Stonham Aspal, Saxtead Green Post Mill and Framlingham Castle.

PUBLIC TRANSPORT

Central Suffolk tends to be best connected by public transport with Ipswich, the county's largest town, which isn't particularly central itself.

The market towns of Stowmarket and Halesworth are minor transport hubs and have decent **bus** links with outlying villages, although many routes require going in and out of Ipswich, an inconvenient dog-leg.

The East Suffolk **train** line, connecting Lowestoft with Ipswich, has stops at Halesworth, Darsham, Saxmundham and Wickham Market along the way, all conveniently close to the area described in this chapter. Stowmarket lies on the main Norwich–Ipswich–London train line and so has frequent connections with Ipswich and Diss (just across the border in Norfolk), as well as a regular service to Bury St Edmunds and Newmarket to the west.

CYCLING

Cycling is good in parts, especially away from the A1120. The A12, A14 and A140 are all also to be avoided for obvious reasons. **National Cycle Route 1** and North Sea Cycle Route (⌀ sustrans.org) pass right through the locale from Hadleigh in the Stour Valley via Ipswich and Woodbridge through Framlingham and Halesworth to Beccles in the Waveney Valley, while National Cycle Route 51 crosses the county from Ipswich to Bury St Edmunds. The waymarked 71-mile circular **Heart of Suffolk Cycle Route**, which takes in parts of National Cycle Route 1, loops through Debenham, Framlingham, Halesworth and the Waveney Valley. A reasonable number of connected bridleways can be used for off-road cycling too.

Cycle hire is available from Suffolk Cycle Hire (⌀ 07852 402587 ⌀ suffolkcyclehire.co.uk), who will deliver within a ten-mile radius of Yoxford, Bicycle Doctor and Hire Service in Ipswich (⌀ 01473 259853) and Byways Bicycles at Darsham near Saxmundham (⌀ 01728 668764). The website ⌀ cycle-route.com has plenty of route ideas for cycling in central Suffolk together with informative maps of the suggested routes. Discover Suffolk (⌀ discoversuffolk.org.uk) also has some suggestions

---

i **TOURIST INFORMATION**

Framlingham ⌀ framlingham.com
Love Halesworth ⌀ lovehalesworth.co.uk
Mid Suffolk District Council ⌀ midsuffolk.gov.uk
Visit Suffolk ⌀ visitsuffolk.com

for cycling in the area. **Cycle Breaks** (𝒹 01449 721555 𝄞 cyclebreaks. com), based in Needham Market, has a number of gentle, self-guided Suffolk cycle tours to choose from, several of which are in central Suffolk or at least include the area as part of the itinerary. These tours offer quality bikes and support that includes accommodation bookings and luggage transfers.

WALKING

Pick your way around carefully and you'll find some worthwhile walking, especially along riverbanks. The **Gipping Valley River Path** (𝄞 rivergippingtrust.org.uk/walking-the-river) follows the route of the old canal towpath between Stowmarket and Ipswich, passing Needham Market, Claydon and Sproughton along the way.

The **Thornham Estate** (𝄞 thornhamestate.com) is large enough for a day's walking, with a good network of publicly accessible paths that stretch over 12 miles through parkland, woodland and water meadows. There is also a surface path for pushchairs and wheelchairs.

HALESWORTH & AROUND

Halesworth, straddling the upper course of the River Blyth, is an attractive market town well worth a visit. In the town's hinterland lie several villages that each have a noteworthy church. This is countryside where it is easy to get pleasantly lost: narrow roads meander and change direction through delightful timeless countryside; villages are elusive and unsigned until you stumble right upon them. It's an area ripe for gentle exploration: perfect Slow territory.

1 HALESWORTH

🏠 **The Barns at Belle Grove** (page 278), **Brights Farm** (page 278)

Tucked away in northeast Suffolk midway between the River Waveney and the coast and roughly equidistant from Beccles, Bungay, Saxmundham and Framlingham, Halesworth is a small market town. It was once the highest navigable point on the River Blyth but that was centuries ago and the river that flows through the town today is pretty insignificant.

Small though it may be, the town has quite a distinct identity and a self-contained feel about it. A lot of this may be due to its location in the county – not quite in the Waveney Valley, not quite in the coastal strip, not quite 'High Suffolk' – which helps give the town its hard-to-pin-down character. Not that the town is isolated – it's on the main road between Bungay and the coastal A12 and also has a station on the East Suffolk rail line.

Having pride of place at the centre of Halesworth is **The Thoroughfare**, a shopping street lined with a charming hotchpotch of Victorian and Georgian buildings that appear fairly unspoiled and satisfyingly removed from any notion of 'clone town Britain'. In fact, the street is resolutely old-fashioned, with a miscellany of independent shops providing small-town needs like food, furniture, haberdashery, hardware and stationery. The 14th-century building at number 6, currently a bistro serving East Asian-influenced food, is especially worth looking out for as it has an intricately carved wooden beam that depicts figures from classical mythology and folklore. The Thoroughfare leads to the **market place** where there is another handful of shops and an art gallery. Market Day is Wednesday. Beyond the market place lies St Mary's Church, with some 17th-century almshouses opposite on Steeple End, the gift of a local benefactor to provide for 12 poor single men and women of the parish. Rather remarkably, these were still

"Small though it may be, the town has quite a distinct identity and a self-contained feel about it."

in use as such right up until the 1960s. The Halesworth Art Gallery (✆ 01986 873064 ♂ halesworthgallery.co.uk) now occupies the upper floor of the almshouses building.

If you are at all curious about Halesworth's history, try the **town trail** that begins nearby on Angel Link close to the Angel Hotel, an old coaching inn. For the town trail, just follow the sign of the duck. This will lead you along Steeple End, along Chediston Street where a policeman was brutally murdered in 1862 – his murderer, John Ducker, being the last Suffolk man to be publicly hanged – then down Rectory Lane, better known locally as Duck Lane. After crossing the bridge and investigating the old brewery and malting buildings near The Cut, the trail returns via the Town Park and The Thoroughfare to its starting point at the Angel. Duck signs, Duck Lane, John Ducker – is there a theme here?

The town's cultural scene is nurtured not just by the odd art gallery and a good bookshop, Halesworth Books (✆ 01986 873840

1 Molly dancers in Halesworth, page 50. 2 The 16th-century Wenhaston Doom. ▶

PHIL BUTLER

MARK DUNN/A

⏂ thehalesworthbookshop.co.uk), at 42 The Thoroughfare, which has regular Friday evening wine events, but also by **The Cut Arts Centre** (⏂ 0300 3033211 ⏂ thecut.org.uk), which occupies some converted maltings just north of the centre. The Cut stages an impressive programme of events for such a small town and as well as a modern theatre and performance area there's also a good café and bar. In addition to hosting regular film shows and musical performances, The Cut also provides a centre for workshops and community events as well as weekly classes in yoga, poetry, watercolour painting and the like. The arts centre is also host to INK Festival (⏂ inkfestival.org) in April, which develops, produces and performs original short plays for stage and radio.

ᵎᵎ FOOD & DRINK

There's a fair choice here given the size of the town. The Thoroughfare has several cafés including **Edwards** (⏂ 01986 873763 ⏂ edwardshalesworth.co.uk) at 59a, which is open at lunchtimes, and the **White Hart** pub (⏂ 01986 873386 ⏂ whitehartpub.uk) at number 10, which has Adnams beers and the usual pub grub choices. The **Angel** (⏂ 01986 873365 ⏂ angel-halesworth.co.uk), also on The Thoroughfare, has bar food and Cleone's, an Italian restaurant. **Focus Organic** (⏂ 01986 872899 ⏂ focusorganic.co.uk) at 14 Thoroughfare, with a good range of organic local produce and artisan bread, is just one of three delicatessens in the town. **The Black Dog Deli** (⏂ 07738 774361 ⏂ theblackdogdelis. co.uk), just over the river on Bridge Street, and which also has branches at Walberswick and Wrentham, is worth visiting for coffee, cakes and sourdough bakes as well as for its award-winning sausage rolls.

The Boarding House 10 Market Pl ⏂ 01986 948306 ⏂ boardinghousehalesworth.com. This family-run café-restaurant located in a handsome Georgian building is probably the best in town. The Boarding House prides itself on its support for sustainable farming practices and offers a weekly changing seasonal à la carte menu that features modern English dishes with meat sourced from Suffolk producers like Emmerdale Farm beef and Blythburgh pork. There are also better-value monthly set menus with a more limited choice of options.

2 WENHASTON

Just outside Halesworth in the direction of Blythburgh, Wenhaston is a pretty village close to the River Blyth. There are plenty of **walking** possibilities in the immediate surroundings of the village. One option is to walk along the south bank of the river from here as far as Blythburgh and return on the opposite bank crossing the second bridge back to

Wenhaston. Blythburgh has its magnificent Holy Trinity Church. If you felt particularly energetic you might even push on to the coast to Walberswick along the footpath that follows the south bank of the Blyth estuary.

As well as the famous 'Doom' painting described below, Wenhaston village also has its so-called 'Devil's Stone', a glacial erratic from the Cretaceous period that sits in a wooded hollow called Devil's Pit just down the road from St Peter's church.

The Wenhaston Doom

The church of St Peter at Wenhaston is known not for its architecture but for its rare 16th-century painting of the *Last Day of Judgment*. This was discovered during restoration work in the late 19th century when a wooden panel was taken down and accidentally left outside overnight in the rain. This resulted in the panel's whitewash being dissolved away to reveal a bright painting beneath.

So-called 'Doom' (Day of Judgement) paintings such as this are very rare because almost all were destroyed during the Reformation. It is likely that this example had long been whitewashed over and forgotten about as early as the mid 16th century, long before the despoilers of the English Reformation would have come to the church. Virtually all Doom paintings were made directly onto walls so the fact that this example was painted onto wooden panels makes it unique.

The Wenhaston Doom is exceptional in its clarity and brilliance, better and brighter than any others in the country. A survivor of both the iconoclastic purges of the Reformation and well-meaning but heavy-handed Victorian restoration, it is a true medieval treasure. These days the Doom can be seen on the wall opposite the door of the church rather than in its original elevated position affixed to the chancel arch above the congregation. The outline of where the wooden figures of the Rood group of Christ, St John and the Virgin Mary would once have been attached can still be clearly made out. On the right-hand panel of the painting, Satan can be seen holding a banner with a Latin prayer that translates to 'Now for what is lacking may you give pardon for sin'.

3 BRAMFIELD

Heading south from Halesworth towards the A12 you pass through Bramfield, a tight cluster of houses and cottages around the church and pub. The church here, **St Andrew's**, is one of just 38 round tower churches in Suffolk. Unlike any of the others in the county, this one has a tower that is completely detached from the rest of the building and always has been, it would seem. The tower is actually older than the main body of the church, a lovely thatched 14th-century building with a wealth of intriguing head stops in a range of styles from ghoulish to cartoon-like. There is also a terrified-looking Green Man playing peek-a-boo from behind oversized oak leaves. The somewhat gloomy interior has wall paintings and some beautiful rood screens too, as well as an exquisitely carved 17th-century memorial to Arthur and Elizabeth Coke.

¶¶ FOOD & DRINK

The Queen's Head ✆ 01986 784214 ⊘ queensheadbramfield.co.uk. This long-established dining pub with scrubbed pine tables, exposed beams and cosy open fires has good-value sandwiches, light meals, daily specials at lunchtime and Sunday roasts. Local meat features strongly, in particular steaks from Emmerdale Farm at nearby Darsham, although there are plenty of tasty vegetarian options too. It's also child-friendly, with a special children's menu and an enclosed garden.

4 WALPOLE & HUNTINGFIELD

Heading southwest from Halesworth along the B1117 you soon come to the small village of **Walpole**. Just arriving at the village you will pass what looks like a fairly typical Suffolk farmhouse on the right of the road. What makes this stand out from the ordinary is the collection of gravestones in its front garden. The clue is there – this is not a house at all but **Walpole Old Chapel** (✆ 01986 783348 ⊘ walpoleoldchapel.org), a farmhouse converted into an independent non-conformist chapel in the late 17th century. Barely altered since it was built, the chapel is considered to be a historic gem by no less an authority than Historic England. If you want to look inside – naturally enough, it is somewhat austere – then timing is of the essence as it is usually only open on Saturday afternoons between Easter and the end of September. The road continues past Heveningham Hall, the biggest stately home in Suffolk, to reach the village of the same name.

---

1 Heveningham Hall. **2** The spellbinding interior of Huntingfield's St Mary's Church. **3** Walpole Old Chapel. **4** One of the unusual head stops on St Andrew's Church, Bramfield. ▶

HELEN CANNON

HELEN CANNON

SIMON WEEKS

MIKE P SHEPHERD/A

Before this a narrow road leads off right to soon arrive at **Huntingfield**, where there is a pub, the Huntingfield Arms, set rather idyllically on the village green, and a most unusual church, **St Mary's**. The story of St Mary's is a very human tale of determination and perseverance. In the mid 19th century the rector's wife, Mildred Holland, took it on herself to repaint the hammerbeam roof of the church in its original 15th-century style – an enormously ambitious undertaking that took her seven years to complete. Between 1859 and 1866 Mildred Holland is said to have lain on her back for much of the time on top of scaffolding, painstakingly painting first the chancel and then the nave. It seems that she had no assistance whatsoever other than having the scaffolding erected for her by workmen and being given some advice on appropriate decoration from medieval expert E L Blackburne FSA. The cost of the whole undertaking is recorded as a little over £2,000, which was almost all paid for out of the rector's own pocket. The result is spellbinding, almost intoxicating: a ceiling of golden-winged angels, apostles and saints painted against a background of brilliant vibrant hues. To get the full psychedelic effect you will need to switch the church lights on, easy enough if you have a pocketful of £1 coins to feed into the slot. You'll need quite a few though, as a pound does not buy you more than a few minutes of neck-cricking marvel time gazing up at the ceiling. Some, of course, will consider this fearless restoration job to be vulgar and garish – certainly, 'bright and colourful' does not really sum it up. Let us not forget that medieval churches would once have looked like this – bright colours on every available surface, unequivocal statements of faith and angels and apostles aplenty.

"To get the full psychedelic effect you will need to switch the church lights on, easy enough if you have a pocketful of £1 coins."

The other remarkable thing about the church interior is the font cover, a veritable indoor steeple that was installed as a tribute to Mildred Holland when she died in 1878 not so many years after completing her arduous labour of love. Both she and her rector husband William are buried in the churchyard close to the entrance gate.

¶¶ FOOD & DRINK

Huntingfield Arms The Street, Huntingfield ✆ 01986 798320 ⌂ huntingfieldarms.co.uk. A decent village pub in a lovely rural situation, this has well-kept Adnams beer and good-value food that usually includes a choice of specials as well as a standard pub menu.

FRAMLINGHAM & AROUND

5 FRAMLINGHAM

🏠 **Boundary Farm** (page 278) 🏰 **The Round House** (page 278)

'Fram', as most local people tend to call it, is a lovely little market town that still functions in the way that a market town is supposed to, providing services to the villages that surround it. Voted among the most desirable places to live in England some years back by *Country Life* magazine, you might think that this would be a rather smug place, but not at all. Framlingham really does not need to try too hard and so it doesn't – the town just goes about its business in the knowledge that while life may be pretty good here it is best not to shout about it too much. The town has been gifted a higher profile in recent years with the world domination of its most famous son, the pop singer Ed Sheeran, and also for its use as a location in the television series *Detectorists*, where it serves as stand-in for a fictitious small town of Danebury in northeast Essex. Neither of these brushes with fame seem to have gone to Framlingham's head, although you might just see jewellery designed by Ed Sheeran's mother in the occasional shop window. If you are a dedicated *Detectorists* aficionado you might find some odd corners of the town unexpectedly familiar, although St Michael's Rooms, the community hall that doubled as the fictional scout hut that served as the meeting place of the DMDC (Danebury Metal Detecting Club), has since been demolished and replaced with the larger, spanking new Castle Community Rooms.

What I find most appealing is that, unlike many other places of a similar size, the town still seems to have a strong sense of community. It's old-fashioned in an unselfconscious way and quite remarkably self-contained for a town of not much more than 3,000 souls. This is mainly the result of its serving a large rural hinterland, and local village folk, when not scurrying off to Ipswich or the supermarkets at Saxmundham, will probably choose to come here to do their shopping and pay their bills. Despite all of this, even in the face of an explosion of new housing, it has more of the character of a big village than a small town. Framlingham

> *"The town just goes about its business in the knowledge that while life may be pretty good here it is best not to shout about it too much."*

DRONEPLANETUK/S

SS

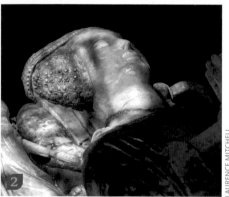

SS

LAURENCE MITCHELL

certainly embodies the spirit of Slow, although I doubt if many town residents have yet heard of the Cittaslow movement.

On top of all those virtues, the town has a couple of splendid sights – a well-preserved castle, the largest in the county, a beautiful medieval church and even a wildlife reserve. Coming along the road from the direction of Dennington, the first thing you will see of the town as you round the bend at Church Farm will be the mock-Gothic spires of Framlingham College, a large independent school. Arriving from the opposite direction, from Parham, is a little less auspicious, as you will pass a batch of warehouses, grain silos and new-build housing as you enter the town. Keep going though and you'll soon reach the **market square** with the church and castle positioned above it: on Tuesday market day and Saturday mornings most of the space is filled by stalls selling meat, bread, fruit and veg, clothes and bric-a-brac.

The Crown Hotel dominates the east side of the square and appears to be so firmly established that you might think that the square grew up around it – it didn't, though. There's a delightfully quirky secondhand bookshop on the south side alongside an Indian restaurant, a café, a butcher's and a deli. Queen's Head Alley leads on to this side of the square through a tiny alleyway. If you go through here, you'll see on the right a timber-framed house that was once an inn called the Blue Boar, an even older establishment than the Crown Hotel, where bears were once tethered outside while their owners slept within. The narrow archway itself is thought to be the original toll entrance into the town. Returning to the square, walk uphill past the Dancing Goat café and you'll soon arrive at the church and the impressive **castle**. Another street well worth checking out along the way is Double Street, which curves between Church Street opposite St Michael's Church and Castle Street close to the castle. This is home to a host of elegant listed Tudor buildings and in the 19th century served as the town's major shopping street. *Detectorists* fans might also come across the property that was used as Lance's flat if they look hard enough.

Elsewhere in town, you might also want to seek out what is probably the smallest house in England: the **Check House** (at Mauldens Mill

◀ **1** Tudor pageantry at Framlingham Castle. **2** The ghostly alabaster Bardolph tombs in Dennington's church. **3** Easton is home to Suffolk's longest crinkle-crankle wall. **4** The 26ft bronze statue *Yoxman*, in the Cockfield Estate.

development off Bridge Street) is now a domestic dwelling of the 'one up, one down' category that even the most imaginative of estate agents would have to describe as 'cosy and bijou'. It used to be the check house for the steam-powered mill that once stood here; later it became a betting shop.

St Michael the Archangel Church

This church contains the **family tombs** of the Howards, Dukes of Norfolk, who used to own the castle. After the Dissolution of Thetford Priory (page 240), Thomas Howard, the Third Duke of Norfolk, rebuilt the chancel here as the new resting place for his family's bones. Thomas Howard was a lucky man as far as timing went. Uncle of both the wives Henry VIII had executed, Anne Boleyn and Catherine Howard, he continually plotted to gain influence through serving up his more desirable female relatives for the king's attention, and was himself eventually condemned to death, but this was commuted to imprisonment when Henry died on the day before the sentence was due to be carried out. His tomb, the most impressive of the group here, dates from 1554, the year before his son upped sticks and moved in with his new wife's family at Arundel in Sussex.

"Two kneeling, praying effigies sporting Elizabethan ruffs and neat beards guard the tomb on one side."

Two kneeling, praying effigies sporting Elizabethan ruffs and neat beards guard the tomb on one side – these are his sons – while his daughters pray together above his head. Henry Fitzroy, a bastard son of Henry VIII, who died aged just 17, has a tomb with a frieze of reliefs from Genesis that was probably once part of Thetford Priory. Another tomb in black marble flanked by angels honours Robert Hitcham, the man who bought the manors of Framlingham and Saxtead from the Second Duke of Norfolk, and bequeathed Framlingham Castle to Pembroke College, Cambridge with the instruction to build a poorhouse.

There's more to St Michael's than just tombs, spectacular though they may be. Jean Coles, a Fram resident who used to sometimes work as a guide in the church, drew my attention towards some of its other treasures. 'When I used to show visitors around I would always show them the tombs first because they are my favourites too. But then I would point them towards *The Glory* – it's a real focal point for the church.' *The Glory* is, in fact, a painting that sits in the reredos above the

A stroll from Framlingham

✸ OS Landranger map 156 or Explorer map 212; start: Castle Street, Framlingham,
♥ TM286636; 2 miles; easy

A circular walk of two miles begins near the castle. This is a good way to see the castle from a variety of different viewpoints and it also gives a flavour of the surrounding countryside.

To start, follow the path down to the mere from the Castle Inn and enter the Suffolk Wildlife Trust reserve. Follow the circular nature trail as far as the footbridge over the River Ore. Leave the trail here and cross the river and follow the left bank to a second footbridge before turning right onto New Road.

After about 500yds, the road turns right at Great Lodge Farm; continue another 200yds until you reach a footpath to the right. Follow this south along a field edge until you reach another footpath branching left.

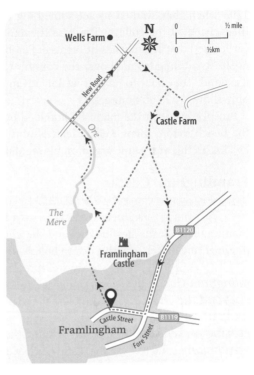

Take this path, crossing another footbridge, until you reach the B1120 Badingham road, where you turn right and follow Castle Street back to the start.

high altar: a bright, mysterious work that has concentric rings of light glowing mystically from its centre, rather like the background for one of William Blake's Old Testament pieces. 'It's a bit of a mystery, that picture. No-one knows who painted it, although we think it dates from the 18th century. It has got the letters "IHS" in the middle of it and I'm told that signifies the name of Jesus.'

The other treasure is the church's **organ**, just one of three built by the craftsman Thomas Thamar that managed to survive the English Civil War – Oliver Cromwell had a bit of a grudge against ornate instruments like this, apparently. 'It was originally made in 1674 for Pembroke College, Cambridge,' Jean told me. 'But they gave it to the church in 1708 when they wanted to get something a bit more up to date for their chapel at the college. The case is even older, from 1630 or even earlier, and that actually has the arms of Pembroke College on it. We get organists coming from all over the country to play it – they really love its sound. They have to book it well in advance, of course, and they are only allowed half an hour each.'

Prospective organists might be humbled by knowing who has sat on the bench before them: Felix Mendelssohn is believed to have given lessons on this very same organ on his regular visits from London.

Framlingham Castle

Framlingham Castle, Church St ✆ 01728 724189 ⊙ Apr–Oct daily, Nov–Mar w/ends only, except half-terms and Boxing Day to New Year's Day when daily; English Heritage

Framlingham Castle lies just beyond the church on top of the hill, a domineering presence with a dozen hollow towers, a deep dry moat and sturdy, well-preserved battlements. It's a very special place for a walk around the walls, taking in the views of the village and the mere. Although fortifications existed here in Saxon times, the present castle dates from the 12th century, the work of Roger Bigod, the second Earl of Norfolk. Generations of Howards, whose graves lie in the church, were later incumbents of the castle before their move south to Arundel in 1555. More famously, Mary Tudor mustered her supporters and proclaimed herself queen while staying here in 1553. Her successor, Elizabeth I, subsequently made use of it as a prison for luckless priests before Pembroke College, Cambridge, took it over, demolished the existing inner buildings and built a poorhouse within its walls that remained in use until 1839. It now serves as a visitor centre and has a display that tells of the various struggles in the castle's history.

"Framlingham Castle lies just beyond the church on top of the hill, a domineering presence with a dozen hollow towers."

For children, there's a specially devised audio tour and a set of giant games. Special family event days are held too, with ghost trails at

Halloween, a time-traveller trail at half-term with clues to solve and prizes to win, and festive family fun trails on weekends leading up to Christmas. William A Dutt writes of rather more vigorous activity taking place within its walls back in 1744, when John Slack the Norfolk champion pugilist fought the Suffolk champion John Smith and won. John Slack went on to meet John James in Broughton, London – they all seem to be called 'John' – and defeated the London champion in less than four minutes.

Just beneath the castle is **Framlingham Mere**, a 33-acre lake that used to be much deeper than it is today. This is in the ownership of Framlingham College but is currently leased to Suffolk Wildlife Trust as a nature reserve for birds and water plants. It's a good place for moisture-loving wild flowers like ragged robin, marsh marigold and irises, and waders like snipe can often be seen here too. Looking at the rather puny River Ore that flows into the lake, it seems hard to believe that this same river once brought ships from the coast. The Caen and Northamptonshire stone used for constructing the castle would have come by this route.

FOOD & DRINK

Of the few cafés around the market square, the **Dancing Goat** (✆ 01728 621434) at 33 Market Hill is as convenient as any, with good coffee and some sunny outdoor tables. **The Common Room** (✆ 01728 768238) at 22 Bridge Street just down from the square is a nice choice for cooked breakfasts and brunches. Staff are pretty flexible about making you whatever you want, too.

Just outside the town along the Badingham road, the **Shawsgate Vineyard** (✆ 01728 724060 ⌂ shawsgate.co.uk) produces dry and medium dry whites along with a red, a rosé and two sparkling wines. There's a shop (☉ Mon–Sat) and you can do a self-guided tour too – the shop will provide a vineyard map and information sheet. Experience days give tours and tastings on most Saturdays and some Fridays between May and August. A special experience day for two that includes lunch is also on offer.

Castle Inn Castle St ✆ 01728 724033 ⌂ castleinnframlingham.co.uk. Just before the castle entrance at the top of the town, this has a pleasant courtyard, Adnams ale, Aspall cyder and decent pub grub at lunchtimes only.

Crown Hotel Market S✆ ✆ 01728 723521 ⌂ crownframlingham.co.uk. This long-established hotel on the market square has a lunch and evening menu that features rare-breed meat from local farmers and Southwold fish. There's also a pleasant courtyard area at the back for alfresco dining.

Station Hotel Station Rd ✆ 01728 723455 🖰 thestationframlingham.com. There's no longer a station here, nor a functioning hotel, but this shabby-chic establishment has been running as a pub since the 1950s. More a gastropub with a wood-fired pizza oven these days – it's not particularly child-friendly or the sort of place to come just for a drink – the Station serves imaginative food with a Mediterranean twist in a comfortable, homely setting and makes full use of locally sourced ingredients. There's a good selection of wines to choose from as well as tasty ales from the nearby Earl Soham Brewery.

221B 1 Bridge St ✆ 01728 723526 🖰 2twenty1b.co.uk. A combined coffee shop and bakery with lovely pastries, cakes and cooked breakfasts. By the roundabout at the corner beneath the market place, this is a popular stop for local sports cyclists.

6 DENNINGTON

Dennington, on the A1120 north of Framlingham, has all the essential ingredients: a good pub, an interesting parish church and a café. It may seem like a fairly small village today but at the time of the 1851 census Dennington was one of the largest villages in Suffolk and had a population considerably bigger than Lowestoft. Until recently, the village had what was one of the oldest post offices in the country, established in 1845. It may be just coincidence but neighbouring Framlingham is also said to have two of the country's oldest pillar boxes, making this area a veritable Shangri-La for postal history anoraks. Most come to see the parish church though, or to have Sunday lunch in the pub.

The church of **St Mary the Virgin** is highly rated by those who make it their business to comment on such matters. It stands out from the crowd thanks to two unique features: a wooden pyx canopy over the altar, and the representation of a sciapod carved onto one of the bench-ends. A sciapod is a mythological desert creature that uses its one enormous foot to shade itself from the sun, an appendage that no doubt comes in useful for leaping too. Mentioned by Pliny in his writings, this is the sole English representation of this curious creature other than appearing as a minor detail on Hereford Cathedral's medieval world map, the Mappa Mundi. Other bench-ends represent creatures that are altogether more commonplace, although not in Suffolk – pelicans, tortoises, lions and even a giraffe with a twisted neck. The pyx, which is one of only four in England, is rather like a hanging spire and was used for storing the sacrament back in Catholic times. There are also some rather beautiful, and somewhat spooky, tombs belonging to the Bardolph family, delicately carved from ghostly alabaster and beautifully preserved.

¶¶ FOOD & DRINK

The Dennington Queen The Square, Dennington ✆ 01728 638241
✆ thedenningtonqueen.co.uk. Next door to the village church, this attractive timber-framed
pub is highly rated locally for its pleasant ambience and quality, reasonably priced food. It is
popular and often full on Sunday lunchtimes.

The Neathouse The Old Post House, Dennington ✆ 01728 638957. On the green opposite
the village church, this small café and community shop has outside tables and excellent
sandwiches, cakes and light savoury dishes.

7 PEASENHALL

🏠 **Sheep Cottages** (page 278)

This village lies further east along the A1120, a little beyond Badingham.
The dead-straight stretch of road offers some lovely views southeast over
the wheat fields towards the coast and even without consulting the map
you can sense that this was once a Roman route. Peasenhall is a pretty
village with a good smattering of Suffolk
pinkwash and neat thatched roofs. There
is also the timber-framed Ancient House,
which, although attractive in a Grade-II-
listed sort of way, is not really that ancient
having a 16th century core and an 18th
century façade. The village derives its name from 'Pisenhalla' meaning
'a valley where peas grow'. On the back of this somewhat tenuous
connection, the village instigated its very own Pea Festival in 2008,
which for several years was an annual July event that included such
leguminous events as the World Pea Podding Championships, the East
Anglian Pea Throwing Championships and the Great Pea Draw. The
really enthusiastic could also enter the pea-eating competition – using
chopsticks. Sadly, this admirably green event only lasted until 2014.

> "The really enthusiastic could also enter the pea-eating competition – using chopsticks."

¶¶ FOOD & DRINK

Emmett's of Peasenhall (✆ 01728 660250 ✆ emmettsham.co.uk), an old-fashioned
food store and smokehouse, is highly regarded for its sweet-cured hams and bacon made
from free-range Suffolk pork. It stocks delicious Suffolk unpasteurised cheeses too, and the
shop also has a small café with an Italian espresso machine.

Sibton White Horse Halesworth Rd, Sibton IP17 2JJ ✆ 01728 660337
✆ sibtonwhitehorseinn.co.uk. A traditional village pub, just a mile from Peasenhall, which

serves seasonal food provided by several local suppliers and its own kitchen garden, plus excellent real ales and a broad selection of wines. There's also a secluded Mediterranean-style courtyard garden area for alfresco dining.

Weavers Tea Room 2 The Knoll ✆ 01728 660548. A popular and cosy village café providing cream teas and good-value three-course lunches.

8 YOXFORD

🏠 **School Cottage** (page 278)

Continuing east along the A1120 from Peasenhall, you pass through Sibton, virtually next door, before arriving at Yoxford. The village hugs the road as far as the junction with the A12 but it is nevertheless a rather quiet place. With an eclectic mix of building styles that blend attractively, the village has the face of something of an artistic centre, with a number of art shops and galleries alongside a couple of antique businesses. The small four-day **Yoxford Arts Festival** (✆ 01728 668401) takes place in August.

Holding a strategic location at the junction of two main roads, Yoxford was an important coach stop on the London to Yarmouth run in the days before steam power. You can see clear evidence of this at the church where a tall iron signpost points in three directions: Framlingham (10 miles), Yarmouth (30), London (93). The signpost stands tall for a reason – for coachmen to read from their high perch. When the railways came to the area in the 19th century, the village was promoted as a tourist attraction for well-to-do urbanites. 'Yoxford: The Garden of Suffolk' became the catchword, referring to the village's location between three country estates. This 'garden' label was hyped by newspaper journalists and also by some interested parties in the village wishing to cash in on the act. William A Dutt, writing in 1901, was clearly not impressed: 'It may be that injudicious advertisement has had something to do with the district's flattering designation, and that if we had never heard of "Poppyland", Yoxford would have remained unknown and its mediocre charms unproclaimed.' This seems a little harsh, as it is quite a handsome village, with some lovely parkland close to hand.

"With an eclectic mix of building styles that blend attractively, the village has the face of something of an artistic centre."

Looking at adverts in the window of Horne's store on the main road probably tells you more about life in the village today than any official account. With flyers for art exhibitions, tree surgery, holistic therapy and painting workshops, and small ads that give details of cockerels ('with bags of character'), boats, chicken huts and an 'ideal family horse' up for sale, you soon get a picture of what modern-day Yoxford is all about now that the Yarmouth stagecoaches have disappeared from the scene.

The Cockfield Estate lies just behind the village – the former family home of the Blois family who give their name to one of the village pubs. The estate takes its name from the Cokefeud family – a name to be conjured with if ever there was one. **Cockfield Hall** served as a high-class prison for Lady Catherine Grey, sister of Lady Jane Grey, in 1567 but she died soon after arrival and was buried in her own private chapel in the village's St Peter's Church. The hall, an impressive 16th-century brick building, has a rooftop forest of tall chimneys and crow-step gables. It is visible from the A12 but you can get a much closer look by following the footpath through the gatehouse just beyond Horne's store opposite the church. Follow the footpath for a short while through a

A LITERARY DIVERSION – HERODS TEMPLE IN SUFFOLK

In his rambling masterpiece, *The Rings of Saturn*, W G Sebald describes walking a stretch of Roman road in east Suffolk. Setting out from Yoxford, he walks for four hours across a sparsely populated landscape in which he sees nothing other than harvested cornfields and a sky heavy with clouds (Sebald's landscapes always seem to be strangely devoid of people).

He ends up at a remote moated house where he encounters Thomas Abrams, a remarkable farmer who has been building an accurate scale model of the Temple of Jerusalem for the past 20 years. Sebald describes Abrams as having spent years studying sources as obscure as rare tracts on Roman architecture and the Mishnah, part of the rabbinic talmud in order to pursue his obsession. Sebald

discovers that Abrams's project has already attracted a number of interested parties: one morning the farmer found that the man who had parked his Rolls-Royce in his driveway was none other than Lord Rothschild.

It's a typically tangential Sebald tale – with singular, Sisyphus-like characters turning up in odd places – but then, who knows what schemes and obsessions are dreamed up on these isolated Suffolk farmsteads?

It turns out that Abrams is, in fact, Alec Garrard, a friend of Sebald's, who subsequently published an illustrated book, *The Splendour of the Temple*, in which his 1:100 scale model is used to describe the history and architecture of the temple that existed between 19BC and AD70. Gerrard died in 2010 aged 80.

dark wood with ancient yews and, after a small footbridge, the wood opens onto open parkland and a clear view of the hall with its large complex of stables and coach houses all bearing similar architectural detail. On a visit to the village a few years back, the gatehouse was covered in scaffolding and builders were hard at work at the hall. 'They sold it off a couple of years ago,' a worker told me. 'I think the plan is to do it up and then put it up for hire.' He pointed out the fancy brickwork on the façade behind Horne's. 'That bit's not actually part of the estate. I think it was just added in the same style as the rest of the buildings so that wedding parties would be impressed when they arrived at the entrance to the hall.'

The estate is now host to a large sculpture called **Yoxman**, which can be seen from the A12 just north of the junction with Yoxford High Street. *Yoxman* is a larger than life naked human figure. Actually 'larger than life' is an understatement as the figure stands 26ft tall and weighs eight tons. This work by local sculptor Laurence Edwards has certainly turned a few heads since its installation in 2021. Made of bronze, the figure, which is made up of 52 individual pieces that each had to be cast separately, took four years to create. Edwards' vision was to create a timeless, sentient watchman for the Suffolk landscape that he stood in. Being made of bronze, *Yoxman* will not rust but in time will be partly reclaimed by nature – weeds will grow at his feet and birds will perch upon his head and limbs as the giant silently watches the Suffolk landscape continue to evolve over the years to come.

¶¶ FOOD & DRINK

Flying Goose Café Yoxford Antique Centre, A1120 ☏ 01728 668844. A small café at the rear of an antique shop with standard tea shop fare and optional outdoor seating.
Satis Main Rd ☏ 01728 668221 ⌂ satishousehotel.co.uk. On the main A14 close to the junction with Yoxford's high street, the restaurant of this Georgian country house hotel has a reasonably varied menu that utilises mostly locally sourced produce.

9 LAXFIELD

Laxfield is a couple of miles north of Dennington on the Stradbroke to Halesworth road. Its 16th-century timbered **Guildhall**, across the road from All Saints' Church, has a small museum devoted to local history. This is the village that William 'Smasher' Dowsing, the puritan iconoclast, hailed from. Dowsing's handiwork extended through much of Suffolk, such was his distaste for religious ornament and what he considered 'superstitious pictures'. There's still a Dowsing Farm in the parish. Religious fervour seems to be a tradition in Laxfield, as a century before Dowsing's church-smashing antics, a village man named John Noyes was burned at the stake here for his opposition to the Catholic faith, a brave if foolhardy stance to have during the reign of ex-Framlingham Castle resident, Queen 'Bloody' Mary. In fairness to the villagers, Noyes's neighbours all dowsed their fires on the day in protest… well, all but one.

¶¶ FOOD & DRINK

The King's Head (The Low House) Gorams Mill Lane ✆ 01986 798395 ⌕ lowhouselaxfield.com. Known to all and sundry – well, locals at least – as 'The Low House', this is an authentic old-school Suffolk country pub with low ceilings, settles, tiny rooms and narrow passageways. There's no bar as such, just a tap room that serves an assortment of real ales straight from the casks like Adnams Southwold Bitter, Earl Soham's Victoria and Green Jack Brewery's Trawlerboys. Nor will you find a juke box or television, as the King's Head prides itself on being a social pub with a sense of tradition. A blackboard menu flags up tasty, rustic, homemade dishes made with local seasonal produce and in summer you might find performing Morris dancers or a horse and trap parked outside. New management took over the pub in 2022 but its authenticity appears to have survived unscathed.

10 SAXTEAD GREEN POST MILL

The Mill House, Saxtead Green IP13 9QQ ✆ 03703 331181 ☉ Apr–Oct Fri & Sat; English Heritage

In Saxtead Green, 2½ miles northwest of Framlingham, this is a fine example of the type of Suffolk mill in which the whole body revolves on its base. It dates from 1796 but was completely rebuilt in 1854 following wind damage, then resurrected yet again between 1957 and 1960. The Saxtead Green post mill also appears on the sign of the 17th-century Greene King pub, the Old Mill House (✆ 01728 685064 ⌕ oldmillhouse-saxtead.co.uk) just east of the mill. Another post mill survives in Framsden, further west along the A1120 and south at the B1077.

If you look in the porch of the tower-less 15th-century All Saints' Church in **Saxtead** village you'll see a set of stocks and a whipping post. The stocks bear the none-too-gentle warning to 'Fear God and Honour the King', which is hardly what one might call a progressive attitude.

THE REAL-LIFE AKENFIELD

Back in 1969, author Ronald Blythe published *Akenfield: Portrait of an English Village*, a classic account of Suffolk country life. The book was an evocative portrait of a rural community told through the eyes of its members, and described a farming economy that had not long made the transition from horses to tractors. *Akenfield* was an immediate bestseller that single-handedly took responsibility for disabusing city dwellers of some of the romantic notions they might have held about country life. *Akenfield* told it as it was: funny in parts but also gritty and unflinching, it spoke of almost unimaginable poverty and the hardship of rural working-class life from the Victorian era up until the 1930s.

There is no such real place as Akenfield, of course, but it isn't too difficult to deduce that the name is an amalgam of two Suffolk villages – Akenham, just north of Ipswich, and Charsfield close to Wickham Market. Indeed, Charsfield was where Ronald Blythe had carried out a series of interviews with locals in the summer and autumn of 1967 prior to writing his book. He spoke to young and old alike, documenting both the frustrations of youth and the bittersweet memories of senior villagers who were still able to remember events that seemed to belong to another age – picking stones by hand from fields and sewing children into their winter underwear.

The book was turned into a film in 1974. Rather than employ professional actors, authentic Suffolk villagers were used instead, a move that angered Equity, the actors' union. The Equity problem was circumvented by doing away with a formal script and having the characters improvising all of their dialogue based upon Blythe's 20-page 'transcript'. It was a neat solution – using locals rather than trained actors ensured authenticity. Ronald Blythe, a lay preacher in real life, played the village vicar. The film was shot over the period of a year in order to reflect the changing seasons, and at weekends only, so that village actors could attend to their usual professions during the week. Once again, the village of Charsfield had a part to play and this was one of several villages in the Wickham Market area, south of the River Deben, that was used as a filming location. Hoo, Debach, Monewden, Dallinghoo, Letheringham and Pettistree were the others.

Like the book before it, the film was also highly acclaimed for its rural realism, and it was watched by 13 million viewers on its first television showing – quite an achievement for a film with no stars and no formal script.

11 EARL SOHAM

Earl Soham lies a mile or two further west, at a point where the A1120 once again regresses to its original Roman form of an unstinting straight line. It's a sprawling, laid-back place with nice old cottages set back from the road. The village was the original home of the **Earl Soham Brewery** ($\mathcal{O}$ 01728 861213 $\mathcal{O}$ earlsohambrewery.co.uk), which started life in an old chicken shed at the village's Victoria pub but now brews at larger premises in Debenham (page 192).

¶¶ FOOD & DRINK

Victoria The Street ✆ 01728 685758 ⏚ earlsohamvictoria.com. This whitewashed local on the village green serves up hearty pub food (Wed–Sun) and its very own excellent ESB Victoria Ale in its sparsely furnished bar. It has an open fire, board games and Queen Victoria-themed pictures.

12 PARHAM & EASTON

⋀ **The Orchard Campsite,** Wickham Market (page 278)

Head south along the B1116 from Framlingham and you soon arrive in **Parham**, a village that gave its name to a World War II US Air Force bomber airbase located between the village and its neighbour, Great Glemham. The airfield has the **Parham Airfield Museum** (✆ 01728 621373 ⏚ parhamairfieldmuseum.co.uk), which stands as a tribute to the 390th Bomb Group that was based here. Between 1943 and 1945, over 300 bombing missions were flown from the base using B-17 'Flying Fortresses', and the bandleader Glenn Miller performed in a hangar here in 1944. The museum is free but has fairly limited opening hours – mostly Sundays and bank holidays from April to October – so check first if you want to visit. For many years now there had been proposals for a wind farm on the airfield – Suffolk's first onshore wind farm – with plans for six turbines. Not surprisingly, this stirred something of a local storm but the proposed scheme was eventually abandoned in favour of further offshore wind farm development.

A wonderful late 15th-century timber-framed fortified manor house lies close to the village: **Moat Hall** is now part of a farm but used to be the residence of the Uffords, the former Earls of Suffolk, and later the Lords Willoughby. You can walk up here along a footpath from the village church of St Mary the Virgin and enjoy some sweeping views along the way.

Little Glemham, a village a couple of miles southeast of the airfield museum, is home to Glemham Hall, which hosts the annual **Folkeast Festival** (⏚ folkeast.co.uk) in August, a three-day event with camping that attracts a number of top folk performers.

In the opposite direction, a little way southwest of Parham, is **Easton**, a village that is home to a fine pub, the White Horse, and Suffolk's

CRINKLE-CRANKLE WALLS

Although they can be occasionally found in other parts of the country, and even overseas, crinkle-crankle walls are very much a Suffolk phenomenon. These walls, often found around gardens, are built in a serpentine pattern of alternating curves that provides greater stability than straight walls of the same thickness of bricks. They also do not require buttresses to support them. Suffolk boasts around one hundred examples of these walls, which is twice as many as the rest of the country combined. It is likely that they were first introduced to the region by Dutch engineers who came to East Anglia to work on Fen drainage.

To build such a wall requires considerable skill and it is likely they were often erected as a sort of status symbol demonstrating the wealth of the owner. The longest wall of this type is believed to be in the village of Easton (page 187), where three-quarters of a mile of an original two-and-a-half mile wall still stands. This once surrounded Easton Hall, which was demolished and transported to the US in the 1920s. Built from the 18th century onwards in England, the same wall design appears to have ancient predecessors: similarly shaped, zigzagging mudbrick walls have been unearthed in the 3,000-year-old ancient Egyptian city of Aten near Luxor.

longest stretch of **crinkle-crankle** wall (page 188). The wall runs along the boundary of Easton Park, past All Saint's Church, where it surrounds three sides of the graveyard. Today, the wall stretches for three-quarters of a mile but originally it was two and a half miles long in its entirety. Interestingly, the wall is pretty much all that remains of the original Easton Hall estate, the former seat of the Dukes of Hamilton. The house was demolished brick by brick in 1924 and its bricks were reputedly transported to the United States to be reassembled as a ranch. If this is true then it would not be the first time that the bricks had been repurposed – the building had started life on Tacket Street in Ipswich before being dismantled and transported to Easton where it was re-erected as the original Easton Hall in 1687.

Close to the village, in a bend of the River Deben, is **Easton Farm Park** (✆ 01728 746475 ⬦ eastonfarmpark.co.uk ⊙ Easter–Sep & school holidays), where there are all sorts of farm-based activities for children to enjoy, such as pony rides, animal feeding, pond dipping and den building. There are also indoor and outdoor play areas, a café and a tea room. Camping facilities are also available, as are glamping pods and holiday cottages.

¶¶ FOOD & DRINK

White Horse The Street, Easton ✐ 01728 746456 ⌂ eastonwhitehorse.co.uk. With a cosy interior and a sunny beer garden outside for fine weather, this traditional white-washed Tudor-period inn serves hearty British pub food with a focus on locally sourced, seasonal produce.

WEST OF EARL SOHAM TO STOWMARKET

Continue west along the A1120 from Earl Soham and you'll soon arrive at Peats Corner, a junction where the B1077 leads south to Framsden, with a recently reconstructed post mill, and past Helmingham Park to Otley, where you'll see a splendid 15th-century moated manor house, rather like the one at Parham. **Framsden** is a small village that has a church with splendid 14th-century misericord carvings, and a corrugated iron village hall. The village's doggy-sounding pub, the Dobermann Inn (it used to be the Greyhound!) is now sadly closed for business. What it is probably best known for though is **Fox Fritillary Meadow**, just north of the village. This is a six-acre unimproved meadow, owned and managed by the Suffolk Wildlife Trust, which is the largest known site for snake's head fritillaries in East Anglia and one of only four such sites in Suffolk. It's undoubtedly a spectacular sight but you'll need to be exact with your timing if you want to see it in its full glory as the meadow is only open to the public on a single annual open event in mid to late April (✐ 01473 890089 for details).

> "It's undoubtedly a spectacular sight but you'll need to be exact with your timing if you want to see it in its full glory."

Otley Hall (✐ 01473 890264 ⌂ otleyhall. co.uk), a Grade I-listed, 16th-century moated hall, is mostly used for retreat days and as a wedding venue these days but is open for pre-booked group tours to both the hall and gardens. The ten-acre gardens at the hall, which contain historically accurate recreations that include an orchard, herber, knot garden and nuttery, are worth a look in their own right and are open to the public between 10.00 and 16.00 Tue–Sat during the summer months (tours are also available). The extensive gardens at **Helmingham Hall** (✐ 01473 890799 ⌂ helmingham.com; ☉ May–Sep 10.00–17.00 Sun–Thu & bank holidays) are also open to the public and the 400-acre park has herds of both red and fallow deer.

13 DEBENHAM

Debenham comes as a surprise from whatever direction you approach. It stands amid an enormous prairie of golden wheat stretching almost as far as the horizon – quite a contrast to the softer, wooded parkland further to the east around Yoxford. It's a peach of a village with something of Lavenham about it, although far less of the touristiness. Its buildings range from magpie-timbered Tudor to Suffolk pink, to solid Georgian brick, while the High Street has some charming gardens open to the street, where roses and hollyhocks reach for the sky in a clash of pinks. Scattered among some pricey-looking Tudor properties are a handful of old-fashioned shops that seem little changed from the 1950s, as well as a clutch of antique shops, galleries and gift shops. Given all the desirable properties on show lining the street, it comes as no surprise that a disproportionate number of estate agents have set up shop here too.

Many buildings in the village that are now private houses also used to be shops, as evidenced by large windows and house names that reflect the property's former function – the Old Cobblers House and so on. The Red Lion on the High Street is a 15th-century jettied building that once served as a guildhall; although it still has its sign, it no longer functions as an inn. Elsewhere, the most substantial medieval buildings on the High Street are the Old House at number 23, which incorporates both of its former neighbours 21 and 25, and number 37, a 16th-century jettied building. The ancient-looking Market Cross, which served as the village's market hall in the 17th century, gets its name from reputedly occupying the site of a former Anglo-Saxon cross. Now an architects' practice and art gallery, its first floor was converted for use as a school by Sir Robert Hitcham in 1668. Leading off from Market Cross at the northern end of the High Street, Gracechurch Street, which has the magnificent jettied cottage Bleak House at its corner, has another splendid parade of handsome half-timbered dwellings.

Offering a break from an almost relentless Tudor-beam theme on the High Street is a large Neoclassical chapel dated 1905 that bears the legend 'The Ancient Order of Foresters' on its portico. It is now an antiques showroom and once featured as the same in the popular 1980s/90s television series *Lovejoy*. For fans of the series, generally women of a certain age if truth be told, Debenham with its Tudor

---

1 Helmingham Hall. 2 The charming village of Debenham. 3 The Mid-Suffolk Light Railway. 4 Thornham Estate in the snow. ▶

HARPUR GARDEN IMAGES

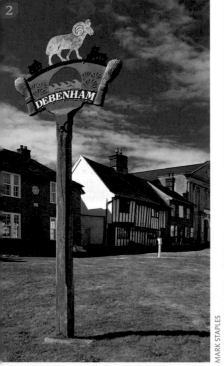

MARK STAPLES

ALEX DUGGAN

THORNHAM WALKS

splendour, antique shops and well-heeled eccentricity must represent something of a spiritual home. It's the sort of place where grandfather clocks, corduroy trousers and Morris Travellers blend into the scenery.

The River Deben rises nearby to give Debenham its name and, known as The Butts, runs as a prolonged ford through the village which is claimed to be the longest of its kind in Britain. The extensive tracts of arable land around the town are relatively new: historical accounts suggest that most of the surrounding land was pasture in the 18th century, but hedges were enthusiastically grubbed up and trees felled later in that century to make way for cereals. Now the heavy, but highly fertile, clay soils produce exceptionally high yields of wheat and barley. If anywhere in the region deserves the epithet 'Suffolk's breadbasket', it is probably here.

The **Cyder House** at Aspall Hall just north of Debenham (✆ 01728 860510 aspall.co.uk) has been producing its own Aspall apple juice, cyder and organic cyder vinegar since 1728 so the Chevallier family who have run the place for eight generations should know a thing or two about what to do with apples. Aspall cyder is made only from freshly pressed apples and the notion of stretching fermentations by eking them out with concentrates is anathema.

A surprising variety of apple types are used for cyder making. There are apples such as Cox or Blenheim Orange for sweetness, cooking apples like Bramley for aroma and acidity, and a mixture of bittersweet apples that might include varieties like Médaille d'Or and Kingston Black to provide perfume, depth and body. The spelling of 'cyder' rather than 'cider' goes back to the 1920s when an earlier member of the Chevallier dynasty, John Barrington ('JB') Chevallier (1857–1940) considered the 'y' version indicative of the style he was producing at the time. And it's not all about alcohol – there's organic vinegar and apple juice too. Aspall apple juice is cold-pressed from a mash made from pre-blended apples that hail from most of the country's prime apple locations – Cambridgeshire, Kent and the Wye Valley. Cox and Bramley form the base and these are supplemented by varieties such as Egremont Russett, Discovery and Crispin to achieve the right balance of flavour and acidity.

If beer is more your thing then the **Earl Soham Brewery** (✆ 01728 861213 earlsohambrewery.co.uk), which started life in an old chicken shed at the back of the Victoria pub in Earl Soham village (page 186) now brews at larger premises in Debenham. The brewery, which has an on-site shop, produces a cross section of ales that give fellow producers Adnams and Greene King a run for their money and range from Victoria, a light 'session beer', to winter-only Sir Roger's Porter and Jolabrugg, a stronger, Christmas-only 'Yule Brew'.

¶ FOOD & DRINK

At one time Debenham had nine pubs; now just one remains open, **The Woolpack** at 49 High Street (✆ 01728 860516), which has local ales and good home-cooked meals. At the time of writing a local community group 'Save the Angel' was attempting to save the **Angel Inn** at 5 High Street, which was up for sale.

Deben Coffee House 7 High St ✆ 01728 861582. A café with sandwiches, scones, freshly baked bread and other locally sourced and home-baked produce.
River Green Café and Deli 21 Cross Green ✆ 01728 860430. Cakes, coffee and sandwiches available here, including several vegetarian and gluten-free options.

14 NEEDHAM MARKET

A small town just southeast of Stowmarket and close enough to the A14, Needham Market's pride and joy is its **church of St John the Baptist**, which has a quite astonishing double hammerbeam roof that has been described as 'the culminating achievement of the English carpenter'; certainly Pevsner waxed lyrical about it in his *Buildings of England: Suffolk*, saying 'the eye scarcely believes what it sees, and has a hard if worthwhile job in working out how this unique effect could be attained'. Roof timbers aside, the church is certainly idiosyncratic – it has no graveyard or tower and only the tiniest of spires atop the porch.

Wool combing became big business here in the 15th and 16th centuries until the arrival of the plague in the 1660s. Chains were fixed at either end of the village to prevent the disease spreading to other communities – a noble gesture that wiped out two-thirds of the town's population. Chainhouse Road in the town commemorates this event, as does another road known as The Causeway, a more palatable variant of 'the corpseway' that was used to move plague victims out of town for burial at the church in nearby Barking.

Meanwhile the **River Gipping**, which flows to the east, makes a rewarding strolling ground. The river was navigable in the medieval period and was used to bring stone for the building of the abbey at Bury St Edmunds. Then, in the late 18th century, the river was canalised and a series of 15 locks were set up between Needham Market and Ipswich so that barges could navigate between Stowmarket and the coast. The towpath of what became known as the Stowmarket Navigation is still in place today and you can walk all 11½ miles to Ipswich from here, or even better, the whole way from Stowmarket. The **Gipping Valley River Path** is a 17-mile walk if done in its entirety from Stowmarket railway station to Ipswich docks, an interesting and peaceful route past locks and old watermills. It's a long way but the beauty of it is that both ends can be easily reached by train. Indeed, the Norwich–Ipswich–London railway line runs parallel to the canal for much of the way.

15 STOWMARKET

It was not at all unusual for towns in East Anglia to be destroyed by fire in the medieval period – the lethal combination of open fires and overcrowding made this a common occurrence, especially in the 16th and 17th centuries when buildings were largely built of wood. Stowmarket bucked this trend and, rather than be razed by fire, it was instead accidentally blown up when a guncotton factory exploded in 1871, taking a lot of the town along with it. Despite this setback, this remains central Suffolk's largest settlement, a pleasant enough market town (with a market on Thursday and Saturday) but with little of special interest.

What stands out here, though, is the **Food Museum** ($\mathscr{O}$ 01449 612229 $\mathring{\partial}$ foodmuseum.org.uk), on a 75-acre site close to the town centre. Its location might be a tad unromantic – next to a large branch of Asda; you can park in the supermarket car park – but the museum, which until 2022 went under the name of Museum of East Anglian Life or MEAL, wonderfully encapsulates all things rural East Anglia, with a range of reconstructed old buildings giving a historic perspective on traditional life in the region. These include windpumps and watermills as well as agricultural buildings. You'll see displays of local trades and crafts like brewing, blacksmithing and rope-making as well as agricultural machinery and a collection of rare-breed animals such as Red Poll cattle and Suffolk Punch horses. The recent change of name to Food Museum has resulted in a slightly different emphasis and a newfound mission 'to connect people with where our food comes from and the impact of our choices: past, present and future'. The museum puts on a number of regular events, talks and activities that include Food from the Hedgerow demonstrations, Food Diversity Days, Forest School for children and Toddler Time activities for the under 5s.

¶¶ FOOD & DRINK

Feast Café Food Museum. With home-cooked food made from locally reared meat and vegetables grown on-site, this is a convenient place for a drink and a snack while visiting the museum.

The Mill Station Rd East ✆ 01449 674674 ⌂ mill.restaurant. A bar-restaurant with an emphasis on British gastro pub-style food that also has a decent choice of vegetarian and vegan options.

Osier Café St Peter's and St Mary's Church ✆ 07873 348584. Now relocated from its original home at the Food Museum, this remains one of the best choices for coffee, cakes and sandwiches in town.

The Shepherd and Dog Lower Rd, Onehouse ✆ 01449 614675 ⌂ theshepherdanddogonehouse.co.uk. Just outside Stowmarket in the curiously named Onehouse (which actually has a couple of housing estates), this country pub has a decent choice of hearty pub grub, Sunday roasts, Aspall cyder and Greene King ales.

Great Finborough, Buxhall & Rattlesden

Just west of Stowmarket, along the minor roads south of the A14 is a handful of attractive villages, and with an intricate spider's web of footpaths linking them. The first village to be reached is **Great Finborough**, which has a pub, the Chestnut Horse, and a flint church with an exotic-looking spire, St Andrew's. John Peel, the BBC DJ and broadcaster, lived for many years in the village in a house he dubbed 'Peel Acres'. His grave (inscribed with his real name of John R P Ravenscroft and the first line of his favourite song, 'Teenage Kicks' by The Undertones) lies in the village churchyard, itself graced with fine views of the surrounding countryside. Every Easter Monday the village hosts a highly competitive event called the Race of the Boggmen, involving the men of the village and from nearby Haughley. The race, a village tradition that began in the late 19th century, starts and ends at the pub and, not surprisingly, a great deal of boisterous drinking generally takes place.

Buxhall lies a little further on, an attractive yet relatively ungentrified village that still mainly serves a farming rather than an incomer community. As well as a pub, The Crown, and a church, it has a converted, capped tower mill. A couple of miles northwest of Buxhall is **Rattlesden**, tucked away in a gentle valley, a gorgeous little place with rows of neat thatched cottages and the church of St Nicholas high on a rise above the village.

NORTH OF STOWMARKET

16 MENDLESHAM

Northeast of Stowmarket close to the A140, Mendlesham is well known locally for its cloud-scraping television and radio mast, an ugly beacon for miles around, but there's more to the village than just towering steel. The **church of St Mary** is large for a village of this size and highly unusual in being the last surviving Anglo-Catholic parish church in the county, where Mass is celebrated daily and the biggest event in the religious calendar is the Feast of the Assumption. Not surprisingly, the airy interior is filled with candles, icons, several altars and the persistent whiff of incense. For those with more interest in cudgel-wielding than Catholic ceremony, there are also two fine and fierce woodwoses (page 56) on the roof of the northern porch, and a village armoury in the room above it that contains armour dating from between the 15th and 17th centuries that was kept for use by villagers in the event of an insurrection. You're supposed to have an appointment to view the armoury, but you might just get lucky.

In the village itself, by the village sign, a **preaching stone** is said to have been used as a platform by mendicant friars in the 14th century and later by followers of the preacher John Wesley in the 18th. No doubt it has also been put to use on occasion by the odd reveller delivering an opinionated rant on his or her way home from the village pub. A large street fayre takes place in the village on May Day bank holiday; the one held in 2023 marked its 40th anniversary.

17 THE MID-SUFFOLK LIGHT RAILWAY MUSEUM

Brockford Station, Wetheringsett IP14 5PW ✆ 01449 766874 ⏚ mslr.org.uk ⊙ Easter & end of May– early Sep Sun & bank holidays

Wetheringsett is Mendlesham's neighbour just across the A140. This is the home of the Mid-Suffolk Light Railway Museum at the village's former Brockford station (there used to be a stop at Mendlesham too). The MSLR, or 'Middy' as it was known, was inaugurated in 1904 and had ten stations along a line that transported passengers between Haughley, north of Stowmarket, and Laxfield. Closure eventually came in 1951, by which time almost all of the passengers were children on their way to and from school. The museum was set up in 1990 and has displays of artefacts, photographs and rolling stock. You also get to take a short ride in one of the carriages, hauled by an Edwardian steam engine.

18 THE THORNHAM ESTATE & THORNHAM PARVA

⋏ **Swattesfield Campsite**, Thornham Magna (page 278)

A little further north and you reach the villages of Thornham Magna and Thornham Parva just west of the A140. Thornham Hall sits between the two villages, the original hall having been demolished in the 1950s, and the Thornham Estate offers 12 miles of waymarked walks through parkland, woods and farmland and water meadows known as **Thornham Walks** (✆ 01379 831242 ◔ thornhamestate.com), with maps available at the information board at the main car park. Thornham Walks also incorporates a Victorian **walled garden** that can be reached by a surfaced path from the car park, suitable for wheelchairs and pushchairs.

For those wanting more than informal self-guided strolls, Thornham Walks' staff are able to organise bespoke guided walks and environmental activities for groups and even 'environmental birthday parties'. With so much management work and maintenance needing to be done, volunteers are always welcome. Helen Sibley, one of two staff members who manage access to the walks, told me, 'We rely heavily on volunteer help. We have a regular volunteer day on the last Sunday of every month and every Tuesday, plus we have a team of probationers who work here once every other week and on Sundays. The Walks always require more volunteers and no experience is needed, just enthusiasm.' Helen went on to explain how the Thornham Walks came into being. 'The late Lord Henniker retired from the diplomatic service and became involved with a variety of grant-making trusts, helping people living in deprived areas of London. He and his wife retired to Thornham Magna in the 1970s, where there was a shortage of both local jobs and affordable housing, and together they began a programme of diversification of the Thornham Estate in order to try to alleviate some of these problems. Redundant farm buildings were turned into reasonably priced workshops for small businesses, others into offices and some into houses.

'The estate had few rights of way at the time and the Hennikers were determined to open it up to the public. Twelve miles of waymarked walks were created and these became known as Thornham Walks, which are now enjoyed by thousands of visitors each year. Lord Henniker's final project was the derelict walled garden. The walls were restored and the garden was planted as a walled orchard with extensive glass houses.' The walled garden now serves as a centre for people with disabilities to learn horticultural skills.

Special events take place throughout the year at the Thornham Walks, such as dawn chorus birdsong walks, butterfly walks and fungi forages, also guided walks in the Upper Waveney Valley and mid Suffolk. Some events, like scarecrow building and pond dipping, are specifically geared towards children's interests.

As its Latin suffix suggests, Thornham Parva is the smaller of the twin villages. 'Little thorny village' has very few houses but it does have a remarkable thatched Saxon church, **St Mary's**, which is renowned not so much for its tiny size, its thatched roof or circular Saxon window, but for its 14th-century retable (altarpiece) – the largest surviving example from the medieval period – which managed to outlive the iconoclast reformers of the 16th century by hiding away, more or less forgotten, in a stable.

Lord Henniker of Thornham Hall rediscovered the work in a pile of wood in 1927 and presented it to St Mary's Church, where his brother was parson. The altarpiece, restored by a Cambridge University team, dates from around 1300 and shows strong Dominican influence with representations of eight saints witnessing the Crucifixion, one of whom is local hero St Edmund. The Musée de Cluny in Paris has another piece that would once have belonged alongside this, but the two sections became separated at the time of Henry VIII's Dissolution. The pronounced Dominican style suggests that both pieces originated from Thetford Friary in Norfolk, a 13th-century Dominican stronghold that has since disappeared and now lies under the foundations of Thetford Grammar School. In the churchyard is the grave of Sir Basil Spence, the architect of Coventry Cathedral.

⁎⁎ FOOD & DRINK

The Forge Thornham Walks ✆ 01379 831053. Close to the beginning of the walks, near the car park. This has plenty of outdoor seating and serves up cakes and coffee, light lunches and ice creams.

Four Horseshoes Wickham Rd, Thornham Magna ✆ 01379 678777 ⬦ thefourhorseshoes. net. An attractive thatched building with plenty of exposed woodwork, this dog-friendly pub serves traditional English favourites and European dishes along with a decent choice of real ales.

Belle Grove

✦ ★ ✦ ★ ✦

In a tranquil corner of rural Suffolk, we are excellently placed for exploring the coast including Southwold, Walberswick & Aldeburgh. Enjoy & explore that special combination of sky, sun, sea, dunes and marshes that has long attracted walkers, artists, musicians & writers. Not to mention the great foodie opportunities!

EXCEPTIONAL
EXOTIC
EXTRAVAGANT

Five star retreat near timeless Suffolk Heritage Coast

www.belle-grove.com

[f] telephone 01986 873124

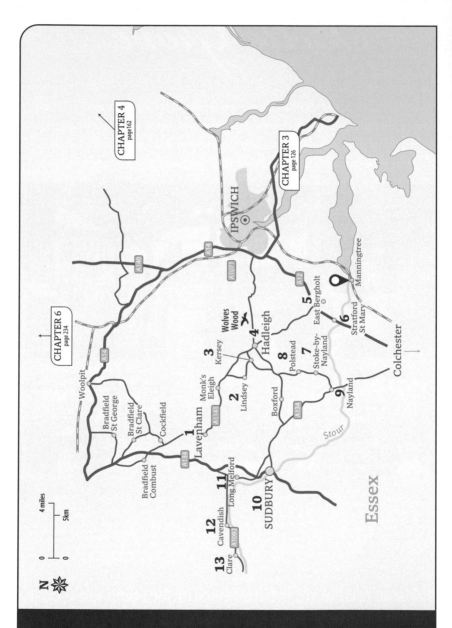

SOUTH SUFFOLK & THE STOUR VALLEY

5
SOUTH SUFFOLK &
THE STOUR VALLEY

This chapter covers the southern part of the county that includes the towns of Lavenham and Hadleigh and their hinterland as well as the Suffolk side of the Stour Valley (from East Bergholt and the Stour estuary in the east as far as Clare in the west) that stretches along the Suffolk–Essex border to the south.

In the south of the county, the Stour Valley is still very much a rural idyll, as the Stour babbles its way through fields of contented cattle and past improbably perfect-looking villages. A chocolate-box scene as painted by John Constable – and it was… many times over. It is not so much that Constable was a great painter – although he undoubtedly was – but what he painted. Though the healthy character of Constable's Suffolk has disappeared, the subject matter of many of his works is still easily identifiable

> *"The Stour babbles its way through fields of contented cattle and past improbably perfect-looking villages."*

almost two centuries later. This gives all of us a warm, fuzzy sense of continuity and tradition, and delights even those who do not normally have much time for paintings. Most of all, it somehow encapsulates the essence of rural England.

The irony is that many who live here among the Stour Valley's timber-framed splendours are also those that have the most tenuous connections to the area – a classic wealthy incomers versus disgruntled locals dilemma. London and the Home Counties are sometimes just a little too close for comfort and the goose that laid the golden egg is in danger of being flattened beneath the wheels of a commuting 4x4. In many cases the commute by car is a short one – just as far as Manningtree railway station, less than an hour from London's Liverpool Street. In the old days, geese would walk all the way to London from the area. There again, it was always just a one-way trip.

GETTING AROUND

It's easy enough in a car although meandering roads often mean that it takes longer to go from A to B than you might imagine. The main road leading to this part of the county from both north and south is the A12, which passes just to the west of Ipswich. The A1062 links the villages of the western part of the Stour Valley; the A134 connects Sudbury with Bury St Edmunds and Colchester across the Essex border; the A1071 connects Sudbury and Hadleigh with Ipswich; Lavenham is linked to Hadleigh and Bury St Edmunds by the A1171.

PUBLIC TRANSPORT

A useful bus route is the Chambers 236 service (Mon–Sat only) between Clare and Sudbury that passes through the villages of the western Stour Valley like Clare, Cavendish and Long Melford. Other services include the Chambers 374 bus that plies four times daily between Bury St Edmunds and Clare, the Ipswich Bus service 90/91 between Ipswich and Sudbury via Hadleigh, and the Chambers 750/3 service between Sudbury and Lavenham via Long Melford. Chambers 84 service connects Sudbury with Colchester via Stoke-by-Nayland three times a day. Sunday services tend to be sporadic or non-existent.

For the Stour Valley, the most useful **railway** station is at Manningtree, which although lying just within Essex is close to East Bergholt, Flatford Mill and the long-distance Stour Valley Path. Manningtree lies on the main Norwich–Ipswich–London line and usually has trains every hour during the day. Sudbury has a branch line from Marks Tey in Essex from where there are connections to London.

CYCLING

Cycling is good in parts, especially away from the main routes that are best avoided. **National Cycle Route 1** and **North Sea Cycle Route** (⊘ sustrans.org) pass right through the locale from Hadleigh in the Stour Valley via Ipswich and Woodbridge to Beccles in the Waveney Valley, while **National Cycle Route 51** crosses the county from Ipswich to Bury St Edmunds. In the Stour Valley is part of the **National Byway** (⊘ nationalbyway.org), still in development in the region, running from Sudbury west along the river. Another option is the 69-mile **Painters' Trail** (⊘ dedhamvalestourvalley.org),

ℹ️ TOURIST INFORMATION

Dedham AONB and Stour Valley Project ⌖ dedhamvalestourvalley.org

Flatford Flatford Lane, East Bergholt ℘ 01206 299460

Hadleigh The Library, 29 High St ℘ 01473 823778 ⌖ visithadleighsuffolk.co.uk

Lavenham Lady St ℘ 01787 248207

Sudbury The Town Hall (Gaol Ln entrance), Market Hill ℘ 01787 372331 ⌖ sudbury-tc.gov.uk/visit

which tours Constable Country in Dedham Vale. The website ⌖ dedhamvalestourvalley.org has several cycle routes with downloadable maps of the Stour Valley, including circular routes that pass through Clare and Stoke-by-Clare, Sudbury and Bures, and Stoke-by-Nayland and Polstead. A reasonable number of connected bridleways can be used for off-road cycling too.

Self-guided tours of the area are offered by Cycle Breaks (℘ 01449 721555 ⌖ cyclebreaks.com) and UK Cycling Holidays (℘ 01379 644818 ⌖ ukcyclingholidays.co.uk), who have a number of itineraries on offer. The Stour Valley Adventure Centre (℘ 01206 700707 ⌖ stourvalleyadventurecentre.com) at Sudbury is the nearest place to the Stour Valley for **cycle hire**. Hadleigh Food Bikes, a charity based at Kersey Mill (℘ 07377 190455 ⌖ freshstartcharity.org/hadleigh-foodbikes) is another option. Bike hire here is not only very reasonably priced but it also helps support the Hadleigh Foodbank and Fresh Start Charity. Rental should be pre-arranged online. Children's bikes, child seats and electric bikes are also available to rent.

WALKING

Pick your way around carefully and you'll find some worthwhile walking, especially along riverbanks. The Dedham Vale AONB and Stour Valley Project (⌖ dedhamvalestourvalley.org) gives a good selection of suggestions for walks in the Stour Valley area and has free downloadable guides on its website. One long-distance footpath passes through the area: the 60-mile **Stour Valley Path**, part of the European Path E2, begins at Cattawade near Manningtree in Essex and loosely follows the River Stour valley west through Sudbury to eventually reach Newmarket. John Harris's Walking in England website (⌖ walkinginengland.co.uk) features a wealth of links to downloadable maps and walk guides for the Stour Valley and other parts of Suffolk.

LAVENHAM, HADLEIGH & AROUND

A little way north of the Stour Valley, this area has at its centre one of the most celebrated villages in the county. Many visitors that come here restrict themselves solely to Lavenham but the surrounding countryside is highly attractive in its own right and there is plenty more to be discovered along the quiet lanes of this corner of Suffolk.

1 LAVENHAM

🏠 **Milden Hall** Farmhouse (page 278), **The Swan** (page 278) 🏚 **Byes Barn** (page 278)

The cherry liqueur in the Suffolk assortment box, Lavenham is the village that has showed up on a thousand calendars, jigsaws and chocolate boxes. With wobbly timber-framed cottages, flower-bedecked gardens and thatch galore, it's even more overwhelmingly gorgeous than the many lovely villages that grace the Stour Valley just south of here. Its beauty makes it almost unreal: the only things that do not seem to be half-timbered are the smart cars lining the cobbles – they are mostly Range Rovers – although you might see the odd Morris Traveller doing its best to complement the vernacular. Like a very rich, celebratory meal, too much exposure might induce a little artery thickening but as a once-in-a-while experience Lavenham is unparalleled – just don't even think of building a bungalow here, or opening a kebab shop.

"It's even more overwhelmingly gorgeous than the many lovely villages that grace the Stour Valley just south of here."

Lavenham grew fat and rich on the medieval wool trade and by the early 16th century had become the 14th wealthiest town in the country, a sort of medieval Knightsbridge, paying more tax than York or Lincoln. Prosperous merchants invested their fortunes in real estate and what would have been considered very desirable properties for the time. Then as now, close-studded timbers spoke of affluence, albeit for rather different reasons; living in a plastered cage of medieval woodwork did not come cheap. A decline in the town's fortunes came with the 16th century, thanks to undercutting by newly arrived Dutch weavers from Colchester, but it was this decline and the transferral of the weaving industry elsewhere that have managed to keep Lavenham so beautifully preserved. If it had had access to the new-fangled water power used in the west and northwest of England, or had been near a coalfield, its buildings would very likely never have survived so intact.

With an astonishing total of 361 listed buildings in the village, there is little point in my directing you to more than one or two: you can just potter around the rest at will. Although they've been meticulously restored, it seems remarkable that some of the timber-framed buildings are actually still standing given the eccentric tilt to the horizontal that some of them have. Some of the wobbliest houses, like the almost cartoon-like 'Cordwainers', can be seen at the corner of the High Street and Market Lane.

The all-white and quite spectacular **Guildhall** dominates the market square across from the Angel Hotel. This was the headquarters of the town's powerful Guild of Corpus Christi, and it's a hugely impressive 16th- and 17th-century building that is whitewashed all over, beams and all. Now it serves as a National Trust museum (page 206). The car park situated directly in front of it is a reminder that, despite an abundance of pristine historical architecture, this is definitely the 21st century. Next door to the Guildhall is a quaint half-timbered Tudor-period cottage that serves as a local estate agent's office – a more idyllic location for such an enterprise is hard to imagine. The **Angel Hotel** on the other side of the square became the centre of a controversy in 2013 when its then owner, celebrity chef Marco Pierre White, repainted the 1420 building in a Barbara Cartland-esque shade of pink that offended locals claimed was neither authentic nor appropriate. Such are the priorities of Lavenham. After bitter accusations that the Angel now 'looked like blancmange', the famously grouchy chef reluctantly agreed to repaint it the correct shade of pink after consultation with English Heritage. This was not the first time the chef had ruffled feathers in the village: when he first took over the Angel he refused to serve lager, claiming this encouraged the wrong kind of clientele. It should be noted that Marco Pierre White is no longer in charge at the Angel and the new owner has been keen to repair ties with the local community. Lager is available in the bar these days but whether or not the original clientele has returned is another matter.

The market square itself has some very fine Georgian houses to complement the Tudor and if you look down the slope of Prentice Street alongside the Angel, you'll see the lush folds of the valleys beyond. So steep and old world in character (apart from the parked cars), this could almost be the street from the well-known Hovis advertisement. Indeed, there's actually a large old-fashioned sign for Hovis on the gable of one of the shops across the square from the Guildhall, although Lavenham is really more a sort of brioche and sourdough sort of place.

The town's church of **St Peter and St Paul** is, as you might expect, large and exceptionally grand. It was rebuilt in the late 15th century by a consortium of local families, who were no doubt willingly converting their wool wealth into what might be termed 'medieval fire insurance' – a generous gift to God to avert any possibility of a fiery afterlife. The flint tower seems enormous, 140ft high and visible for miles, while the interior is lavish, with a chantry dedicated to St Catherine and St Blaise, the latter, having been martyred by being 'combed to death' by the emperor Diocletian, ended up becoming the patron saint of the wool trade.

"To keep things real and bring a bit of muddy-booted rusticity into town, a farmers' market is held in the village hall."

To keep things real and bring a bit of muddy-booted rusticity into town, a **farmers' market** is held in the village hall and in the adjoining field on the morning of the fourth Sunday of each month. This has all manner of local products like bread from Sparling and Faiers, pork products from Clavering Pigs and free-range eggs from Manor Farm. There are also home-baked pies, local cheeses and Suffolk honey on sale. Sometimes the falcons, owls and hawks from Lavenham Falconry (✆ 01787 249691 ⌖ lavenhamfalconry.co.uk), based at nearby Monks Eleigh are on display outside – a rare opportunity to ruffle the feathers of a real-life raptor.

The Guildhall

Market St ✆ 01787 247646 ⊙ Apr–Jul Tue–Sun, Aug daily, Sep & Oct Wed–Sun, Nov–mid Dec Thu–Sun; National Trust

Otherwise known as the Guildhall of Corpus Christi, one of five guilds in the town, this dramatic white building is the jewel in the crown of Lavenham's Tudor heritage. The guildhall was built around 1530 but

---

1 & **2** Lavenham has a grand 15th-century Guildhall and plenty of 'Suffolk pink' cottages.
3 Monks Eleigh's village green. **4** The 13th-century chapel of St James in Lindsey. ▶

LAVENHAM ON THE SILVER SCREEN

If the village seems to be something of a living museum or film set then it will not come as any surprise to learn that Lavenham has featured as a backdrop for period dramas like Stanley Kubrick's *Barry Lyndon*, Michael Reeves's *Witchfinder General* and even Pasolini's *The Canterbury Tales*. In the case of *Witchfinder General*, a witch-burning scene was shot in the market square, the same location as real burnings in the past.

Most famously, the village was used in recent years as a stand-in for Godric's Hollow, the fictitious West Country village birthplace of both Harry Potter and his headmaster, Albus Dumbledore, and made an appearance in the film *Harry Potter and the Deathly Hallows, Part 1*. Any modern buildings caught messing up the magical Potter aesthetic were digitally edited from the final print, although there probably wasn't much to do given the homogeneity of the architecture here. The 'Potters' Cottage in Godric Hollow', a Grade I-listed 14th-century building known as the De Vere House, has since become the second most-photographed doorway in the UK after 10 Downing Street. The house changed hands for a little less than £1 million in 2012. Lavenham's timber-framed other-worldliness certainly makes a convincing setting for schoolboy wizardry action – if you were looking to catch a game of Quidditch anywhere in England then this would probably be the first place you'd look. It almost goes without saying that episodes of *Lovejoy* were also filmed in the village in the past. Most recently, Lavenham was one of two Suffolk villages (the other was Kersey) used as a location for the 2023 Netflix film *The Strays*.

by the end of the following century it was in use as a jail, a use that continued until the end of the 18th century when it was closed before later serving as a workhouse and almshouse. During World War II the building received evacuees and served as a restaurant and nursery before coming into the National Trust's care in 1951. As well as the timber-framed main hall, the first floor has an exhibition of Lavenham's wool-trade history and building tradition. You'll also find a tea room, a gift shop and a courtyard garden.

¶ FOOD & DRINK

Angel Hotel Market Pl ☎ 01787 247388 ⌂ theangellavenham.co.uk. Lavenham's oldest inn, overlooking the splendid market place and guildhall. The kitchen here offers a regularly changing seasonal menu with all dishes making use of locally sourced ingredients where possible. Food is served in either the restaurant or in the cosy bar, which comes complete with fireplace and comfy Chesterfield sofas. There's a comprehensive wine list, a wide-ranging gin selection and Suffolk ales on handpump.

Blue Vintage Tea Room Market Pl ✆ 01787 248285 ⌂ lavenhambluetearooms.com.
Popular tea room on the market square with a vintage atmosphere and little courtyard
garden. Good sandwiches, cakes and scones, plus ploughman's lunches and afternoon teas.
The Greyhound High St ✆ 01787 249553 ⌂ greyhoundlavenham.co.uk. Probably the
closest it gets to a straightforward drinking pub in Lavenham yet still geared mostly towards
food. This has good beer and a varied Mediterranean-influenced menu offering a range of
sharing plates and tapas-style 'small plates'.
The Swan High St ✆ 01787 247477 ⌂ theswanatlavenham.co.uk. Various dining options
are available here: lunch or dinner in the relaxed surroundings of the Mess Call 487 brasserie
or top-range fine dining in full medieval style in the Gallery, a high-ceilinged room with a
minstrels' gallery. Afternoon tea in the lounge, garden or gallery here is quite special too.
There is also the option of a slightly more economical set lunch in the brasserie from Mon–
Thu. See page 278.
Tatum's Teahouse 17 High St ✆ 01787 249674. A popular Lavenham tea room with good
scones, sandwiches and homemade cakes.

2 LINDSEY

The countryside around Lavenham is rolling and picture-postcard
pastoral, especially along the narrow country lanes that lead off the main
A1141 to Hadleigh. If you turn right after Monks Eleigh the chances are
that after negotiating a few single-track roads that seem to go nowhere
you'll end up in the hamlet of Lindsey.

Similar to Worstead in Norfolk, this tiny village is associated with a
variety of cloth and Lindsey gave its name to a coarse cloth made of
linen and wool known as linsey-woolsey. It's hard to credit it with such
importance in the past given what you find on the ground – a tiny and
very attractive cluster of thatched cottages with a modest rustic church
that has no tower.

Head south from the village and at Rose Green veer east to discover
some barely visible earthworks and, hidden behind a hedge, the thatched
13th-century **chapel of St James**, now in the care of English Heritage.
The chapel was formerly the chantry of Lindsey Castle, of which the
aforementioned earthworks – effectively just a trace of motte and bailey
– are now the only reminder. The chapel, which is lit by narrow lancet
windows, is not really visible from the road and so quite easy to miss.
You can park at the small lay-by next to the English Heritage sign and
then go through the gate that leads to the entrance. Inside, it is bare but
highly atmospheric.

SUFFOLK PINK

Suffolk cottages are typified by their pastel pinkwash, a colour not generally common elsewhere in the country. Historically, the distinctive colour is said to be the result of adding pig or ox blood to traditional lime whitewash, the exact shade varying considerably according to the quantity added and because of natural pigments in the daub beneath.

Sometimes juice from sloe berries was also added to produce a richer tone – there are some who argue that blood was never used and it was solely juice and red ochre that was used to create the colour.

Whatever the truth of this, these days the colour is far more standardised and widely available, blood-free, from Dulux and other proprietary paint manufacturers. The correct colour is important to both villagers and local authorities, and certainly not just any shade of pink will do as chef Marco Pierre White discovered to his cost when he repainted his hotel in Lavenham (page 205).

Interestingly, it would appear that Suffolk pink is a relatively new tradition, and the colour-washing of external walls was not widely practised until the late 19th century. Constable's Suffolk landscapes of the early 19th century show white or off-white plastered buildings, with not a hint of 'Suffolk pink' to be seen. So for true 'heritage' Suffolk read white, not pink.

Tracts of ancient woodland can also be found in the area. **Groton Wood**, managed by the Suffolk Wildlife Trust, a couple of miles south of Rose Green, is noted for its coppiced small-leaved limes and wild cherry trees, one of the few woods in the county where this species grows wild. In spring, you can expect to see bluebells and early purple orchids, and in the shadier areas you might even come across scarce species like violet helleborine and herb-paris. Fifteen species of butterfly have been recorded here, including purple hairstreak.

North of Lindsey, downstream from Lavenham along the valley of the River Brett as it meanders southeast towards Hadleigh, is the village of **Monks Eleigh.** Often overlooked in terms of its illustrious and more-visited neighbours, here you'll find an attractive scattering of houses around a village green. Some of the village houses date back to the 16th century or earlier, and the parish church of St Peter's that stands on the site of a former Saxon church is 15th century. The church's tower is quite a conspicuous landmark around these parts and can be seen long before you arrive in the village. An independently minded sort of place, Monk's Eleigh has its own well-stocked community shop and post office located next to the Swan pub (page 211), although, like many other non-profit rural enterprises, in recent years there have been threats of closure.

¶¶ FOOD & DRINK

Bildeston Crown High St, Bildeston ☏ 01449 740510 ⏚ thebildestoncrown.com. The sister pub of the Lindsey Rose, this hostelry east of Monks Eleigh and a few miles north of Lindsey and Kersey dates from 1529 and makes the most of the ancient beams, open fires and flagstones. Very much a pricey (and award-winning) gastropub, with an ambitious menu that makes use of locally sourced products where possible; a range of Suffolk real ales are on offer.

The Cock Inn Lavenham Rd, Brent Eleigh ☏ 01787 247371. A mile or two west of Monk's Eleigh on the Lavenham road, this delightful pink-washed and thatched 'parlour' pub is like stepping back to another age – in a good way. An old-fashioned 'proper' pub (a rarity in these part), The Cock has no electronic gadgets, no TV or music, just two cosy rooms with excellent beer and friendly locals. There's Greene King and Adnams ales on tap, and good-value, honest food too, including doorstep sandwiches and an excellent ploughman's lunch. Meals may be eaten at a shared table indoors or in the small beer garden.

Lindsey Rose Lindsey Tye ☏ 01449 741424 ⏚ thelindseyrose.co.uk. With open beamed partitions and rich red décor, this 15th-century food-oriented inn has a varied main menu and a set 'locals day menu' available for lunch and dinner (Wed–Sun). The house beer is Mauldons ales from Sudbury.

Swan The Street, Monks Eleigh ☏ 01449 403828 ⏚ swaninnmonkseleigh.co.uk. Reopened in 2023 after undergoing a makeover, this traditional oak-beamed 16th-century inn with inglenook fireplace and log burner has long been the focal point of the village.

3 KERSEY

Like its neighbour Lindsey, the village of Kersey has given its name to a type of cloth and 'kersey' describes a lightweight, coarse broadcloth of the sort used in military uniforms. Although the cloth was made in many other places it probably originated here. Kersey is widely regarded as one of the county's most photogenic villages. With an assortment of timbered weavers' cottages strung along its high street, a large wool-trade church and a quaint water splash at the bottom of the hill, it is a delightful scene on arrival from the north. The only thing that detracts from Kersey's Hovis-advert wholesomeness is the line of Range Rovers and their ilk parked along the street. Blame the Tudors – they were never very forward-thinking when it came to 21st-century parking arrangements.

BOXFORD'S LIONESS & THE WALL OF DEATH

Just west of Hadleigh, the old weaving village of Boxford was once the home of George 'Tornado' Smith (1908–71), who was one of the first Englishmen to perform the gravity-defying 'Wall of Death' on a motorcycle in this country in the early 1930s.

As well as taking his act to the Essex coastal resorts, Smith would also perform the feat in the local pub garden for the amusement of the villagers.

To spice up his already quite spectacular act, he also sometimes carried a lioness in his sidecar. The lioness, Briton, who was taken for walks through the streets of Boxford, now lies buried in the pub garden; there's even a plaque to her memory.

Edit this unavoidable modernity from your mind's eye and Kersey is indeed gorgeous. With pinkwashed cottages, pargeted walls, time-hardened beams and thatched roofs on show, it's an assembly that shouts out iconic Suffolk. The hill that dips down to the ford and then rises sharply up the other side to the church at the top is perhaps more archetypal Dorset but does set the scene off beautifully. Cue Hovis music… or the *Lovejoy* theme tune if your memory stretches back that far.

The ford at the bottom of the hill – a tributary of the River Brett and usually a damp squib of a thing that is just deep enough to wet your tyres – has a footbridge to one side of it. Next to this stands River House with a huge Elizabethan door. Just up from here is the village pub, The Bell, with bright hanging baskets prettifying its already handsome magpie-beam exterior. Across the ford at the top of the hill stands the church of **St Mary's**, which as so often in former wool towns and villages seems supersized in terms of a village of this size's needs.

¶¶ FOOD & DRINK

Bell Inn The Street ✆ 01473 823229 ⟨ thebellinnkersey.co.uk. A lovely old inn dating from the 13th century that offers a choice of real ales and wines, Aspall cyder and eclectic, locally sourced homemade food; also daily specials and Sunday roasts.

4 HADLEIGH

East of Lavenham, halfway to Ipswich, Hadleigh is a small town set in gently rolling countryside. The River Brett flows through the town,

1 The picturesque village of Kersey dips down to a ford. **2** Hadleigh's handsome Guildhall. **3** Stroll beside the River Brett to the medieval Toppesfield Bridge. ▶

LAURENCE MITCHELL

ALAN COPSON/AWL

PAUL WISHART/S

rather wider here than it is at Lavenham and Monks Eleigh upstream. From Hadleigh the river flows due south to reach its confluence with the River Stour near Stratford St John.

Like Lavenham, this compact market town has plenty of timber-framed wool-trade buildings, although Hadleigh is much less of a museum piece and more an everyday lived-in sort of place. Despite a considerable expanse of new estates north of the centre close to the A1071 bypass, there's much of interest in the compact centre and it is worth making a diversion to look at the town's three-storeyed 15th-century Guildhall that once served as a poorhouse.

The most rewarding area for a stroll is along High Street, Queen Street, Church Street and Angel Street, which have a plethora of eye-catching old houses, some with pargeting. The church, as with all these wool towns, is very grand and St Mary's is the only large church with a spire in the county. The exterior bell, in situ since at least the late 16th century, is also East Anglia's oldest and inside the church you'll find a painting, *Head of Christ*, by Maggi Hambling, who was raised in Hadleigh – a far less controversial work than her Aldeburgh steel scallop sculpture (page 58). There's also a fine modern stained-glass memorial window in memory of the parish's former rector, John Richard Betton. Facing the western end of the church is the distinctive Deanery Tower, actually two connected towers, which was built as a gatehouse to the new rectory in 1495.

The aforementioned **Guildhall** (⊘ hadleightownhall.co.uk), a handsome half-timbered complex, lies on the south side of the graveyard. It currently serves as offices for the town council and an events centre; guided tours are available by prior arrangement. **Market day** in the town is on Friday morning.

A pleasant stroll along the **River Brett** can start from the medieval Toppesfield Bridge, the oldest working bridge in Suffolk, from where there is a signed riverside walk. This follows the river along a peaceful willow-shaded path before emerging at Corks Lane next to a recreation ground and returning to High Street via a Victorian iron bridge. An alternative here is to turn left from the riverside path to climb up to the wooded Broom Hill nature reserve and on to reach Constitution Hill. Another enjoyable walk leads along a **disused railway track** that passes through Raydon Great Wood and serves as an alternative detour for National Cycle Route 1.

♙ FOOD & DRINK

The George 52 High St ☎ 01473 822151 ⊘ georgehadleigh.co.uk. A former coaching inn with decent, well-priced pub grub, made mostly using local produce, and Suffolk ales on tap.
Paddy & Scott's Café 72 High St ☎ 08444 778586 ⊘ paddyandscotts.shop. A coffee specialist with other branches in Ipswich and Colchester, this relaxed place has, as you might expect, a wide range of coffees to choose from, in addition to sandwiches and pastries.

Wolves Wood

This RSPB reserve, three miles east of Hadleigh just north of the main Ipswich road, is a rare remnant of ancient woodland that is managed by traditional coppicing. The dawn chorus is said to be quite something here in spring, with up to 30 species of bird singing, including garden warblers and nightingales, best heard in late April and early May. In the summer months, butterflies and dragonflies abound in the rides around the ponds. In autumn, there's a plethora of colourful fungi to be found alongside the tracks. A one-mile nature trail leads from the car park. It can get muddy here following wet weather, so wellingtons are a good idea. Dogs are not allowed.

THE STOUR VALLEY: EAST BERGHOLT TO SUDBURY

Working east to west along the Stour Valley, Suffolk's southern border with Essex, I begin with what is one of Suffolk's best-known villages, East Bergholt, before following the valley west through Nayland to Sudbury.

5 EAST BERGHOLT

Forever remembered as John Constable's birthplace, East Bergholt, and Flatford Mill in particular, are major honeypots for visitors to Suffolk. East Bergholt is both a beginning and an end: for walkers, the **Constable County Trail** starts here and passes past Flatford Mill and across the Stour on its way to Dedham in Essex. Flatford village is also the last place along the river's Suffolk bank before it widens to an estuary at Manningtree, although you might argue that the bridge at Cattawade, where the Stour starts to become tidal, has this honour.

East Bergholt is a largish village, just north of the river but close enough to Essex to have a Colchester postcode. Although the village also deserves a place in history for its tradition of Protestant radicalism

EAST BERGHOLT & JOHN CONSTABLE (1776–1837)

As a schoolboy, Constable would have crossed the Stour and walked through the meadows from East Bergholt to the grammar school in the square at Dedham. One of his earliest paintings is of the headmaster, who encouraged his pupil's artistic potential, though it is hard now to imagine that Constable's masterly landscape paintings were once so little appreciated that he sold only 20 in England in his lifetime, and had to wait until the age of 52 to be elected to the Royal Academy.

As a young man he loved to paint the details around his home of Flatford Mill – 'willows, old rotten planks, slimy posts and brickwork' – subjects so far from the more fashionable subjects of brooding forests, mountains and medieval ruins that they were scarcely considered picturesque at all. At the same time he was disinclined to emulate fellow Suffolk artist Thomas Gainsborough (page 225), born some 50 years before and whom he much admired, in using his landscapes as the backgrounds to portraits of fashionable folk: he preferred (and was criticised for) showing farm workers and animals going unselfconsciously about their daily business in a real setting. As his own brother commented, 'When I look at a mill painted by John I see that it will *go round*, which is not always the case with those by other artists.'

Constable returned to East Bergholt each summer, renewing his happy associations with the place: 'I love every stile and stump, and every lane in the village,' he remarked. It was here that he developed his very individual techniques for painting directly from nature: he was probably the first artist to sketch in oils in the open air, and he influenced many successors including the French Impressionists of the late 19th century. Constable's towering trees in full leaf and huge skies with rolling, stormy clouds are still a very recognisable part of the late summer scene.

in the 16th century, it is, of course, the painter John Constable who has really put the place on the map by not only being born here but also immortalising numerous local views in his paintings. His place of birth was demolished years ago and now just a plaque marks the site – but you can see a memorial window to the artist and his wife in the tower-less church of **St Mary** (with its unusual 16th-century wooden bell house, apparently constructed when the church ran out of money for the proposed bell tower) next door.

If you venture down the high street towards the Red Lion, you can also see Constable's first studio next to a garage and engineering workshop. The cottage opposite the pub has a sign that says 'Dealer in Hatts' and another that says 'Ye Olde House', just in case you weren't sure.

There's a handy bus stop by the pub with services to Colchester, Ipswich, Manningtree and Hadleigh.

Many visitors to East Bergholt head straight to **Flatford** by the river, down a narrow, leafy lane that follows a one-way system, a sensible precaution given the numbers that come here. At the end of the lane are a large car park and a path down to the river where you'll find a small Constable museum, a tea room and, a little further along, Flatford Mill itself and **Willy Lot's cottage**. Both the mill and the cottage are immediately identifiable from the paintings.

The best view of the mill is from across the river, so cross over on to the Essex bank and walk a little way along it. You are unlikely to be alone, especially in summer, especially on a Sunday. **Rowing boats** for hire can be found at the bridge alongside, quite likely, aspiring artists with easels doing their own take on the Constable theme. Pollarded willows and cud-chewing cows in the fields help complete the bucolic setting.

It is only a two-mile walk from here into **Dedham**, which has a fine wool-trade church and **Castle House**, an art museum ($\mathcal{O}$ 01206 322127 $\mathcal{O}$ munningsmuseum.org.uk) dedicated to the work of Sir Alfred Munnings in the artist's former home, where there is also a tea room, shop and gardens.

¶¶ FOOD & DRINK

The Carriers Arms Heath Rd, East Bergholt $\mathcal{O}$ 01206 298392 $\mathcal{O}$ thecarriersarms.co.uk. This family-run local has good-value home-cooked food. There's a large garden for outdoor dining on fine days and a cheerful log fire inside for cooler weather.

Essex Rose Tea Room High St, Dedham $\mathcal{O}$ 01206 323101. Across the river in Essex, this is a good place to stop for a snack, homemade cakes or an afternoon cream tea.

Oranges & Lemons Burnt Oak, Flatford $\mathcal{O}$ 01206 299000 $\mathcal{O}$ orangesandlemonscafe. com. A little way north of Flatford Mill, this tea room is a decent choice for breakfasts, light lunches and afternoon teas.

6 STRATFORD ST MARY

This village, which featured in many of Constable's paintings, is the most southerly village in Suffolk (although Landguard Point near Felixstowe is slightly further south). It lies along the old London coaching road and so used to be a popular stop for herders marching their geese, turkeys and cattle south to market at London. Such was the volume of trade here in the past that the largest of the village's four inns was reputed to have

A walk in Constable Country

✽ OS Explorer map 196; start: Manningtree station, ♀ TM094322; 7 miles; moderate

Τhis seven-mile walk sneaks into Essex. Actually that's an understatement: most of it is in Essex, but it sums up the gentle charms of the Stour Valley so well that it's well worth the stray over the county border. Also, despite its requiring quite a bit of field-crossing, the southern part of the route follows the Essex Way, which is mostly waymarked (it's still a good idea to take the OS map).

The route starts at Manningtree station, and heads out through the car park on the south side, where a rising path leads up to Lawton church. Here you join up with the Essex Way, which traces an intricate and nicely varied route past Lawford Hall, a Georgian-looking pile concealing an Elizabethan core, and over the Shir Burn and railway to reach Dedham. In this gorgeously handsome village street, you can take a look at the fine wool trade church of St Mary's and perhaps also visit **Castle House** (𝒟 01206 322127 ⊘ munningsmuseum.org.uk), the former home of painter Sir Alfred Munnings and now an art museum open to the public on three or four afternoons a week in summer; it has the largest collection of Munnings' paintings anywhere.

Dedham has plenty of places to stop for a drink or a bite to eat, although they tend mostly to be rather upmarket: **Essex Rose Tea Room** (𝒟 01206 323101) on the high street is a good choice, or for something smarter and more formal, the **Boatyard Eatery** (𝒟 01206 323153 ⊘ theboatyarddedham.co.uk) or the **Sun Inn** (𝒟 01206 323351 ⊘ thesuninndedham.com), which although a distinctly elegant (and much-liked) dining venue is also a place where you can just pop in for a pint of Adnams or one of the other regional brews on offer.

extensive stabling for up to 200 horses, while another had 20 acres of pasture for cattle passing through.

The trade has now gone, but the through road remains – the frenetic A12, which unhappily divides the bulk of the village from its church. Stratford St Mary is certainly a pretty village, with plenty of splendid half-timbered Tudor buildings, but you cannot quite escape the rumble and swish of lorries and cars speeding past on their way to and from Colchester. These days, two pubs remain – The Swan and The Anchor.

⟨ FOOD & DRINK

Hall Farm Stratford St Mary CO7 6LS 𝒟 01206 322572 (shop), 01206 323600 (café) ⊘ hallfarmshop.co.uk. Close to St Mary's Church, this combined farm shop, delicatessen and butcher has won several food awards. This has an excellent choice of quality local meats,

Leaving Dedham, head north on the B1209, past Dedham Mill and over **Dedham Bridge**; follow the Stour Valley Path along the famous water meadows of **Dedham Vale** immortalised by Constable; kingfishers make the occasional appearance, and snipe and redshank frequent the marshes. Recross the river just before Flatford Mill and follow the St Edmund Way back to Manningtree station.

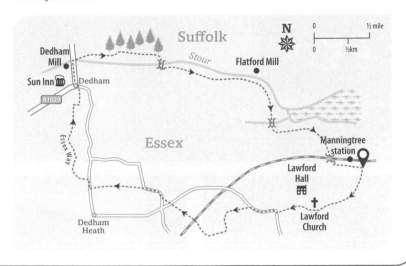

free-range poultry, home-grown seasonal vegetables, freshly baked bread and all manner of deli items. A café serves meals and snacks made with seasonal local produce from the farm shop.

7 STOKE-BY-NAYLAND

♠ The Angel Inn (page 278)

Continuing west, either by road or on foot along the Stour Valley Path, you soon arrive in Stoke-by-Nayland, set away from the river on top of a hill. The church of **St Mary** here, with its 120ft tower, is a beacon for miles around and Constable featured it in a number of his paintings, although not necessarily in exactly the same landscape. One of his most famous paintings, *Stoke-by-Nayland*, features the church illuminated beneath a dramatic rainbow. An earlier visitor, the puritan William 'Smasher'

MARTIN HATCH/DT

NEAR THIS PLACE LIE
THE REMAINS OF

MARIA MARTEN

WHO DIED IN
THE RED BARN
POLSTEAD

AND WAS BURIED ON
APRIL 20th 1828
AGED 26 YEARS

R·I·P

HOLMES GARDEN PHOTOS/A

RAMBO80/S

RICHARD BILLINGHAM/DT

Dowsing, was less enthusiastic about art and destroyed countless 'superstitious' pictures within the church along with some 15th-century glass. Someone, perhaps Dowsing, perhaps another puritan, has also done their best to damage the alabaster tomb of Lady Anne Windsor, leaving a chipped nose and broken hand.

The village is peaceful and highly good-looking, glowing with Suffolk pink; the churchyard is a lovely spot to watch the swallows and house martins that swoop around the tower. A footpath leads between some handsome timbered houses opposite and, if you ignore the sign pointing to 'Cherry Wood', you can continue across the tops of fields and enjoy a view down to the valley below. Seen from here, you realise that Stoke-by-Nayland is quite an elevated village by East Anglian standards. If you retrace your steps and then follow the sign and footpath down to the valley, you'll eventually end up in Nayland, albeit by a rather circuitous route.

¶¶ FOOD & DRINK

The Angel Inn ✆ 01206 263645 ⊘ angelinnsuffolk.co.uk. A gastronomically inclined restaurant with rooms in a converted 16th-century coaching inn, this luxurious establishment has walls bedecked with paintings that range from Old Masters to modern British. The top level, Michelin-standard (and price) cuisine here makes use of seasonal, sustainable produce from the local area.

The Crown Park St ✆ 01206 262001 ⊘ crowninn.net. With low-ceilinged, rambling rooms, The Crown offers a seasonal menu combining traditional and contemporary dishes made with regional produce where possible. More prosaically, there are also regular 'Pizza Friday' evenings. It has an outstanding wine list, Adnams, Woodforde's and Humpty Dumpty ales in the bar, and a sunny terrace for warm weather. In summer, there is also a garden tipi, field kitchen and shed bar set up under a mature willow tree for special events.

8 POLSTEAD

Just north of Stoke-by-Nayland, on the other side of the shallow valley of the River Box, a tributary of the Stour, is Polstead. The village is infamous as the location of the **Red Barn Murder** of 1827 in which a local farmer's boy, William Corder, murdered his lover. The story captured the imagination of the people thanks to its publication in the penny dreadfuls, and when Corder was later caught and subsequently hanged

---

◀ **1** Hire a rowing boat on the River Stour near Dedham. **2** A plaque marking the infamous Red Barn Murder in Polstead. **3** Flatford Mill. **4** East Bergholt's unusual wooden bell house.

at Bury St Edmunds his execution attracted a huge audience. Given the macabre tastes of the time, this wasn't the end of it: his skin was used to bind a copy of the trial proceedings (which can be seen along with his scalp in Moyses Hall Museum, Bury) and souvenir hunters squabbled over pieces of the hangman's rope, which sold for a guinea an inch, and even chipped away the victim's tombstone. A melodramatic play based on the events, *Maria Marten or The Murder in the Red Barn*, remained hugely popular throughout the mid 19th century and was resurrected as a 1935 British film.

A more cheerful association is the small sweet cherry variety, known as **Polstead Black**, that used to grow here and which is thought to have originally been brought to the area by Romans. Cherries are commemorated in several place names around here: Cherry Meadow, Cherry Farm, Cherry Billy's Lane; and there used to be a cherry fair too, on the village green each July. Cherry growing is, alas, no longer big business, although some local gardens still have their own Polstead Black cherry trees.

Even without any interest in murder or cherry trees, Polstead is a highly attractive village worthy of a visit in its own right. From the green where the pub and shop are located the road dips sharply down into the valley to reach the village pond and a T-junction. St Mary's Church stands above here at the top of the opposite slope, well worth the brief climb up to see it. There used also to be an ancient oak tree nearby – the **Gospel Oak** – that was considered to be the oldest tree in Suffolk at around 1,300 years old and the scene of Saxon worship back in the 7th century when it may have been planted by St Cedd or one of his followers. The oak collapsed in 1953 but its stumpy remains can still be seen between St Mary's Church and Polstead Hall in the grounds of the hall. St Mary's Church is distinguished in not only having a beautiful location but also in being the only surviving medieval stone spire in Suffolk. The graveyard holds an impressive war memorial, one of the largest church war memorials in England. It also affords excellent views over the surrounding countryside. The pub on the village green, The Cock Inn, dates from the 17th century, although the original pub was next door. The Cock Inn once served as premises for the local assizes and the Red Barn murder inquest took place here. Alongside all this talk of long-standing tradition, it's worth mentioning that the **community shop** on the green next to the village hall is the oldest in Suffolk and second oldest in England, dating from 1984. The shop also doubles as the village post office, open weekday mornings only. You can buy local **apple juices** here, made from Polstead apples at nearby Willow Farm, which also has its own farm shop (✆ 01787 211883) at Polstead Heath, north of the village. In recent years, the village playing field, known locally as the pitch, has been host to 'Polstice', an annual music festival of local bands around the time of the summer solstice.

⊓⊔ FOOD & DRINK

The Cock Inn The Green ✆ 01206 263150 ⌖ thecockinnpolstead.co.uk. This old village inn has real ale, an open fire and a decent pub food menu (Wed–Sun) featuring locally sourced produce. There's also a tea room serving light bites at lunchtimes (Tue–Fri) and full afternoon tea on Saturdays (booking required).

9 NAYLAND

Down in the valley itself on a lovely stretch of the Stour, Nayland is another fine village of timbered and colour-washed cottages. It's not quite Lavenham but it's not that far off in visual appeal, with timber-framed and pinkwashed cottages every way you look.

Across the Nayland Bridge, a footpath along the opposite bank follows the river west past a weir – part of the Stour Valley Path that leads to Wissington, with its Norman church, where the path crosses into Essex. As a reminder that you are still in Constable Country, St James's Church has an altarpiece by the artist: *Christ Blessing the Bread and Wine.*

⊓⊔ FOOD & DRINK

Anchor Inn 26 Court St ✆ 01206 262313 ⌖ anchornayland.co.uk. This traditional pub has a delightful setting next to the bridge over the River Stour. There's plenty of local produce on offer like home-reared lamb, duck, pork and beef, and, usually, at least one guest ale on tap, although, rather than beer, the pub adheres to the modern fashion of providing a wider choice in the gins and cocktails on offer.

THE STOUR VALLEY: SUDBURY TO CLARE

Continuing west along the Stour Valley, Sudbury, Long Melford, Cavendish and Clare come in fairly fast succession. Sudbury is by far the largest of these.

10 SUDBURY

🏠 **Mill House** (page 278)

The largest of the wool towns in this part of Suffolk, Sudbury is a busy place, with traffic streaming through its centre and local shoppers competing for parking spaces in the central square below the church. Despite the town's glorious wool-trade past and its later artistic connections, Daniel Defoe was not at all impressed with what he found at Sudbury when he visited here in the early 18th century, 'I know nothing for which this town is remarkable, except for being very populous and very poor.' Clearly he came to the town prior to what must have been a considerable revival as the town is a wealthy-enough-looking place today, with plenty of showy civic buildings and solid private dwellings on show.

"Daniel Defoe was not at all impressed with what he found at Sudbury when he visited here in the early 18th century."

Among a rich mix of architectural styles Georgian buildings tend to dominate. One fine example of these is **Gainsborough's House** (see opposite), the solid 18th-century house that now serves as a museum to the town's most famous son, Thomas Gainsborough, born here in 1727. A prominent bronze **statue** to the artist, palette and paintbrush in hand, stands at the top of the market square next to the imposing tower of the **church of St Peter**.

One of three medieval churches in the town centre, St Peter's was built as a chapel of ease to **St Gregory's Church**, which stands some distance away close to the river. St Peter's is no longer used for religious purposes but it still has a role to play in town life serving as an occasional venue for concerts, craft fairs and farmers' markets. At the time of writing, the church was closed for repair and would be reopening as a cultural venue in autumn 2023. Check ⊘ stpetersudbury.co.uk for further information. The market square next to the church hosts a twice-weekly market on Thursdays and Saturdays.

The third of Sudbury's churches, **All Saints'**, can be found a little way south of the centre. The churchyard here has a large mausoleum to the Gainsborough family, who were wealthy merchants in the town long before Thomas took up a paintbrush, although Thomas himself is buried in London.

It is easy to escape Sudbury's gentle bustle. As well as the river stroll outlined below there is also a very pleasant 3½-mile **Meadow Walk**, the first part of the longer **Gainsborough Trail** (⊘ gainsboroughtrail.org.uk) that starts at Friar's Meadow and follows the old railway track over the river to reach a pumping station before following the river north through water meadows to arrive at Brundon Mill. Here the trail rejoins the old railway track that is followed south back to the starting point. The trail is signed with waymarks and you have a reasonable chance of seeing wildlife like kingfishers, grass snakes and water voles along the way. A map of the walk can be downloaded from the Gainsborough Trail website.

Gainsborough's House
46 Gainsborough St, CO10 2EU ⊘ 01787 372958 ⊘ gainsborough.org

This museum and art gallery occupies the house where the artist was born and fittingly the walls are filled with his paintings, both commissioned portraits of the gentry and local landscapes painted at various times in his career. The complex has been redeveloped in recent years and now includes a purpose-built three-storey wing that provides the largest gallery space in Suffolk. There is also a café that overlooks the 18th-century walled garden.

Although the collection does not include masterpieces like *The Blue Boy* and *Mr and Mrs Andrews*, which are on display in leading art galleries elsewhere, this is the largest collection of Gainsborough paintings on show in any one place, and the setting of the house where the artist grew up provides added poignancy. Its Gainsborough memorabilia include his books and studio cabinet on which he would grind colours, as well as personal items like his swordstick and pocket watch. Special exhibitions, printmaking workshops and lectures are held here. There's also a gift shop close to the visitors' entrance.

THOMAS GAINSBOROUGH, LANDSCAPE ARTIST

Although he is generally better known as a society portraitist, Thomas Gainsborough started his career as a Suffolk landscape artist and his early works such as *Cornard Wood* (now hanging in the National Gallery), with its waving trees and stormy sky, were a great influence on the younger artist John Constable (page 216).

Gainsborough remained fond of including landscapes as backgrounds to his portraits: in *Mr and Mrs Andrews*, also in the National Gallery, the fashionably dressed sitters are off to one side of the painting, while their newly harvested cornfield – at the Auberies, a farm estate near Sudbury – glows equally prosperously alongside them.

The walled garden has as its centrepiece a 400-year-old mulberry tree that was planted during the reign of James I, who used to encourage the planting of such trees with the aim of establishing a silk industry in England. Unfortunately, the king was unaware that it was the white mulberry tree that fed silkworms, not black mulberries like this one, which supplies edible fruit. The tree still produces a fine crop most years.

The visitor information centre at the Town Hall, which doubles as the Sudbury Heritage Centre (⌂ sudbury-tc.gov.uk), has a **Town Trail** that describes the town's buildings, and the **Talbot Trail**, a series of 14 small bronzes to follow around the centre of town, tells of Sudbury's past.

A riverside stroll is hard to beat on a fine summer's afternoon. Continue down Gainsborough Street past the museum and you'll soon arrive at a footbridge across the River Stour from where you can wander south down to Ballingdon Bridge or north to Brundon Mill. At the Quay, south of Friars Street, you can take river trips on one of several boats that go downriver to Great Cornard, with its visitor centre, and on to The Swan at Great Henny. The boats that ply the river here are: the *Rosette*, an electric boat that can accommodate eight passengers; *Edwardian Lady*, an Edwardian-style electric boat that can take up to 12 passengers; *John Constable*, a restored Stour Lighter that can accommodate 12; and *Francis J Batten*, an adapted pontoon-style boat taking a maximum of eight and suitable for those with impaired mobility. All of these are run by the River Stour Trust (✆ 0844 8005015 ⌂ riverstourtrust.org ⊙ Easter–Oct Sat, Sun & bank holidays).

❦ FOOD & DRINK

Sudbury has a decent choice of pubs, restaurants and cafés. The suggestions listed below tend to stand out from the crowd in one way or another. **Sudbury Farmers' Market** takes place on Market Hill, on the last Friday of the month.

The Brewery Tap 21 East St ✆ 01787 370876 ⌂ thebrewerytapsudbury.co.uk. Sudbury's only real ale pub, serving a a choice of Mauldons Brewery beers on tap alongside a number of guest ales. There are also snacks that include gammon baps, pork pies and homemade Scotch

---

1 The town of Sudbury is set among meadows. **2** Gainsborough's House. **3** A heron in flight near Sudbury. **4** Long Melford's Holy Trinity Church features medieval stained glass. **5** Kentwell Hall holds Tudor re-enactments. ▶

LOVE ALL THIS PHOTOGRAPHY/S

GAINSBOROUGH'S HOUSE/A K PURKISS

RICHARD GIFFORD/S

LAURENCE MITCHELL

NIGEL NUDDS/DT

eggs. You can also order cooked food from a nearby take-away and the pub will provide plates and cutlery.

David's of Sudbury 51 Gainsborough St ✆ 01787 373919 ♂ davidsofsudbury.co.uk. A relaxing peaceful place for coffee, pastries, breakfasts or light lunches, this is a bit of a haven for adults as children under 13 are not allowed admittance.

Painters at the Angel 43 Friars St ✆ 07380 988224 ♂ paintersattheangel.co.uk. A dog-friendly independent café in the premises of a former pub, with an outdoor seating area at the back. Run by a husband and wife team, there's a good breakfast menu among other things on offer. Most ingredients are locally sourced, with bread from Weston's bakery and meat from Wicks Manor Farm in Maldon.

Secret Garden Tea Room 21 Friars St ✆ 01787 321301 ♂ tsg.uk.net. A quality tea room with a strong French theme and a blackboard offering daily specials, plus set-price three-course lunches; there's also a changing à la carte menu in the evenings. Local seasonal produce is used as much as possible, and work by local artists and photographers is usually displayed on the walls.

11 LONG MELFORD

As you head north from Sudbury, Long Melford is almost like a continuation of the same place: a long, linear village of thatched Suffolk pink with more than a few antique shops and booksellers lining the high street. **Melford Hall** (☉ Apr–Oct Wed–Sun & bank holidays), an Elizabethan country house belonging to the National Trust, lies north of the village next to a large open green that was the site of a Whitsun horse fair, the largest in East Anglia, in the 19th century. Beatrix Potter was once a regular visitor to the hall and Elizabeth I stayed here in 1578.

The village's **Holy Trinity Church**, an enormous 15th-century Perpendicular edifice brimming with medieval stained glass, lies north of the green – you need to get quite close before it reveals itself fully. Here is living proof that Long Melford was once one of the very richest places in the land thanks to the success of the wool trade. The church contains chapels to three of its wool tycoon benefactors – the Cloptons, the Cordells and the Martyns – and with an attached Lady Chapel, it's effectively two buildings in one – more like a cathedral than a parish church. This is the longest church in Suffolk but scale is not the only thing that makes this church exceptional. Holy Trinity's setting is noteworthy too, standing proudly on the highest ground in the village. As well as a vast quantity of beautiful medieval glass, the exterior walls also boast a fine array of intricate flint flushwork. Simon Jenkins gives it a five-star rating in his book *England's Thousand Best Churches*, the only church in Suffolk to rate so highly. Given Holy Trinity's grandeur and exceptionally opulent detail, it is hard to argue against such an appraisal.

Kentwell Hall & Gardens

Long Melford CO10 9BA ✆ 01787 310207 ⊗ kentwell.co.uk ☉ Easter–late Jul & Sep Sat–Thu, late Jul–Aug daily

A little way north of Long Melford's Holy Trinity Church, Kentwell Hall is a grand moated Tudor mansion complete with a brick rose maze and a walled garden containing a herb garden, a potager and a large variety of espaliered apples and pears. The extensive grounds hold ancient yews and cedars, a shrubbery, a ha-ha wall and a three-quarter-mile-long avenue of lime trees. An unhurried wander through the **grounds** reveals an ice house, a camera obscura and even an 'alchemist's hut' tucked away in a clump of yews. In the **rare-breed farm** based in the old dog kennels by the moat, you'll find Norfolk Horn sheep, Longhorn cattle and Suffolk Punch horses.

The hall and gardens host plenty of **special events** like Tudor re-enactment days, May Day celebrations, Hands-on History days and a History Festival for schoolchildren.

¶¶ FOOD & DRINK

Crown Inn Hall St ✆ 01787 377666 ⊗ thecrownhotelmelford.co.uk. A free house with a fine selection of ales and a daily changing seasonal menu with contemporary British cuisine, as well as sandwiches and baguettes in the bar. The large courtyard garden is ideal for alfresco dining.

Tiffin's Tea & Coffee House Drury House, Hall St ✆ 01787 827911. The place to come for homemade cakes, scones and, naturally, tea, of which you have a bewildering number of varieties to choose from – all loose leaf, of course.

12 CAVENDISH

Cavendish, further along the Stour Valley due west of Long Melford, is exceptionally pretty and, understandably, perhaps just a little bit given to vanity, with neatly grouped thatched pink cottages facing a large village green with the church juxtaposed behind them. Dotted along the high street are a handful of smart eating places, a pub above the green and an antique shop or two.

The village was not always so peaceful. During the Peasants' Revolt of 1381, John Cavendish, who came from the village, killed the rebel leader Wat Tyler with his sword at Smithfield in London. Irate local peasants decided to take their revenge on Cavendish's father, Sir John Cavendish, who was lord of the manor in the village. Sir John attempted to plead for sanctuary at **St Mary's Church** while hanging onto the door handle but was finally caught up with at Bury St Edmunds where he was beheaded by the mob. The very same handle supposedly hangs from the door of the village church today.

Both Sue Ryder, who founded her international charitable organisation, the Sue Ryder Foundation, here and Leonard Cheshire, her husband, the World War II pilot who set up homes for disabled people, are buried in the village.

¶¶ FOOD & DRINK

Tea on the Green The Green ✆ 0775 7355872 ⌘ teaonthegreencavendish.co.uk ☉ Wed–Sun. Facing the green, as its name suggests, this small tea room has a wide array of cakes and scones to choose from, as well as sandwiches, sausage rolls and ploughman's. Ingredients are sourced from local suppliers where possible.

13 CLARE

🏠 **Cobbles** (page 278)

Another fine medieval wool town, this is perhaps my favourite of all the places along the Stour Valley. Particularly striking is the 15th-century **Ancient House** (✆ 07483 310634 ⌘ clare-ancient-house-museum. co.uk) which has luxuriant white pargeting (page 150) like the sugar icing on a fancy cake. A date of 1473 on the wall no doubt refers to the date of the house itself rather than the pargeting, which would be at least a couple of centuries later. The house now serves as a **museum** with local history displays and exhibits from archaeological digs in the area. Part of the house is also available to rent as a Landmark Trust (⌘ landmarktrust.org.uk) property.

Directly opposite is the church of **St Peter and St Paul**, a fine 15th-century Perpendicular building in which Henry VIII and Catherine of

1 The pretty village of Cavendish. **2** The sundial on St Peter and St Paul Church in Clare. **3** The motte and moat of Clare Castle. **4** The view across town from Clare Castle Country Park. ▶

MARK STAPLES

RAEDWALD/S

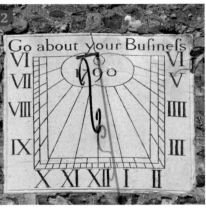

CLARE CASTLE COUNTRY PARK TRUST

CLARE CASTLE COUNTRY PARK TRUST

Aragon have bespoke pews bearing their crests. On the wall next to the porch a sundial dated 1790 is inscribed 'Go about your business', which might be interpreted as 'Back to work, peasants, now that you have paid your respect to God'. I found that the sundial seems to tell the time with uncanny accuracy (once you allow for correction to British Summer Time), as does the chiming clock on the tower. Inside the porch is a Green Man boss and, even more mysteriously, above the entrance to the church, an upside-down figure that some consider to be a rare example of a Green Woman.

The **town centre** is compact and businesslike, and wears its history lightly. Daniel Defoe, writing back in the early 18th century, described Clare as 'a poor town and dirty' but neither of these adjectives applies today. Thankfully, neither can Clare be described as a museum piece, which some of the settlements further east along the Stour Valley are in danger of becoming as locals move out and Home Counties money moves in. This is commendable when you consider that despite being the smallest town in the county, Clare has the third-largest number of listed buildings in Suffolk (after Bury St Edmunds and Lavenham) and has

"Despite being the smallest town in the county, Clare has the third-largest number of listed buildings in Suffolk."

somehow managed to hang on to its identity without polishing it up for the tourist market. This is no Tudor Disneyland. Walking up the high street past the Swan Inn you will find all the outlets and amenities you'd expect in a self-contained and not particularly touristy market town: an independent bookshop, Harris and Harris Books ($\mathscr{O}$ 01787 277267 $\mathscr{O}$ harrisharris.co.uk), a couple of antique shops and an old-fashioned ironmongers, the sort of place you can buy individual nuts, bolts and door hinges. Around the corner, surrounding the market place on Market Hill, is a traditional butcher and what appears to be the town's liveliest pub, the Bell Hotel.

A couple of minutes' walk from the town centre, **Clare Castle Country Park** has the stone remains of a 13th-century Norman castle keep on top of a mound overlooking the town. A footpath spirals up to the top and, although there is not much to see in terms of historic remains, it is worth the climb for the view south over the rooftops of Clare back to the church of St Peter and St Paul, and north across the valley into the sheep-grazed fields of Essex beyond. Clare's former railway station stands within the inner bailey of the castle; a small display on the town's railway history is inside a former goods shed. The park is also the gateway for a 3½-mile waymarked circular walk and a shorter historic town trail.

If you return to the entrance of the country park and take the footpath that leads down to the river by the antique shop you'll soon come to the entrance to **Clare Priory** (⌀ 01787 277326 ⟨ clarepriory.org.uk) after crossing the river (the Essex border diverts around this so you are actually still in Suffolk). Clare Priory was founded in 1248, the first house of Augustinian friars to be set up in England. As with most other religious houses it was suppressed by order of Henry VIII in 1538 and it was not until 1953 that Augustinians returned. Today it serves as a retreat centre for a mixed community of friars and laypeople. Access is free but limited to the priory grounds and a walled garden that includes a ruined 13th-century church nave as part of its structure. It is a strikingly peaceful spot, its isolated benches dotted between the apple trees offering the perfect setting for quiet reflection.

ᵗ┦ FOOD & DRINK

The Cock Callis St ⌀ 01787 277391. Very much a local pub, which serves decent good-value bar meals. There's a large beer garden at the back.

Platform One Café ⌀ 01787 277850. Located in the grounds of Clare Castle Country Park, this small café with indoor and outdoor seating has a choice of snacks, cakes and light lunches.

The Swan Inn 4 High St ⌀ 01787 278280. A conveniently located pub with a large outdoor dining area, cask ales and tasty pub grub.

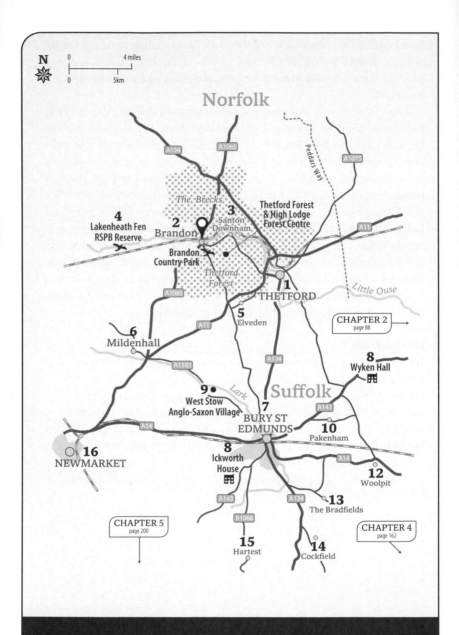

N
0 ___ 4 miles
0 ___ 5km

Norfolk

A134   A1065

Peddars Way

A1075

The Brecks

4
Lakenheath Fen
RSPB Reserve

2
Brandon

3
Santon
Downham

Thetford Forest
& High Lodge
Forest Centre

A11

Brandon
Country Park

Thetford
Forest

A1065

1
THETFORD

Little Ouse

5
Elveden

CHAPTER 2
page 88

A11

A134

6
Mildenhall

8
Wyken Hall

A1101

Lark

Suffolk

9
West Stow
Anglo-Saxon Village

A143

A14

7
BURY ST
EDMUNDS

10
Pakenham

16
NEWMARKET

8
Ickworth
House

A14

12
Woolpit

A143

A134

13
The Bradfields

B1066

CHAPTER 5
page 200

15
Hartest

14
Cockfield

CHAPTER 4
page 162

WEST SUFFOLK & THE BRECKS

6
WEST SUFFOLK & THE BRECKS

This chapter covers two distinct regions: the Brecks, the arid, sandy heath and forest region that straddles the county boundary in the northwest of Suffolk, and the western region of the county that lies immediately south of this and has Bury St Edmunds at its centre. Both regions have historical interest well beyond what one might expect. Thetford, the Brecks's largest town, just over the border in Norfolk, was once home to the monarchs of East Anglia and the seat of a bishopric. Brandon nearby has long been a centre for flint mining, an industry that dates back to Neolithic times. Bury St Edmunds is a place apart, the capital and burial site of the Saxon King Edmund. The area south of Bury St Edmunds is home to some of Suffolk's most enchanting countryside, a rural landscape of rolling farmland, sleepy tucked-away villages, narrow country lanes and high hedgerows – an area ripe for Slow exploration. Although focusing primarily on Suffolk, this chapter will occasionally make brief inroads into Norfolk in order to get a fuller understanding of what the Brecks region has to offer.

GETTING AROUND

Both of the main towns of this region lie on major trunk roads: Thetford on the A11, which connects London with Norwich, and Bury St Edmunds on the A14, which links the Midlands with Felixstowe. South of Bury St Edmunds, the A143 leads to Haverhill and the A134 to Sudbury.

PUBLIC TRANSPORT

This is far from wonderful but it is usually possible with careful planning to just about get to where you want providing you do not wish to travel on a Sunday. The main towns, at least, can easily be reached by bus or train. Thetford stands on the Norwich to Cambridge rail line and has a regular **rail service** with Greater Anglia (⌀ greateranglia.co.uk) to both cities – almost hourly during the day. Some Cambridge trains will stop at Lakenheath for the RSPB reserve at weekends – just one in each direction on a Saturday, three each way on Sundays. Bury St Edmunds has regular rail links to Ipswich, and to Newmarket and Cambridge too, although no direct service to Norwich: you need to change at Stowmarket. Trains to Ely link with national services north and south.

Surprisingly, there are no direct **bus services** between Ipswich and Bury St Edmunds – to travel between the two requires a change in either Diss (in Norfolk) or Stowmarket. Simonds bus service 304/338 runs fairly regularly between Bury St Edmunds and Diss via Ixworth, Stanton and Redgrave in the Waveney Valley. Between Stowmarket and Bury St Edmunds there is one bus a day with Dan's Coach Travel service 386, via Rattlesden and Rougham. There's a decent service between Bury St Edmunds and Mildenhall with Mulleys Motorways service 355/357 and Coach Services bus 84 runs frequently between Bury St Edmunds and Thetford, while service 86 continues on to Brandon. Mulleys Motorways 312 service operates throughout the day between Bury St Edmunds and Newmarket, and Stephensons of Essex service 11 connects Newmarket with Cambridge hourly through the day.

Local services also run from the larger towns to outlying villages. The Coach Services 200/201 route between Thetford and Mildenhall, calling at Santon Downham, Brandon and Lakenheath along the way, is especially useful for the Brecks, while Chambers 374 service between Bury St Edmunds, Cavendish and Clare via Hartest and Boxted is a convenient – and scenic – way to reach the Stour Valley. Less convenient than scheduled buses because they need to be booked at least 24 hours in advance, Suffolk Links Brecks (✆ 01638 664 304 ⊙ 08.00–16.00 Mon–Fri)

---

i TOURIST INFORMATION

The Brecks Fen Edge & Rivers Landscape Partnership ⌀ brecks.org

Bury St Edmunds The Apex, Charter Sq (with another branch at St Edmundsbury Cathedral shop on Angel Hill) ✆ 01284 764667 ⌀ visit-burystedmunds.co.uk

Newmarket Palace House, Palace St ✆ 01638 667314 ⌀ discovernewmarket.co.uk

Thetford Belmont House, 20 King St ✆ 01842 751975 ⌀ leapinghare.org

provides an on-demand service between villages in the Mildenhall, Thetford, Brandon and Lakenheath area.

Unfortunately, there are no buses on Sundays for any of these services.

CYCLING

Given a general lack of traffic and quiet roads, the Brecks have plenty of potential for cycling. Thetford Forest has lots of off-road choices too. For those who want to go farther afield, Sustrans National Cycle Route 13 (𝒿 0845 1130065 ⬧ sustrans.org.uk) connects Thetford with National Cycle Route 1.

The Brecks Tourism Partnership website (⬧ brecks.org) has information on cycling in the Brecks and on Thetford Forest Park cycle trails. More information on cycle trails can be found at the Forestry Commission website (⬧ forestry.gov.uk). **Thetford Forest Park** has three waymarked forest trails of varying difficulty between 6½ and 8 miles long that start from the High Lodge Forest Centre, where bike hire is also available at Bike Art (𝒿 01842 810090 ⬧ bikeartthetford. co.uk). Harling Drove, just north of Thetford over the Norfolk border, is a fairly long easy route through the heart of Thetford Forest, suitable for both cyclists and walkers. The 14-mile Brecks Trail between Brandon Country Park and West Stow Country Park is another suggested route that can be used by walkers, horseriders and cyclists alike.

HORSERIDING

There's scope to abandon two wheels for four legs in the Brecks region too and the potential for riding is probably the best in East Anglia. Horseriders have free access on all Forestry Commission freehold land. The Thetford Forest area also has stables where horses may be hired, such as Forest Park Riding and Livery Centre at Brandon (𝒿 01842 815517), which also organises riding lessons and 'own a pony' days. There is even scope for experienced riders to bring their own horse to the region – a list of 'horse-friendly' bed and breakfast accommodation is available from the Brecks Tourism Partnership website (⬧ brecks. org), although much of this tends to be in Norfolk.

WALKING

There's some excellent walking to be had. In the Brecks, one obvious choice for **long-distance** hikers is the **Peddars Way**, which begins in

Suffolk at Knettishall Heath just south of the Norfolk–Suffolk border, close to Thetford, before crossing west Norfolk to reach The Wash at Holme-next-the-Sea. Other long-distance routes that spend more time in Suffolk are **St Edmund Way** (Brandon to Flatford via Thetford and Bury St Edmunds – 81 miles) and **Iceni Way** (Knettishall Heath to Holme-next-the Sea via Brandon and the Fens – 83 miles). Shorter routes in the west of Suffolk include the aforementioned 14-mile **Brecks Trail**, the 13-mile **Lark Valley Path**, which leads from Bury St Edmunds to Mildenhall, and the ten-mile **Little Ouse Path** between Thetford and Brandon.

You can walk anywhere you like on **Forestry Commission land** and numerous circular walks are waymarked from all the main parking areas. Thetford Forest High Lodge has four waymarked forest trails between one and 7½ miles in length, and Knettishall Country Park has four trails through heath, woodland and along riverside. Further suggestions for shorter walks are made in the appropriate places in this chapter.

THE BRECKS & THETFORD FOREST

Although the Brecks border the pancake-flat region of the Cambridgeshire Fens to the west, it really could not be more different. The Brecks, in contrast to the fertile black soil found in the Fens, have light, sandy soil that is far less ideal for intensive farming. The word 'breck' comes from a word that means land that becomes quickly exhausted. It's the closest thing that Britain has to a desert and this is really not so far-fetched, as the rainfall is the lowest in the country, summer temperatures can be among the highest, and winter frosts, the hardest. The sand that covers the chalk was originally wind-blown, but trees have since been planted to stabilise the soil. Back in the days before such enlightened ideas, when large estates sought to maximise their profits by introducing sheep, the sand blew freely around causing untold damage, depleting thin topsoil in one place and covering up fertile land in another.

Naturally, what is a shortcoming today was actually a boon in the distant past. In Neolithic times, Britain's very first farmers were drawn to the region because the light soil of the Brecks was easy to work with their limited stone tools, and because there was no dense forest needing to be cleared with nothing other than brute strength and a hand axe.

The region had a plentiful supply of flint too, the machine steel of the Neolithic Age.

With careful farming, the Brecks became reasonably prosperous and **Thetford**, its capital, became an important regional capital in the Anglo-Saxon period. It was later, in the medieval period, when the real damage was done. Sheep were introduced to the land in large numbers and allowed to roam freely, overgrazing and damaging the soil with their hooves. In other parts of Suffolk and Norfolk, sheep may have brought fortune but here they just heralded disaster. The Brecks became increasingly depopulated as a result – the area is still sparsely populated today – and rabbits and pheasants became the land's only bounty.

The vast **Thetford Forest**, flanking the A11 around Thetford itself, is a relatively recent innovation, planted by the Forestry Commission after World War I to provide a strategic reserve of timber. The forest area spans both Suffolk and Norfolk, and the county boundary, largely defined by the course of the Little Ouse River, passes right through it. In the Norfolk Brecks, much of what is not forest goes to make up the **Stanford Battle Area**, established in 1942, and marked on OS maps as 'Danger Area', where the army practises manoeuvres and test ordnance.

Vast stands of Scots and Corsican pine may be what most people immediately associate with the Brecks these days but it is a very recent trend. Step back just a hundred years in time and you would see only sandy heathland, gorse and rabbits – lots of rabbits. It almost goes without saying that this is a part of East Anglia that many speed through without stopping. Consequently, it is not as well known as perhaps it deserves to be. Outside the few towns, the Brecks's distinctive habitat is a prized haven for wildlife: it is home to several species of plant, insect, bird and mammal that are found almost nowhere else in the country.

It may seem perverse to start a chapter on West Suffolk in Norfolk but I do this purely because Thetford lies at the very heart of the Brecks region, historically, politically and geographically.

1 THETFORD (NORFOLK)

Sometimes dismissed as a 'London overspill town', Thetford tends to get overlooked. While it is true that it does have some large and unlovely housing and industrial estates built for an influx of workers from the south in the 1960s, this is just part of the picture. Thetford was hugely important before the Norman invasion and even held the bishopric of

East Anglia before Norwich did. Whether or not Thetford was the royal seat of Boudica, the Iceni queen, is highly uncertain but it was certainly an important centre during the late Iron Age and early Roman period. In Anglo-Saxon times, Thetford became the home of the East Anglian monarchs and seat of a bishopric, and King Canute made the town his capital too in 1015, half a century before the Norman Conquest. Despite the religious focus being transferred to Norwich after the conquest, a Cluniac priory was established here in the 12th century that lasted until the Reformation.

Ignore the outskirts and head straight to the centre and you encounter some striking medieval architecture and a heady sense of history. The bus station is right in the centre next to the Little Ouse River. It's reached by way of the same narrow medieval street that has Thetford Grammar School. Beyond the lacklustre shopping precinct, just across the river from the bus station, the town centre has a good assortment of medieval and Georgian buildings in timber and flint. The best of these is the **Ancient House**, now the Museum of Thetford Life ($\mathscr{O}$ 01842 752599 $\mathscr{O}$ museums.norfolk.gov.uk), in a 15th-century timber-framed building on White Hart Street, which has exhibitions on Thomas Paine and Maharajah Duleep Singh as well as jewellery from the 'Thetford Treasure' hoard that was discovered locally in 1979.

The stonework of the town's Norman castle is long gone but the motte remains to provide a satisfying mound to climb up and get a view over the town. There is rather more to see at the site of the **Cluniac priory** west of the centre by the river. This was founded in 1103–04 by Richard Bigod to become one of the largest and richest priories in East Anglia. The priory was torn down after the Dissolution but there are still some impressive flinty remains and even bits of original tile flooring in places. The towering remains of the arch of the massive presbytery window are particularly striking and give a real sense of the original scale of the priory.

Nearby, **Thetford Grammar School** dates back to Saxon times, was re-founded in 1566 and is still active today. Its most famous ex-pupil is **Thomas Paine** (1737–1809) who had the distinction of being involved in both the French Revolution (where he only escaped execution by a

---

1 The River Little Ouse, which runs through Thetford. **2** The ruins of Thetford's priory.
3 Cycling in Thetford Forest. ▶

MARIA SCHEPERS/S

JASON SALMON/DT

IAN DAGNALL/A

whisker) and the American War of Independence; he was one of the original signatories to the Declaration of Independence and invented the term 'United States of America'. Born in the town (as Thomas Pain; the 'e' was added later when his squiggly signature was misinterpreted as Paine), he attended the school between 1744 and 1749 before going on to be apprenticed to his father as a corset maker. Paine's gilt **statue** by Sir Charles Wheeler, President of the Royal Academy, stands outside the King's House, with the radical thinker clutching a copy of his revolutionary book *Rights of Man* upside down. Why he holds the book upside down is open to speculation. The Leaping Hare (∂ leapinghare. org) shop at Belmont House on King Street can provide leaflets for a self-guided **Tom Paine Trail** through the town. There are also occasional guided tours that can be booked at the shop.

Tom Paine aside, Thetford's other associations include the television series *Dad's Army*, much of which was recorded in and around the town. A *Dad's Army* tourist trail highlights spots that became the fictitious Sussex town of Walmington-on-Sea. In 2010, the Thetford Society erected a bronze statue of Captain Mainwaring (the Arthur Lowe character) seated on a bench next to the River Ouse by the bus station. There's the **Dad's Army Museum** ($\mathcal{O}$ 07562 165795 ∂ dadsarmythetford.org.uk $\odot$ 10.00–15.00 Sat, plus Aug 10.00–13.00 Sun) at the back of the Guildhall on Cage Lane, and you can see Jones's butcher's van at the nearby **Charles Burrell Museum** ($\mathcal{O}$ 01842 751166 ∂ charlesburrellmuseum.org.uk) on Minstergate, which has a collection of steam traction engines and agricultural machinery.

"Ignore the outskirts and head straight to the centre and you encounter some striking medieval architecture and a heady sense of history."

Nearby, and reached by means of a footbridge, **Maharajah Duleep Singh**, the former squire of the nearby Elveden Estate (page 251), a little further down the A11, has a very fine equestrian statue set among the shady willows of **Butten Island** in the midst of the Little Ouse River.

Outside the town, some good **walks** are to be had around Thetford. The most obvious route is along the **Little Ouse Path** that links Thetford with Brandon, most of which follows an old towpath. It's about ten miles of easy walking in total and if you are up to this you could walk all the way then catch a bus or train back from Brandon. Even if you walk just a short distance along the river path past the abbey ruins you get a sense of being in open countryside despite the proximity of the town's council estates.

¶¶ FOOD & DRINK

Bell Hotel King St 𝒥 01842 754455. This 15th-century inn, right in the heart of town, was where the *Dad's Army* cast and crew used to stay. The hotel, now part of the national Greene King chain, tends to make the most of this association as well as its reputation for being haunted but serves decent enough pub food and Greene King ales.

Tall Orders 22–4 King St 𝒥 01842 766435. Probably the best of the town centre cafés, this is conveniently situated on the main pedestrian street and has a reasonable choice of coffees, teas, cakes and light meals.

2 BRANDON

West of Thetford, on the southern, Suffolk bank of the Little Ouse, is Brandon. If the presence of Grimes Graves, a little way north back over the Norfolk border, is not enough to attest that the town was once central to an important **flint industry**, then take a look at the buildings here. The black flint typical of the area can be seen to good effect in the Victorian houses down Thetford Road as well as in many of the town's modern buildings. The flint trade was big business locally as far back as the late Neolithic period and returned to prominence with the invention of the musket and the need for gun flints. It is interesting to reflect that, given the area's USAF and RAF bases, the war industry has long played a part in the region and, in addition to forestry, much of Brandon's present-day economy is focused upon servicing the nearby airbase at Lakenheath. Brandon is not a tourist town by any stretch of the imagination.

"The black flint typical of the area can be seen to good effect in the Victorian houses down Thetford Road."

Brandon's flintknappers had their work cut out back in Napoleonic times when the town grew quite prosperous through supplying the essential parts for the British Army's muzzle-loaders. Virtually all the shots fired at Waterloo from the British side would have involved Brandon flint to spark them off. Brandon flint was considered far superior to any that the French troops had at their disposal. In fact, it is said that a single Brandon flint was reliably good for dozens of shots whereas the French equivalent would only last for a few – a serious disadvantage for Napoleon's infantry. The invention of the percussion cap saw the demise of this trade but, according to John Seymour, flintknappers were still active in the town in the 1960s, when he witnessed men in leather aprons chipping away in the back yard of the Flintknappers Arms pub – where else indeed? The 1960s would, in fact, have been the very tail end of the industry, when the only demand would have been from replica gun enthusiasts. The very last of the Brandon flintknappers finally hung up their hammer for good in 1975.

You can get a good idea of the town's flintknapping past by visiting the **Brandon Heritage Centre** (✆ 07882 891022; ⏲ Apr–Oct Thu, w/ends & bank holidays) on George Street. Staffed by knowledgeable volunteers, this has several displays on the town's main industry, as well as the original deeds of the Brandon Flint Company written on vellum and kept in a wooden box. The museum also possesses a lengthy list of all the flintknappers that lived and worked in the town from the 19th century onwards.

A Little Ouse Walk – Brandon to Santon Downham & back

❋ OS Landranger map 144 or Explorer map 229; start: Brandon railway station ⚲ TF784872; 6 miles; moderate

This peaceful walk beside water and through woodland takes in both banks of the Little Ouse River along the Suffolk/Norfolk boundary, keeping to the Suffolk side of the border on the way out and the Norfolk bank on the return. For a longer walk, it could be combined with the suggested route from Santon Downham to All Saint's Church at Santon House, outlined on page 248.

From Brandon railway station, turn left to walk towards the town and cross the bridge over the Little Ouse. Continue a little further; after passing the supermarket car park, turn left along White Hart Lane. Keep straight on as it continues along Gas House Drove, which turns into a track along the bottom of gardens and then past isolated bungalows and paddocks. After about a quarter of a mile, this becomes a sandy track between paddocks and a conifer plantation. The narrow path continues alongside mixed woodland to meet a larger path with a St Edmund Way sign. Turn left here, to pass another paddock and continue along the footpath through conifers. Follow this path, crossing a couple of wide woodland rides, all the way into Santon Downham.

At Santon Downham, follow the road at the bottom of the green to reach St Mary the Virgin church, before turning left along the road to reach the Little Ouse. Cross the river by the bridge.

Brandon's other main business in the past was the production of rabbit furs for the hat trade, a lucrative enterprise in the late 18th and 19th centuries. It was an industry that gave the town a notorious and unenviable aroma back in the day. The pelts were initially obtained from rabbits supplied by the extensive warrens that used to characterise this part of the Brecks, where the light sandy soil was fit for little else. In time, the demand for fur grew to such an extent that rabbit skins had to be imported from as far away as Australia and New Zealand in order to provide an adequate supply for the busy Brandon workshops.

The Little Ouse River used to be of far more importance here in the days when Brandon served as the port for nearby Thetford. Today it is forestry that rules supreme and it is articulated lorries and the A11, not boats and water, that are the means of distribution for Brandon's produce.

(Here, if you wish, you can turn right along the northern, Norfolk-side riverside path to visit All Saint's Church at Santon House before heading back towards Brandon.) On the Norfolk bank, turn left to follow the river path all the way back to Brandon. When you reach the main road by the bridge at Brandon, turn right to return to the railway station or left to visit the town centre.

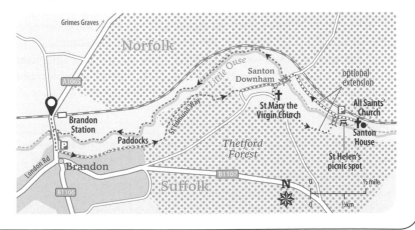

Brandon Country Park

Bury Rd, Brandon 🕿 01284 757088 ⌖ brandoncountrypark.org.uk; free entry

Just a mile or so south of Brandon, this used to be the grounds of a country house that is now a private nursing home. The park has three waymarked forest walks, an 'intermediate' cycle trail, a tree and history trail, an orienteering course, a restored Georgian walled garden and a visitor centre with a café. It's well set up with picnic areas too, one beside a lake, another in an old orchard. A very Gothic-looking – and supposedly haunted – mausoleum to Edward Bliss, the original owner of the estate, can be seen alongside the red walking trail not far from the house. Naturally enough, given that this is Brandon, knapped flint features heavily in its construction.

Thetford Forest & High Lodge Forest Centre

Thetford Rd, Brandon 🕿 01842 815434 ⌖ forestry.gov.uk/highlodge; Forestry Commission

A little way east of Brandon, along the B1107 to Thetford, this offers free entrance to cyclists and walkers arriving without a car. There's an information point with leaflets and maps, a picnic area and a café serving homemade, locally sourced food. Four waymarked walks of varying length explore the forest area from the visitor centre, and the four cycling routes include a family route as well as more challenging mountain-bike rides. **Cycle hire** is available from Bike Art (page 237). There are also opportunities for adults and children over five to participate in archery lessons (🕿 07729 402009) at weekends and during school holidays, as well as weekend Back to Wilderness (🕿 07833 182180) courses on bushcraft and survival skills. Go Ape! (⌖ goape.co.uk), also based in the park, provides adventurous zip-wire and treetop activities for children. The centre also organises special summer wildlife events such as dusk nightjar rambles and moth expeditions.

⑂ FOOD & DRINK

Flintknappers 1–3 Market Hill, Brandon 🕿 07935 088685. This is nothing fancy – just a town pub with Adnams and Greene King ales. Currently there is no food on offer but it's a convenient enough place for a drink if visiting the town.

Number 30 Coffee Lounge 30 High St, Brandon 🕿 01842 266433 ⌖ no30.coffee. Probably the cosiest of Brandon's cafés, this relaxed place has pastries, cakes and sandwiches as well as decent coffee.

3 SANTON DOWNHAM

Halfway between Thetford and Brandon along the Little Ouse River, this small village mostly revolves around the sawing and carting of the forestry business – the headquarters of the East England office of the Forestry Commission is based here. Don't let this put you off though – Santon Downham really deserves a look. Tucked away deep in the heart of the forest, the village is little more than a handful of cottages, a wide green and a small flint church at its eastern end. The village effectively occupies a small clearing in what is the largest forest in England. Tall dark pines are never far from sight – this is definitely Hansel and Gretel territory. There

"The carving is ancient, worn and undeniably mysterious, but its symbolism is anybody's guess."

are no facilities in Santon Downham – no pub, shop or café – but the village makes an ideal setting-off point for a stroll along the bank of the Little Ouse or a walk in the forest, or, best of all, both. The thing to do is bring a picnic or packed lunch with you as you'll have no trouble finding a peaceful spot to enjoy it. Hopefully the weather will be good but you might want to bear in mind that the village's weather station, actually just across the Little Ouse in Norfolk, has the distinction of having recorded some of the highest and lowest temperatures ever reached in England. It's mostly to do with the area's sandy soil, which cools down quickly during cold nights and heats up rapidly on hot days.

Before forestry took over the area, the village was part of the Downham Estate, which was at one time owned by Charles Sloane, who later became Lord Cadogan. Downham Hall was demolished in 1925 and most of the buildings in the village date from just after this, constructed as homes for forestry workers. The exception is the flint-built parish **church of St Mary**, which is mostly Norman with some later additions. Sometimes referred to as the 'Church in the Forest' for fairly obvious reasons, this has a curious figure carved above its south door that may or may not depict a wolf (or perhaps a lion) with what appears to be a lily sprouting from its tail. The carving is ancient, worn and undeniably mysterious, but its symbolism is anybody's guess. Inside, there's a commemorative stained-glass window that depicts St Francis surrounded by the sort of birds that you might expect see locally: a heron, a kingfisher and a barn owl with a mouse in its mouth, along with a crossbill and a golden pheasant, both specialities of the Brecks.

Like all of the Brecks, the soil around here is very light and sandy, and before being stabilised by the planting of conifers in the early 20th century had a tendency to blow around quite a lot, especially after overgrazing by rabbits. Extreme sandstorms were not unknown in the past. Records show that the village was almost completely overwhelmed by sand in the late 17th century when cottages were buried and the navigation of the river so dramatically affected by drifting sand that its course was altered considerably (and by definition that of the boundary of the Suffolk–Norfolk border).

For an enjoyable **walk** of a couple of miles along the valley of the Little Ouse, turn left out of the Forestry Commission car park and walk downhill and you'll soon come to a bridge across the river to the Norfolk bank. Cross over and take the track on the right that runs along the riverbank to soon arrive at a footbridge close to St Helen's picnic site, where there is a car park, noticeboard and trestle tables. You can cross here and follow the St Edmund Way between paddocks and then right along a broad forest track to climb gently through thick forest to return to the village. Before you cross the bridge, you might first want to continue a little further along the Norfolk side to reach **All Saints' Church** adjacent to Santon House. This miniature flint church exudes quaintness, with an equally tiny octagonal tower; although no longer in use, it is usually open. Constructed in 1628 from materials salvaged from demolished buildings, the building was partly rebuilt in the mid 19th century. Curiously, because it once belonged to the parish of Santon Downham, this is the only church in Norfolk that ever belonged to a Suffolk diocese, that of St Edmundsbury.

Another option is to combine this with a walk along the River Little Ouse from Brandon (page 244).

4 LAKENHEATH FEN RSPB RESERVE

IP27 9AD ✐ 01842 863400; RSPB

This RSPB Reserve lies just north of Lakenheath on the road to Hockwold cum Wilton and is accessible from a railway station on the Norwich to Cambridge line. The reserve has a wonderful array of birdlife that includes honey buzzards, hobbies, bitterns and those most exotic of birds, golden orioles. Cranes have bred here in recent years too – the first time in 400 years in the region – and it's also a good place to see cuckoos, which are commonly heard but generally hard to see. The reserve, created from 740 acres of carrot field nearly three decades ago, has reverted into a typical fen landscape of reedbeds and grazing marshes.

Speaking of golden orioles, I recall that it used to be possible to see these gorgeous, rather exotic birds swooping across the Cambridge train line somewhere in this vicinity. This was back in the 1980s when they bred in the poplar plantations that lined the tracks. I never did see them from the train but I did once travel to the plantation with birder friends, where we were charmed by the birds' fluting calls and astonished to discover that a brilliant yellow-and-black colour scheme is actually good camouflage for the dappled light of poplars. The trees eventually disappeared as they ended up – quite literally – as matchwood. It's good to know that the birds are back.

There's a visitor centre and loos, and a number of guided walks and child-friendly events are put on throughout the year. A number of **trains** on the Norwich–Cambridge line stop here at Lakenheath station at weekends, one each way on Saturdays, three each way on Sundays. It's a request stop so you'll need to tell the conductor in advance and flag down the appropriate approaching train when leaving. A footpath links the station with the RSPB visitor centre and there's a convenient cycle link to the Hereward Way. Getting here during the week without a car is more problematic as the nearest working station is Brandon, nearly five miles away. The on-demand Suffolk Links Brecks Bus (✆ 01638 664304) can be used to reach the reserve from Brandon or Thetford but you need to book it by noon the day before at least

> "The reserve has a wonderful array of birdlife that includes honey buzzards, hobbies, bitterns and those most exotic of birds, golden orioles."

(bookings must be made 08.00–16.00 Mon–Fri). Alternatively there is a bus service to Lakenheath village every hour or so from Mildenhall and Brandon but it is still a three-mile walk from the village to the reserve.

Lakenheath itself is dominated by RAF Lakenheath, the home of the largest US Air Force fighter base in Britain. A near nuclear accident took place here in 1956 at the height of the Cold War when a B-47 bomber crashed into a storage igloo containing three nuclear warheads. It was a close thing but thankfully (to put it mildly!) no detonation occurred. If it had, then it is very doubtful that there would be a bird reserve in the area today, even more than half a century later, or even a village at all.

NIGEL WALLACE/S

CDK PHOTOS/S

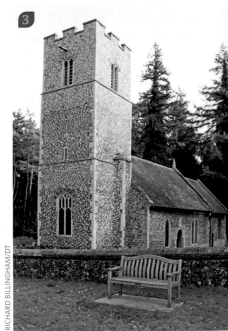

V 4 RY TO SOURCE EVERYTHING WHEREVER POSSIBLE
FROM OUR ESTATE & THE LOCALITY

BUTTERNUT
SQUASH

HISPI
CABBAGE

LEEKS
£2.40

SWEET
POTATOES
£2.50 ea

ALENAKRAVCHENKO/DT

RICHARD BILLINGHAM/DT

The village that gives the base its name is not particularly attractive and very much given over to the everyday needs of a USAF base. What it does have is the large medieval **church of St Mary**, which has some wonderful bench ends and well-preserved wall paintings of St Edmund. Like its sister in neighbouring Mildenhall – another St Mary's – the church still bears scars from the Civil War, with vandalised corbel angels in the roof. Life was evidently tough for angels in the mid 17th century in northwest Suffolk.

5 ELVEDEN

Situated close to a crossroads a little way south of Thetford, to most people this used to be little more than a sign on the A11 and an inconvenient bottleneck for traffic. It used to be an accident black spot too before traffic-calming measures were introduced. Some will tell you that there have been more people killed on the A11 since World War II than there are names on the obelisk-like war memorial south of the village. All this changed in 2013 when, after years of planning delays, numerous media campaigns, a massive amount of soil-shifting and tarmac-laying, the spending of many millions of pounds and a huge amount of disruption, the A11 at Elveden was finally bypassed by a dual-carriageway so that travellers between London and Norwich could make the journey a little quicker than before and Norfolk businesses could reap the benefits of improved accessibility.

Elveden is a small estate village centred upon **Elveden Hall**, a somewhat bizarre private residence. The estate (⊘ elveden.com), which has the largest arable farm in the country, is in the possession of the Earl of Iveagh but the hall itself was emptied of its contents in 1984 and stands empty. You can just about get a glimpse of the hall from the rear of the village churchyard and make out its green dome. The hall was the home of Maharajah Duleep Singh, a deposed Sikh prince from the Punjab who was exiled to England for his part in the Sikh Wars during Queen Victoria's reign. He purchased the estate in 1863 and refurbished the Georgian hall in lavish Moghul style using Italian craftsmen. An equestrian statue of the maharajah stands in Thetford (page 242) and,

◄ **1** & **2** Lakenheath Fen RSPB Reserve, where you might spot kingfishers such as this one. **3** Santon Downham's 'Church in the Forest'. **4** The Elveden Estate shop stocks plenty of local produce.

although he died in Paris in 1893, his surprisingly modest grave lies in the churchyard of Elveden's St Andrew and St Patrick Church. Elveden Hall passed into the hands of the Guinness family after Duleep Singh's death and the first Earl of Iveagh went even further, building a new wing and adding a replica Taj Mahal to the complex. Since its interior was emptied in 1984, Elveden Hall has become much used as a film set: it has appeared as a location for *Tomb Raider*, the Bond movie *The Living Daylights* and Stanley Kubrick's *Eyes Wide Shut*. Most recently it was used for the 2017 film *All the Money in the World* directed by Ridley Scott. The bad news is that the hall is not open to the public.

St Andrew & St Patrick Church

A bit of a Victorian–Edwardian Gothic extravaganza this one; with a double apse, a long cloister that connects a priest door to the bell tower and some lovely modern stained-glass windows that include a memorial window to Maharajah Duleep Singh. He transformed the original Victorian church of St Andrew on taking over the estate, ploughing money into it for its beautification. When the estate passed into the hands of the Guinness family, the first Earl of Iveagh built an entirely new church alongside that effectively created a south aisle. Naturally, in the turn-of-the-century world of the landed gentry, church attendance was compulsory for all estate workers, even Nonconformists (the Guinness family did not employ Catholics). The church is usually open between Easter and September on Wednesdays, Fridays and Saturdays, although it is probably better to check beforehand by phoning the churchwarden Mrs Janice Flack on ✆ 01842 890540.

⁑ FOOD & DRINK

The Courtyard Elveden Estate ✆ 01842 898068 ⌖ elvedencourtyard.com. An outdoor café and restaurant (with seats inside for less clement weather) set in a stable courtyard surrounded by estate shops. Snacks, light bites and main courses using meat from the estate. The estate shop has a delicatessen that sells estate game and venison and over 20 varieties of British cheese.

6 MILDENHALL

I have passed through this town many times on the National Express coach trip between Norwich and London. To be honest, it always felt like a bit of an unnecessary detour. Mildenhall has long been an air-force service town – a large RAF airbase just up the road is used by the US Air Force – and the town seems so resolutely focused on performing this function that it has little truck with any unnecessary frills. The town has something of a listless air about it – the fate perhaps of towns that are dominated by a military base of one sort or another. Historically though, Mildenhall was important as a market town long before people took to the skies, and it was also the place where a large Roman hoard – the Mildenhall Treasure, now kept in the British Museum in London – was discovered in 1945.

Connoisseurs of medieval church architecture will want to check out the enormous **St Mary's Church**, which has one of the largest porches in Suffolk, a glorious west window and a splendid hammerbeam roof of carved angels that are said to be riddled with shot left by trigger-happy puritans during the Reformation.

BURY ST EDMUNDS & AROUND

Immediately south of the Brecks region, the landscape becomes more undulating with mixed farming and pockets of deciduous woodland. At the heart of this region lies Suffolk's third-largest town, Bury St Edmunds, an ancient place that was once one of the royal towns of the Saxon kings.

7 BURY ST EDMUNDS

🏠 **Angel Hotel** (page 278), **Ickworth Hotel** (page 278) 🏡 **East End House** (page 278)

One of several jewels in Suffolk's crown and, according to the 19th-century writer William Cobbett, 'the nicest little town in the world', Bury St Edmunds has received much admiration over the years for its special character and, as well as Cobbett, has been lauded by other literary luminaries such as Charles Dickens and Daniel Defoe. Even the name, Bury St Edmunds, has a timeless, quintessentially English appeal that something more humdrum like Ipswich struggles to achieve. Much of the town's history is encapsulated in its very name: St Edmund, that sainted hero of the Anglo-Saxons, was, in fact, buried here and his subsequent canonisation brought almost cult-like status… and pilgrims. Bury St Edmunds is a place of great historical interest, of course, but its one-time draw as a medieval pilgrimage centre is just part of the picture.

Bury remains affluent and well-to-do today and, even without its St Edmund connections, the town has an undeniable appeal with its unhurried, old-fashioned pace and rich array of Georgian and Victorian architecture. It is quite a mysterious place too, filled with architectural nooks and crannies and occasional murky historical cul-de-sacs.

If you arrive by car and park at the old cattle market, the first thing you'll come to is its shopping centre, The Arc, which has a futuristic-looking store – formerly Debenhams – that looks a little like a cut-price version of Birmingham's silver-buttoned Selfridges. It is a bold design that may not be to everyone's taste but keep going past the glitzy new shops and you'll soon arrive at the **Butter Market** and Neoclassical **Corn Hall**. The rectangular square around the Corn Hall is filled with traders and shoppers on Wednesday and Saturday market days and is the best place in town to buy fresh fruit and vegetables. Beyond this, along Abbeygate Street, lie the Abbey Gardens and cathedral on Angel Hill. The helpful **tourist information point** at the cathedral shop next to the entrance to St Edmundsbury Cathedral can help with recommendations and orientation, as can the tourist information centre at The Apex on Charter Square, which is located just

"It is quite a mysterious place too, filled with architectural nooks and crannies and occasional murky historical cul-de-sacs."

west of St Andrews St South – the thoroughfare lies immediately south of both bus and train stations. If you would like a guided tour of the town's historic centre, there are good-value and informative 90-minute tours that begin at 11.00 and 14.00 daily. These should be booked online in advance at ☙ burystedmundstourguides.org.

St Edmund's Abbey is little more than an appealing ruin these days, having been destroyed at the time of the Dissolution, but the pleasant **Abbey Gardens**, created in 1831 with flower beds and ornamental trees, that occupy its former expansive grounds provide a restful space to wander in and contemplate the time when the site may have been the East Anglian equivalent of Glastonbury. The ornamental beds are lovingly tended and are some of the most colourful plantings I have ever seen – even on a cloudy day you might require a pair of sunglasses. The River Lark flows through the gardens – a river as picturesque as its name suggests. Strolling around the gardens and seeing the extent of the ruins it is astonishing to realise just how large the original abbey church must have been before it was destroyed during the reign of Henry VIII, its stone cladding plundered for use in other buildings around the town. Before its destruction the abbey would have been the largest Romanesque church in Europe, something akin to Ely Cathedral today. A model of how the abbey complex would once have looked can be seen in the gardens. All that remains intact of the original complex are St Mary's Church south of the gardens, which was also once part of the abbey complex, and two gatehouses: Abbey Gate, rebuilt in the 14th-century, the main entrance into the gardens, which was formerly the secular entrance to the abbey used by servants, and the earlier Norman Gate, which served as the gateway into the abbey church and St Edmund's shrine, and which still serves as the belfry of St Edmundsbury Cathedral. A momentous historical event took place at the abbey here in 1214 on St Edmund's feast day when a gathering of barons and the Archbishop of Canterbury swore on St Edmund's shrine that they would force wayward King John to accept the Charter of Liberties, a document that led the way for the creation of the Magna Carta. A plaque on one of the ruined walls near where the event took place records the event. Another portentous event took place just over a century later in 1327 when townsfolk angry with the power and corruption of the monastery attacked and half-destroyed the Abbey Gate, necessitating its rebuild.

St Edmundsbury Cathedral, with its intricate, angel-bedecked hammerbeam roof, started life in the 15th century as the Church of St James and was only granted cathedral status in 1914 – to form one of a quartet of cathedrals in East Anglia alongside Norwich, Ely and Peterborough. In keeping with the myth of the protective wolf, the bishop's throne has details of wolves guarding St Edmund. The cathedral was extended in the 1960s and commemorated with a fanfare specially composed by Benjamin Britten. A Gothic-style tower was added as part of a millennium project in 2005. A modernist bronze statue of St Edmund by the sculptor Elisabeth Frink stands just outside the cathedral; accompanying this is, appropriately enough, an iron wolf.

"The ornamental beds are lovingly tended and are some of the most colourful plantings I have ever seen."

St Mary's, the sister parish church just to the south, with another hammerbeam roof, poppyhead pews and 11 pairs of flying angels, is even finer according to the discerning eye of Simon Jenkins, who describes St Mary's as being 'left like Cinderella up the road, rather

A WOLF, A CORPSE, PILGRIMS & WITCHES

Edmund came to East Anglia from Germany in the mid 9th century to become the King of East Anglia, the last Saxon king before Danish and Norman rule. The Danes, always keen to have things their own way, tortured and killed Edmund in AD870 because of his refusal to disavow Christianity. The story goes that his head went missing after his death until it was discovered 40 days later lying between the protective paws of a wolf (a wolf is represented on the town crest in remembrance of this). Once his head had been seamlessly reunited with its body, Edmund's corpse was buried at a place called Haegelisdun – possibly modern-day Hoxne – but was dug up 30 years later to be taken to the monastery of Beodricsworth, which later became known as St Edmundsbury in his honour.

In 1032, the monastery was granted abbey status by the Christian Dane, King Canute, and St Edmundsbury Abbey became an important place of pilgrimage following Edmund's canonisation. St Edmund was the patron saint of England for many years but somewhere along the line he was replaced by St George, a historical figure who, if truth be told, may be little more than a myth and has more connections with Turkey and Palestine than with England.

The Normans enlarged the abbey church and the surrounding town, Bury St Edmunds, developed around it to become a prosperous trade and weaving centre. In the 17th century, the town found fame as a centre for its witch trials, in particular that of the year 1645, in which the self-proclaimed Witchfinder General, Matthew Hopkins, saw to it that 18 people were executed in a single day. Bury's prosperity continued through to the 18th century, although the town failed to be caught up in the Industrial Revolution in the same way that Ipswich did in the Victorian age.

forlorn'. The church's stained glass is probably its most immediately striking feature, especially the west window, which is the largest in any English parish church and was paid for by local landowners in thanks for a bumper harvest in 1854. The chancel arch has a window in the form of a pilgrim's badge that shows Edmund being killed with arrows. For a modern take on the Saxon king's martyrdom, head for the Risbygate Street roundabout where you can see a modern sculpture of woven stainless steel that depicts Edmund trussed in captivity, punctured by Viking arrows.

Modern-day, secular Bury St Edmunds owes as much to brewing as to anything else and the **Greene King Brewery** has stood in the town since 1799. There's a museum, beer café and a shop on-site, and brewery tours can be arranged (✆ 01284 843326 ♂ greeneking.co.uk), although bear in mind that taking a tour will require a climb of over one hundred steep steps to reach the brewery roof. The brewery is also the landlord of **The Nutshell**, which, until it lost its crown in 2016 to an establishment called The Little Prince in Margate, was Britain's smallest pub. The pub can be found just off the market place on The Traverse, close to the Victorian Corn Hall. There's a desiccated cat on display here that was found bricked up behind a wall during building repairs; you cannot really miss it as it dangles from the ceiling like a ham in an Andalusian bar. It's a black cat but certainly not a very lucky one. I will admit to initially being sceptical about the pub's claim to be the smallest in the country. I remember The Vine in Norwich also being rather 'bijou' (as an estate agent might put it) but The Vine, a tiny Thai restaurant these days, is a veritable coaching inn in comparison with The Nutshell. The Nutshell was not always just a pub: in the late 19th century it was also billed as a 'Museum of Art and Curiosities', with a display of old musical instruments, works of art in ivory and cardboard and cork models of local buildings. It still has its offbeat items – as well as the dead cat, there are historical photos, a vast array of currency notes, a few miscellaneous animal heads and an aeroplane propeller to look at while you are supping your pint at the bar, elbows drawn in. Less is more, as they say, but sometimes more is less.

The Greene King Brewery, which did admirably to maintain its real ale business through the lean times of the 1970s, has grown in recent years to become the largest British-owned brewery and managed pub company in the country. However, it has its critics for its active acquisition policy of taking over smaller breweries and their pub estates, ironically resulting in less choice of real ales for the consumer.

If small breweries are your preference then you might be better off seeking out Greene King's main local competitor; the **Old Cannon Brewery** (✆ 01284 768769 ⌂ oldcannonbrewery.co.uk), opened in 1999, has a range of its own ales like Hornblower, Rusty Gun, Blond Bombshell and Gunner's Daughter. The Victorian building that houses the brewery-pub was the home of an earlier Cannon Brewery that closed during World War I. The premises now also multi-task as a brasserie, a bed and breakfast and a hire venue for meetings. Tours of the brewery are available.

Returning from thoughts of beer to architecture once more, the **Moyse's Hall Museum** (✆ 01284 706183 ⌂ moyseshall.org) on Cornhill

MARK STAPLES

CHRIS DORNEY/DT

MARK STAPLES

at the top of Butter Market is widely believed to be one of the oldest stone-built domestic buildings in the country. Built sometime around the end of the 12th century, it is something of a mystery why it was constructed of imported flint and limestone rather than the cheaper and far more readily available wood normally used. It was probably done as a show of wealth, and quite a lavish one considering that some of the materials had to be brought from quarries far away. There's considerable debate about the building's original use: there are some who contend that it was originally a synagogue or 'Jew's House', although this seems unlikely; others point to it being used as a tavern from around 1300 onwards but this too is uncertain. It's now a museum, with interesting Bronze Age, Anglo-Saxon and Roman exhibits, but has served as a prison, a police station and a workhouse in the past. The Suffolk Regiment Gallery is based here too and there is also an interesting display of rare timepieces bequeathed by the musician and town benefactor Frederic Gershom Parkington. The collection relating to the notorious Red Barn Murder at nearby Polstead (page 221) is certainly well worth seeing for those who have a taste for the macabre.

The town has a fair number of literary connections. A century or so before William Cobbett visited the town, Daniel Defoe came here to stay at the Cupola House, a former 17th-century inn on The Traverse. **Charles Dickens**, too, spent time at the ivy-covered Angel Hotel and even gave it a mention in *The Pickwick Papers*. Rock musician Nick Cave lodged here awhile and penned songs during his stay that mentioned 'the ivy-covered windows of The Angel' and 'the bell from St Edmunds'.

Another well-known Bury St Edmunds landmark that is considerably less refined (although you cannot say the same thing about its product) is the BSC **sugar beet factory** on the A14. This is the biggest of its type in the country and in season – around midwinter – is the destination for hundreds of clanking lorries delivering beet from the frozen fields of west Suffolk and beyond. Sugar beet is hardly the most beautiful of crops and its processing machinery is anything but lovely too. So, if you detect a slightly cloying smell in the air during your visit then this is its source (if you can detect hops or malt then that is the Greene King Brewery, of course). In fairness, the factory, which has its own power

◄ BURY ST EDMUNDS: **1** St Edmundsbury Cathedral and the Abbey Gardens. **2** Nearby Ickworth House. **3** Elisabeth Frink's bronze statue of St Edmund.

station on-site supplying the National Grid with renewable energy, is a town icon in its own way, a reminder that for all its quaint museum-piece qualities and rarefied medieval atmosphere, this is a major market town in agribusiness country.

¶¶ FOOD & DRINK

Baileys2 5 Whiting St ☎ 01284 706198 ⌂ baileys2.co.uk. In the medieval grid of streets in the centre of town, this coffee shop and tea rooms offers breakfast, light meals and nibbles, all home-cooked using local produce where possible. Excellent homemade biscuits, cakes and puddings, and imaginative sandwiches and salads. Also plenty of gluten-free options.

Bay Tree Café 11 St John's St ☎ 01284 700607. A cosy independent café with good homemade salads, sandwiches and snacks, as well as cooked breakfasts and daily specials.

The Beerhouse 1 Tayfen Rd ☎ 01284 766415 ⌂ burybeerhouse.co.uk. A challenge to the Greene King hegemony in town, this pub near the railway station has at least eight cask ales from its own Brewshed Brewery on handpump, in addition to cask ciders, draught stout and even lager. No proper meals but bar snacks are available and on Wed–Sat evenings there are wood-fired pizzas from the adjacent Pizzashed.

The Eaterie @ The Angel Hotel 3 Angel Hill ☎ 01284 714000 ⌂ theangel.co.uk. The restaurant at this Bury institution serves modern British food created by award-winning chefs and cooked largely using ingredients from Suffolk smallholders and independent producers. It's quite expensive but the food is decent and the place has a nice ambience. Also has accommodation (page 278).

Harriet's Café Tearooms 57 Cornhill ☎ 01284 756256 ⌂ harrietscafetearooms.co.uk. A worthwhile choice for afternoon tea, with old-fashioned service and surroundings that, although perhaps a little self-conscious, are charming nevertheless. A live pianist is often present to provide a musical background.

The Nutshell 17 The Traverse ☎ 01284 764867. You may well be tempted to have a drink in what is claimed to be the second smallest pub in Britain (page 257). There's a choice of Greene King ales of course, but no food – it's far too small to have a dining area or even much elbow space. Don't attempt to swing a cat, especially the one hanging above the bar.

Old Cannon Brewery 86 Cannon St ☎ 01284 768769 ⌂ oldcannonbrewery.co.uk. A Victorian brewhouse-pub with excellent beer and modern pub food, a five-minute walk from the centre.

Pea Porridge 28–9 Cannon St ☎ 01284 700200 ⌂ peaporridge.co.uk. Next to the Old Cannon Brewery, this popular Michelin-recommended restaurant has a highly imaginative Mediterranean- and Middle East-influenced menu that offers dishes cooked in 'Grizzly', an indoor charcoal oven that imbues an aromatic smoky flavour. There's also a three-course fixed menu at lunchtimes.

Pilgrims' Kitchen St Edmundsbury Cathedral, Angel Hill ✆ 01284 748720. Conveniently tucked away among the cathedral cloisters, with an additional peaceful seating area outside, this serves snacks, breakfasts and light lunches mostly sourced from local ingredients.

8 ICKWORTH HOUSE

Horringer IP29 5QE ✆ 01284 735270; ⊙ Rotunda mid-Mar–Oct Thu–Tue; Italianate gardens, park, woods & children's playground open all year; National Trust

Amid sugar beet fields a few miles outside Bury in the village of Horringer, Ickworth House is an extraordinary rotunda of a house that is now in the ownership of the National Trust. It was built at the beginning of the 19th century by the fourth Earl of Bristol and Bishop of Derry as a storehouse for his art collection and a place for his estranged wife and family to live; but some of the intended works of art never arrived because they were taken by Napoleon. Notwithstanding this setback, a collection was amassed that includes Gainsborough, Titian and Hogarth paintings as well as a vast array of Regency furniture. The exhibition in the basement beneath the rotunda depicts 1930s life in domestic service at Ickworth.

The surrounding park, open all year, was landscaped by Capability Brown between 1769 and 1776, although the basic design goes back to around 1700 when the first Earl of Bristol carved out the landscape to his own requirement after the original Ickworth Hall was demolished in 1701. A herd of deer was introduced in 1706. Also seek out the Italian-style garden with its terrace walk created in 1821, the walled kitchen garden and the Victorian stumpery that contains a large fern collection and stones from the Devil's Causeway in Northern Ireland. There are two cafés on-site, one in the West Wing and another in the Porter's Lodge.

9 WEST STOW ANGLO-SAXON VILLAGE

Icklingham Rd, West Stow IP28 6HG ✆ 01284 728718 ⊘ weststow.org; a Bury St Edmunds Heritage ticket allows entry to both this & to Moyses Hall in the town

This lies seven miles northwest of Bury St Edmunds, signposted from the A1101. Excavations here in the 1960s revealed the remains of the buildings from an Anglo-Saxon settlement as well as a cemetery with over one hundred graves. A reconstructed wooden village has been erected on part of the site, constructed using the technology and techniques of the Anglo-Saxon period. It's all fascinating stuff, with costumed Anglo-Saxon villagers played by knowledgeable enthusiasts occupying the village at the busier times of year. Even if the idea of interpreters spelling out the history for you is anathema, it is undeniably a great hands-on way for children to learn about the past. Numerous special re-enactment activities in summer are mostly geared towards children, along with demonstrations for all ages of Anglo-Saxon pursuits like fletching.

West Stow Country Park, beyond the car park, visitor centre and village, with its mixture of heath and woodland over an area of 125 acres, is a good place for a picnic or a walk along the River Lark. There's a lake and a choice of heath and woodland walks as well as two bird hides and a bird feeding area for wildlife enthusiasts.

EAST OF BURY ST EDMUNDS

The A14 that thunders through Bury St Edmunds continues east to bypass Stowmarket on its way to the coast. It is worth avoiding this busy highway if you can and instead make use of the lesser roads that lead to all sorts of worthwhile villages and hidden-away places. The destinations described here are all fairly close to Bury.

10 PAKENHAM

Just six miles northeast of Bury, Pakenham glows with pride in being the last parish in England to have a windmill and a watermill both working. The 2003 village sign will remind you of this just in case you weren't aware. There's even a book, *Pakenham – Village of Two Mills* by N R Whitwell, which you can read in full on the village website (⌂ pakenham-village.co.uk) if your eyes are up to it. The **windmill**, which is black-tarred and dates from 1830, was still in use up to the 1950s. It underwent full refurbishment of its sails in 2000 but, although the sails still turn, it no longer grinds. The **watermill** (✆ 01359 230275 ⌂ pakenhamwatermill.org.uk ⊙ Apr–Sep Thu, Sat, Sun & bank holiday afternoons; Oct–Mar Thu mornings only), a gleaming white building built in 1814 that, despite its name, is actually located closer to Ixworth than to Pakenham, is by contrast still fully functional. Guided tours are

---

1 Pakenham's historic windmill. **2** The intricate hammerbeam roof in St Mary's Church, Woolpit. **3** Woolpit's wrought-iron sign showing a wolf and two children. **4** The beautiful gardens at Wyken Hall. ▶

GRAHAM WILLIAMS/S

MICHAEL BROOKS/A

PETER BRIDGE

CHRIS CULLEN/A

available during opening hours until 45 minutes before closing. The mill shop sells stoneground wholemeal wheat, rye and spelt flour milled on the premises. There's also a tea room serving cakes and scones made using the mill's flour.

Pakenham village, which has plenty of pretty thatch, also has an unusual cruciform church, St Mary's, with a stubby octagonal tower and a lovely stone font that has carvings of unicorns and pelicans.

For windmill aficionados, **Bardwell Windmill** (✆ 01359 251331), just north of Ixworth, dates from the 1820s. The mill has been fully restored in recent years and is now home to **Wooster's Bakery** (✆ 01359 408409 ⌖ woostersbakery.com), which in addition to cakes and pastries produces a wide range of artisan bread that ranges from sprouted rye sourdough to focaccia. The bakery also has a branch in Bury St Edmunds and the bread is on sale at a number of local farmers' markets.

¶¶ FOOD & DRINK

Fox & Hounds Barton Rd, Thurston IP31 3QT ✆ 01359 232228 ⌖ thurstonfoxandhounds. co.uk. In Thurston, less than two miles south of Pakenham, this several-time winner of CAMRA Suffolk Pub of the Year award is not only a good choice for Cask Marque-approved real ale but also for meals. The claim is that the pub does not serve fast food but 'good food as fast as we possibly can' and there's a well-priced menu of pub classics like steak and ale pie and cod in Adnams batter, as well as baguettes and wraps at lunchtimes.

The Six Bells Inn The Green, Bardwell IP31 1AW ✆ 01359 250820 ⌖ sixbellsbardwell. co.uk ⊙ 18.00–23.00 Mon–Fri, noon–23.00 Sat & Sun. This 16th-century country inn in Bardwell village, just north of Ixworth and the A143 Bury to Diss road, featured in *Dad's Army* and there's a photograph of the cast in the bar. The food is fairly standard pub fare with meat, poultry and vegetables mostly locally sourced. The pub also offers B&B accommodation in a converted courtyard block.

11 WYKEN

On the other side of Ixworth, a couple of miles to the east, **Wyken Hall** is an Elizabethan manor house central to an ancient estate and 1,200-acre farm that has Shetland sheep and a herd of Red Poll cattle as well as a seven-acre vineyard. **Wyken Vineyards** (⌖ wykenvineyards.co.uk), planted in 1988 on the site of what is thought to be a Roman vineyard, has won several awards for its white wines – Wyken Bacchus was winner of English Wine of the Year in 2009 and Best East Anglian Wine in 2013, while the sparkling Moonshine won East Anglian Wine of the Year in 2017.

A CHURCH WALK IN CENTRAL SUFFOLK

A decade or so ago, Hilary Bradt spent a considerable amount of time sniffing out Suffolk churches on an epic Land's End to Lowestoft bus journey, together with Janice Booth whose *Green Children of Woolpit* box is on page 266. Here's a brief description of how they spent their day in the Woolpit area.

'We'd already done a wonderful church walk near Bury. Then it was our last day, with some final churches to visit and footpaths to walk. We'd selected Beyton, Hessett and Woolpit, linked by lanes and paths. All were special: Beyton for its round tower and carved pew-ends, Hessett for its wonderful 14th-century murals showing the Seven Deadly Sins and tradesmen's tools (a warning not to work on Sundays) and Woolpit – wonderful Woolpit – which was so crammed with angels you felt the whole church might take to the wing.

We sat on a bench at the village pump and waited for the bus for Stowmarket. The sun was warm, there were no cars, few people and even the pub was sleeping. At that moment, I would have been happy to travel this way forever, just catching the next bus to wherever I fancied. The feeling didn't last, however. By the time we reached Diss, having stopped to explore Eye, we'd seen the last bus of the day leave for Beccles without us.'

Wyken Hall Gardens, a pleasing blend of topiary, herb gardens, rose beds, perennial borders and fruit trees, surround the house. It is open from Easter until the end of September every day except Saturday, when a **farmers' market** is held here in the morning.

The vineyard restaurant, the Leaping Hare (see below), is highly rated, and its shop, the Leaping Hare Country Store, is full of crafts, pottery, books, clothing and naturally wines.

¶¶ FOOD & DRINK

The Leaping Hare Wyken Vineyards, IP31 2DW ✆ 01359 250287 ⚲ wykenvineyards. co.uk ☉ Wed–Sun lunch, Fri & Sat dinner. Serving sumptuous three-course meals, this well-regarded restaurant is located in a 400-year-old timbered barn on the estate. Ingredients are sourced from as nearby as possible – beef and lamb from Wyken's own farm, game from the estate, fruit and veg from the kitchen garden. As well as à la carte, a set lunch menu is available from Wed–Sat. Another option here is the Outside Moonshine café, open lunchtimes only Fri–Sun, which offers sourdough pizzas, sandwiches and croque monsieurs.

12 WOOLPIT

The name Woolpit is a bit of an odd one, and nothing to do with the wool trade. It first appeared in a document in 1005, long before the wool

THE GREEN CHILDREN OF WOOLPIT

Janice Booth

A wrought-iron sign in Woolpit village centre shows a wolf, a church and two children. The wolf and the church are easy to interpret, but the children are part of a more curious tale.

Sometime in the mid 12th century, so the story goes, harvesters found two frightened children crying in a field: a girl of about ten years old and a boy who was younger. They wore strange clothes, spoke in an unknown language and their skins were green. Although clearly famished, initially they refused all food – until offered some raw beans. They seized on these with great delight and tried to open the stalks, thinking that was where the beans lay. When villagers split the pods and gave them the beans inside, they ate them greedily.

They were taken to the home of Sir Richard de Calne, who cared for them. Gradually their green colour faded. The boy was always sickly and soon died, but the girl survived to normal adulthood and eventually married.

When she had learned enough English, she explained their origins: she and her brother had come from a land of perpetual twilight, where the sun never shone and the people (Christians) were green. Far away across a broad river, they could see another land that glowed with light, but their people did not travel there. In one version of the legend, she claims they were swept up by a whirlwind; in another, she and her brother wandered into a cave, mysteriously drawn by the distant sound of bells, when

trade started to flourish in the region. One suggestion is that it may derive from the Old English *wulf pytt* (a pit for trapping wolves).

Woolpit was a place of pilgrimage in the medieval period, with pilgrims coming to pay their respects to the Shrine of Our Lady of Woolpit that was probably housed in what is now the vestry of the village's Church of St Mary – there's still a well called Our Lady's Well in a field just northeast of the church. The early 16th century and the Dissolution brought an end to the pilgrimage trade, so the village shifted its economy to the more prosaic

"The brick industry produced a very distinctive and elegant type of brick known as 'Woolpit white.'"

pursuit of manufacturing bricks. Woolpit's first brick kilns and pits were recorded in 1574, and by the 18th century a large number of villagers were employed in three pits here. This brick industry's unique selling point was that it produced a very distinctive and elegant type of brick known as 'Woolpit white'. Many of the village's buildings are built of these 'whites' but many thousands more – millions probably – left the

they were tending the family's sheep, and after many days lost in the dark passages they emerged at Woolpit.

The main sources of the legend are Ralph, Abbot of Coggeshall, and William Newburg, both contemporary chroniclers probably born within a decade or so of the alleged event but writing about it some years after. It's not impossible that one copied details from the other. The words they put into the mouth of the girl are improbably complex for a child who knew no English before she was ten; but both claim that the children spoke a strange language, and were green.

The colour might perhaps be explained by vivid green clothing – its vegetable dye could have run and stained their skin – and/or the sickly pallor of anaemia.

As for the language, could they somehow have come from across the English Channel? Or, language apart, were they linked to the old legend of the Norfolk man who was appointed guardian to his wealthy brother's two children, whom he then tried to murder in order to gain their inheritance? Having failed, he later abandoned them in Wayland Wood near Watton in Norfolk and they're said to be the original 'Babes in the Wood'. Choose your own theory!

A similar event allegedly occurred seven centuries later, in Spain, but descriptions of it are suspiciously like those of the Woolpit tale.

See ⊘ anomalyinfo.com and other such websites for more about this legend and other tales.

village to be shipped to provide fancy brickwork elsewhere. The local clay is not exactly white but it is paler than usual, and the subsequent pale brick became highly sought after and widely used locally. It is even rumoured that Woolpit whites were used in the construction of George Washington's first White House. You can browse a permanent display on Woolpit brickmaking in Suffolk's smallest museum, the **Woolpit and District Museum** (✆ 01359 240822 ⊘ woolpit.org/information-2/museum), on the upper floor of a 16th-century timber-framed cottage. The museum, which is open at weekends and bank holidays from April to the end of September, also has a display on the myth of the Green Children of Woolpit (see above).

As Hilary Bradt attests (page 265), Woolpit's **church of St Mary** really is quite exceptional. Its double hammerbeam roof has a whole squadron of angels, and there's also a magnificent Tudor eagle lectern and what writer Simon Jenkins describes as 'a church within a church' – a sumptuous two-storey porch. The spire, with its flying buttresses, is a Victorian replacement.

¶¶ FOOD & DRINK

The Bull Inn The Street ✆ 01359 240393 ⌖ bullinnwoolpit.co.uk. Woolpit's only pub now that the Swan Inn has closed, this has standard pub classics that make use of locally sourced ingredients wherever possible.

SOUTH OF BURY ST EDMUNDS

You have a choice of roads to take heading south out of Bury towards the Stour Valley. The A134 through Bradfield Combust follows the route of a Roman road for a while before meandering in a distinctly un-Roman manner to reach Long Melford. The A143 from Bury passes through Horringer and past Ickworth Hall before passing through of some of Suffolk's highest land to arrive at somewhat unprepossessing Haverhill, an overspill town rather like a smaller version of Thetford in Norfolk but without the latter's rich history. Threading between these two main routes, the ultra-quiet B1066 leaves the market town behind to plunge through some of west Suffolk's most overlooked countryside passing delightful villages like Hartest, tucked away in folds of the landscape along the way.

13 THE BRADFIELDS

West of Woolpit and closer to Bury St Edmunds, the Bradfields consist of three appealing villages: **Bradfield St George**, **Bradfield St Clare** and **Bradfield Combust**. All are sprawling parishes with narrow, twisting lanes that lend themselves perfectly to bicycle outings. Bradfield St Clare is yet another candidate for the actual site of St Edmund's martyrdom, although you'd be wise not to mention this to anyone in Hoxne (page 116).

The parish of Bradfield St George is the setting for *Corduroy* by the Suffolk country writer Adrian Bell (father of journalist Martin Bell) who named it Benfield St George in his semi-fictional account of Suffolk rural life. 'Corduroy' is quite an apt term to describe the gentle green furrows and folds of this landscape in spring.

Bradfield Woods (✆ 01473 890089 ⌖ suffolkwildlifetrust.org/bradfieldwoods) nearby, close to Felsham Hall, has been coppiced traditionally for firewood and hazel rods since the 13th century. Some of the ash coppice stools in the wood are thought to be over 1,000 years old. These woods once belonged to the abbey of St Edmundsbury but these days are managed as a nature reserve by the Suffolk Wildlife Trust. As with most ancient woodland, it is a wonderful refuge for wildlife, with a broad variety of plants, plenty of migrant songbirds like garden warblers and blackcaps, woodland mammals such as stoats and badgers, and scarce white admirals among its 24 species of butterfly.

"In spring the coppiced areas are awash with flowers like early purple orchid, and bluebell and wild garlic."

Spring is the perfect time to visit, when the coppiced areas are awash with flowers like early purple orchid, bluebell and wild garlic, and the newly arrived birds are in full song. The chances of hearing nightingales singing are fairly good at this time of year although their numbers have declined in recent years. Three coloured trails lead along the rides – you can pick up a trail guide from the visitor centre or by the noticeboard.

▌▌ FOOD & DRINK

The Manger Bradfield Combust IP30 0LW ✆ 01284 386516 ⌾ themanger.online. The only pub left in the Bradfields since the closure of the Fox and Hounds at Bradfield St George, this has a decent selection of dishes on the menu with some vegetarian choices.

14 COCKFIELD

South of the Bradfields, just off the Bury to Sudbury road, Cockfield is composed of nine small hamlets widely spread out around the central village of Cockfield with its 14th-century St Peter's Church. Each of the hamlets takes its name from the green that it lies next to – Colchester Green, Buttons Green and so on. Great Green, a little way northeast of the main village of Cockfield, more than lives up to its name in having an enormous triangular green as its focal point. Another of the hamlets, Parsonage Green, has a literary connection as Robert Louis Stevenson wrote *Treasure Island* while staying at the Old Rectory here.

As elsewhere in the less populated parts of Norfolk and Suffolk, ghosts of the recent past lurk here in the form of a disused US Air Force airfield from World War II. Lavenham airfield close to Smithwood Green was the base of the 487th Bomb Group from 1944 to '45 and B-24 Liberators and B-17 Flying Fortresses rumbled out of here on their way to bombing targets in Germany. Part of the airfield taxiway now serves as a public footpath. With scattered greens, moated farmhouses and gently undulating terrain, this is a marvellous area to spend awhile exploring on foot, although Lavenham (page 204) just down the road to the south might prove to be just too much of a temptation.

¶ FOOD & DRINK

The Horseshoes Stow's Hill ✆ 01284 828177 ⌂ thehorseshoes-inn.co.uk ⊙ closed Mon except bank holidays. A long, thatched 14th-century building with exposed beams and a crown-post roof that is one of the oldest pubs in Suffolk. As well as Adnams ale, Greene King IPA and at least one guest beer, there's homemade British pub food like steak and ale pie.

15 HARTEST

⌂ **Appleby Cottage** (page 278)

It takes a while to reach Hartest whichever way you arrive at the village. The village lies on the B1066 midway between Long Melford and Bury but if you come here from Shimpling to the east you will arrive at the village green after careering down Hartest Hill, considered by some to be the steepest descent in all Suffolk. Relative isolation such as this has certainly not led to neglect: Hartest is a highly attractive village of brightly painted cottages and other desirable real estate clustered around a village green. For pure good looks, it gives Kersey a run for its money as the perfect rural Suffolk idyll.

"The first impression that the village makes is that of a mix of the traditional, the plain old-fashioned and the gentrified."

The first impression that the village makes is that of a mix of the traditional, the plain old-fashioned and the gentrified. In the last category, the village local, The Crown, has clearly been rebranded as a stylish gastropub for the discerning visitor. But if the pub looks as if it might have ideas above its station, it might well be because the building was formerly Hartest Hall, the seat of the squire in these parts.

The upper part of the village green has a curious large boulder known as the **Hartest Stone** sitting on it, a glacial erratic dumped unceremoniously in the vicinity during the last ice age. The stone is said to have been hauled here on a wooden sledge from a field on top of nearby Somerton Hill on 7 July 1713 by 'twenty gentlemen and twenty farmers' and a team of 45 horses – no mean feat as this was quite some distance even if it was largely downhill. The stone was relocated to celebrate the Peace of Utrecht and the Duke of Marlborough's victories in the War of Spanish Succession. Rumour has it that after the stone had been successfully shifted to its new location an 'erotic debauch' took place among the villagers. In July 2013, celebrations in the village paid tribute to the 300-year anniversary of the stone, with bell-ringing, maypole dancing, and a deputation from Somerton asking for the stone to be returned. A symbolic 'stone' was then collected from a barn at Place Farm and taken to Hartest to be paraded around the green before being placed beside the original stone and given a parking ticket. No erotic debauch, though.

South of the village at the top of a hill on the Shimpling road, **Giffords Hall Vineyard** (⌀ 01284 830799 ⌀ giffordshall.co.uk) is a medium-sized vineyard that produces a range of English wines from grape varieties that include Bacchus and Pinot Noir. Planted in the late 1980s, the vines are now fully productive; the 2010 vintage received several gold awards, and subsequent years have also received medals. Giffords Hall is a signed-up member of the Sustainable Wines of Great Britain programme and is working towards natural methods of weed control and disease prevention – a flock of rare breed black sheep is employed to help graze the weeds and improve the soil of the vineyard. Guided private tours of the vineyard with cellar tasting session for groups of between two and 60 people are possible anytime, while lower-cost 'grand tours' are run once a month in summer. A vineyard shop is open throughout summer, closing for harvest but reopening in November until January (⊙ 11.00–16.00 Tue–Sun). A small café is open 11.00–16.00 on weekends and bank holidays from Easter onwards.

¶¶ FOOD & DRINK

The Crown The Green ⌀ 01284 830250 ⌀ thecrownhartest.co.uk. A stylish village pub owned by the Brewshed Brewery in Bury St Edmunds, who have another property, The Cadogan, at Ingham on the other side of Bury. Naturally, this has a good choice of real ales along with an extensive wine list and various tempting food options: grilled sandwiches at lunchtime, seasonal menus with the emphasis on local produce, 'pie and pint Wednesdays' and Sunday roasts.

WEST OF BURY ST EDMUNDS

West of Bury St Edmunds, the A14 and the railway line run more or less parallel on their way to Cambridge through a gently undulating landscape of cereal and beet fields. At Kentford the county boundary narrows dramatically to a pinch before widening again like the

MARK STAPLES

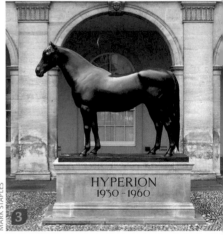

DAVID KNIGHTON/A

PETER MOULTON/S

PETER MCLEOD

protuberance of a jigsaw piece to incorporate the horseracing town of Newmarket. Halfway between Kentwell and Newmarket, astride the quieter B1085, is the pre-Domesday Book village of Moulton, best known for its 15th-century **packhorse bridge**, a photogenic flint and stone structure with four pointed arches that spans the River Kennet beside what was once the main Bury St Edmunds to Newmarket road.

16 NEWMARKET

🏠 **Packhorse Inn** (page 278)

Newmarket is not that large but it could never be described as a one-horse town. Horses are the town's raison d'être; as a major centre for thoroughbred horseracing, racehorse breeding and training, the mere utterance of the name brings to mind sleek horses, velvet green paddocks and thin, short men. Newmarket first came to prominence in the early 17th century, when James I built Newmarket Palace in the town, a small estate that established the town as a royal resort. It was also in Newmarket that Charles I had a lodge built for him by Inigo Jones, and where he was later imprisoned by Cromwell's New Model Army before his subsequent beheading in 1649. Following the Restoration in 1660, King Charles II became a frequent visitor to the town and in 1670 commissioned a new palace to be built, part of which remains today as **Palace House**, now home to the National Heritage Centre for Horseracing & Sporting Art, the town's main draw for those who don't come simply for a flutter on the horses.

Like it or not, it is hard to escape the overriding equestrian theme of the town as almost everywhere you look you'll find evidence of some sort of horsey connection – saddlers' shops, a coffee bar called 'The Stables', and the splendid Georgian **Jockey Club Rooms** on the High Street that has a life-size statue of the prizewinning thoroughbred Hyperion (1930–1960) adorning its courtyard. And, just in case you were in any doubt, The Shoes pub near the clock tower at the top end of the High Street has stencilled horseshoes climbing its walls and a life-size multicoloured fibreglass horse on its roof. In fairness, the High Street does have points of non-equestrian interest too, like the King Edward VII Memorial Hall, next to the White Hart Hotel, which

◀**1** Brightly painted cottages in Hartest. **2** Moulton's 15th-century packhorse bridge.
3 Newmarket's life-size statue of prizewinning Hyperion. **4** Giffords Hall vineyard.

now serves as offices for the town council. Closer to the clock tower at the eastern end of the High Street, is the **Rutland Arms Hotel**, a grand Georgian building that gives the impression of being somewhat oversized for a small town such as this. At one time it no doubt fitted the bill perfectly – built in the early 19th century as a coaching inn, it once enjoyed a thriving trade with the great and the good of the horseracing world. The clock tower itself commemorates Queen Victoria's Jubilee in 1887. Palace Street runs from the clock tower diagonally to the High Street, past an annexe of the Rutland Arms Hotel and two half-timbered cottages named 'Nell Gwynne's Cottage' and 'Nell Gwynn House' respectively – a speculative claim but undoubtedly highly convenient lodging for King Charles II's mistress considering that Palace House is only a little way down the road. Palace House is but part of **The National Horseracing Museum** (✆ 01638 667314 ♂ nhrm.co.uk), a five-acre site that has three complementary attractions. Palace House has the Fred Packard Museum & Galleries of British Sporting Art, while across Palace Street is the entrance to the main complex, which has the National Horseracing Museum in the Trainer's House and King's Yard Galleries, and live former racehorses that you can get up close to in the Rothschild Yard. Another life-size horse statue, this time of Frankel, now retired but still the highest-rated racehorse in the world, has central pride of place in the yard. There's also a restaurant, The Tack Room, which is accessible to the public, not just museum visitors, by way of the gates on Palace Street. When I visited on a warm late summer day most of the tables on the outdoor terrace were occupied by muscular men in Lycra rather than small men in silks – a road cycling group had stopped by. King's Yard also has a café, The Bakery, which can provide drinks, cakes and snacks.

For a taste of Newmarket's pre-equestrian, indeed pre-Norman, past you might wish to venture a little way southwest of the town to take a look at the **Devil's Dyke** that cuts a groove and ridge across the landscape. This Anglo-Saxon defensive ditch stretches for seven miles from the Fen edge at Reach in Cambridgeshire to Ditton near Stechwort (also in Cambridgeshire). The mile-long section between the racecourse on Newmarket Heath and the National Stud forms part of the Suffolk–Cambridgeshire boundary. The best place to get an idea of its size and extent is on Galley Hill near Burwell just over the Cambridgeshire border, where it stands 34ft high from base of ditch to top of bank.

¶¶ FOOD & DRINK

The Bull 62 High St ☎ 01638 662534. This conveniently located, traditional pub on the high street has a choice of cask ales and serves highly rated cooked breakfasts and good-value pub meals.

The Packhorse Inn Bridge St, Moulton CB8 8SP ☎ 01638 751818 ⌂ thepackhorseinn. com. Next to the eponymous bridge in the village of Moulton, a little way to the east of Newmarket, this smart traditional inn has a fairly pricey Modern European à la carte menu in addition to 'sharing roasts' for four to six people on Sundays. There's an extensive wine list with plenty of three-figure champagnes on offer for those who have been lucky on the horses. Also has accommodation (page 278).

The Pantry Unit 17 & 18 The Guineas ☎ 01638 661181 ⌂ thepantryfinefoods.com. Tucked away in The Guineas shopping centre, opposite The Bushell pub, this deli and restaurant with open-plan kitchen and minimalist décor seems a little incongruous in a location like this. Nevertheless, it is a pleasant place to linger over a coffee, and the menu offers a wide range of snacks and meals as well as tempting daily specials and a fixed price, two-course evening menu on weekdays. There's even a gin and tonic menu that features a couple of locally produced gins.

ACCOMMODATION

The places to stay listed below have been selected for their good location and because they embrace the Slow mindset, either in terms of their overall feel or because they embody a 'green' approach. Prices for hotels vary considerably, but two people sharing a room in a B&B can usually expect to spend around £80–100 per night. Holiday cottage prices also cover a wide range, depending on capacity, season and location. There is plenty to be said for visiting out of season in order to save money. Campsites run the gamut from no-frills to luxurious 'glamping' options.

The accommodation selection here is just a small assortment of selected places. These have been ordered according to geographical area. The list is not meant to be in the least bit exhaustive but rather just a small personal selection. The hotels and B&Bs featured in this section are indicated by 🏠 under the heading for the town or village in which they are located. Self-catering options are indicated by 🏡 and campsites by 🏕. For complete listings, go to ⏻ bradtguides.com/suffolksleeps.

1 THE SUFFOLK HERITAGE COAST

Hotels

The Crown and Castle Market Hill, Orford IP12 2LJ 🕿 01394 450205 ⏻ crownandcastle.co.uk

The Ship St James St, Dunwich IP17 3DT 🕿 01728 648219 ⏻ shipatdunwich.co.uk

The Swan Market Pl, Southwold IP18 6EG 🕿 01502 722186 ⏻ theswansouthwold.co.uk

B&B

Argyll House B&B Yoxford Rd, Westleton IP17 3AE 🕿 01728 649054 ⏻ argyllhousebnb.co.uk

Self-catering

Aldeburgh Cottage High St, Aldeburgh IP15 5D 🕿 01728 638962 ⏻ bestofsuffolk.co.uk

The Balancing Barn Near Walberswick ⏻ living-architecture.co.uk

The Dune House Near Thorpeness ⏻ living-architecture.co.uk

Five Acre Barn Aldeburgh Rd, Aldringham IP16 4QH 🕿 07788 424642 ⏻ fiveacrebarn.co.uk

The Found Bawdsey 🕿 01637 881183 ⏻ uniquehomestays.com

The Gallery Blythburgh 🕿 01728 440981 ⏻ bestofsuffolk.co.uk

Martello Tower Aldeburgh 🕿 01628 825925 ⏻ landmarktrust.org.uk

Campsites

Harbour Camping & Caravan Park Ferry Rd, Southwold IP18 6ND 🕿 01502 722486 ⏻ southwoldcamping.com

Mill Hill Farm Caravan & Campsite Westleton Rd, Darsham, Saxmundham IP17 3BS *☎* 01728 668555 *☝* suffolkcamping.webs.com

2 THE WAVENEY VALLEY

Hotel
Waveney House Hotel Puddingmoor, Beccles NR34 9PL *☎* 01502 712270 *☝* waveneyhousehotel.co.uk

B&B
Cowpasture Barn The Common, Mellis, Eye IP23 8EE *☎* 01379 788196 *☝* bedandbreakfasts.co.uk

Self-catering
Fritton Lake Woodland Lodges Church Lane, Fritton NR31 9HA *☎* 01493 484008 *☝* frittonlake.co.uk

Campsite
Outney Meadow Touring & Camping Park Outney Meadow, Bungay NR35 1HG *☎* 01986 892338 *☝* outneymeadow.co.uk

3 SOUTHEAST SUFFOLK

Hotels
The Crown Thoroughfare, Woodbridge IP12 1AD *☎* 01394 384242 *☝* thecrownatwoodbridge. co.uk

Kesgrave Hall Hall Rd, Kesgrave, Ipswich IP5 2PU *☎* 01473 333741 *☝* milsomhotels.com/kesgrave-hall

B&Bs
Grafton Guesthouse 13 Sea Rd, Felixstowe IP11 2BB *☎* 01394 284881 *☝* the.graftonguest.house
Station Guesthouse Station Rd, Woodbridge IP12 4AU *☎* 01394 384831 *☝* stationguesthouse.co.uk

Self-catering
Freston Tower Near Ipswich *☎* 01628 825925 *☝* landmarktrust.org.uk
Jasmine Cottage Woodbridge *☎* 03330 151348 *☝* suffolk-secrets.co.uk
Teachers House Shottisham Rd, Alterton, Woodbridge IP12 3DE *☎* 01728 638962 *☝* bestofsuffolk.co.uk/properties

Campsites
Secret Meadows White House Farm, Hasketon, Woodbridge IP13 6JP *☎* 01394 337337 *☝* secretmeadows.co.uk
Suffolk Yurt Holidays Ufford Rd, Bredfield, Woodbridge IP13 6AR *☎* 07976 613602 *☝* suffolkyurtholidays.co.uk

USEFUL WEBSITES

BedandBreakfasts.co.uk (*☝* bedandbreakfasts.co.uk/suffolk) has details of a large number of properties that can be searched for online by list or map view. **Best of Suffolk** (*☝* bestofsuffolk.co.uk) has a large number of self-catering holiday cottages to choose from and you can search by size and facilities. **Suffolk Secrets** (*☝* suffolk-secrets.co.uk) and **Suffolk Cottage Holidays** (*☎* 01394 389189 *☝* suffolkcottageholidays.com) are other options that offer plenty of choice, as are the Suffolk entries for **Country Cottages Online** (*☝* countrycottagesonline.net/england/cottages-in-suffolk) and **Heritage Hideaways** (*☎* 01502 322405 *☝* heritagehideaways.com).

4 CENTRAL & EAST SUFFOLK

B&Bs

Boundary Farm Framlingham IP13 9NU ℘ 01728 885422 ⌂ boundaryfarmcottages.co.uk

Self-catering

The Barns at Belle Grove Bell Grove Farm, Halesworth IP19 8QU ℘ 01986 873124 ⌂ bellegrovebarns.com

Brights Farm Bramfield, Halesworth IP19 9AG ⌂ suffolk-secrets.co.uk

The Round House Station Rd, Framlingham ℘ 07968 711565 ⌂ theroundhousesuffolk.co.uk

School Cottage Yoxford IP17 3EU ℘ 07986 812851 ⌂ suffolkcottagefor2.co.uk

Sheep Cottages Bruisyard Rd, Peasenhall IP17 2HP ℘ 07768 693548 ⌂ sheepcottages.co.uk

Campsites

The Orchard Campsite 28 Spring Lane, Wickham Market IP13 0SJ ℘ 07818 034729 ⌂ orchardcampsite.co.uk

Swattesfield Campsite Gislingham Rd, Thornham Magna IP23 8HH ⌂ swattesfieldcampsite.co.uk

5 SOUTH SUFFOLK & THE STOUR VALLEY

Hotel

The Angel Inn Stoke-by-Nayland CO6 4SA ℘ 01206 263645 ⌂ angelinnsuffolk.co.uk

The Swan Lavenham CO10 9QA ℘ 01787 247477 ⌂ theswanatlavenham.co.uk

B&Bs

Cobbles 26 Nethergate St, Clare CO10 8NP ℘ 01787 277539 ⌂ cobblesinclare.co.uk

Milden Hall Farmhouse Milden, Lavenham CO10 9NY ℘ 01787 247235 ⌂ thehall-milden.co.uk

Mill House Cross St, Sudbury CO10 2DS ℘ 01787 882966 ⌂ millhouse-sudbury.co.uk

Self-catering

Byes Barn Prentice St, Lavenham CO10 9RD ℘ 01787 247833 ⌂ suffolk-secrets.co.uk

6 WEST SUFFOLK & THE BRECKS

Hotels

Angel Hotel 3 Angel Hill, Bury St Edmunds IP33 1LT ℘ 01284 714007 ⌂ theangel.co.uk

Ickworth Hotel Horringer, Bury St Edmunds IP29 5QE ℘ 02080 765555 ⌂ ickworthhotel.co.uk

Packhorse Inn Bridge St, Moulton CB8 8SP ℘ 01638 751818 ⌂ thepackhorseinn.com

B&B

Appleby Cottage The Green, Hartest IP29 4DH ⌂ clickbedandbreakfast.co.uk

Self-catering

East End House 140 Eastgate St, Bury St Edmunds IP33 1XX ℘ 02081 234532; ⌂ oldschoolhouseholidayproperties.com

NOTES

INDEX

Page numbers in **bold** refer to main entries; *italics* refer to walk maps

Y

Z

INDEX OF ADVERTISERS

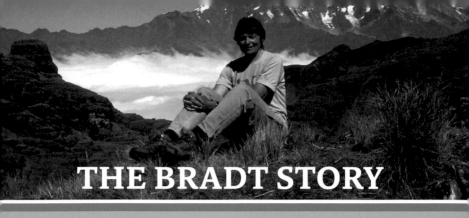

THE BRADT STORY

In the beginning

It all began in 1974 on an Amazon river barge. During an 18-month trip through South America, two adventurous young backpackers – Hilary Bradt and her then husband, George – decided to write about the hiking trails they had discovered through the Andes. *Backpacking Along Ancient Ways in Peru and Bolivia* included the very first descriptions of the Inca Trail. It was the start of a colourful journey to becoming one of the best-loved travel publishers in the world; you can read the full story on our website (**bradtguides. com/ourstory**).

Getting there first

Hilary quickly gained a reputation for being a true travel pioneer, and in the 1980s she started to focus on guides to places overlooked by other publishers. The Bradt Guides list became a roll call of guidebook 'firsts'. We published the first guide to Madagascar, followed by Mauritius, Czechoslovakia and Vietnam. The 1990s saw the beginning of our extensive coverage of Africa: Tanzania, Uganda, South Africa, and Eritrea. Later, post-conflict guides became a feature: Rwanda, Mozambique, Angola, and Sierra Leone, as well as the first standalone guides to the Baltic States following the fall of the Iron Curtain, and the first post-war guides to Bosnia, Kosovo and Albania.

Comprehensive – and with a conscience

Today, we are the world's largest independently owned travel publisher, with more than 200 titles. However, our ethos remains unchanged. Hilary is still keenly involved, and **we still get there first**: two-thirds of Bradt guides have no direct competition.

But we don't just get there first. Our guides are also known for being **more comprehensive** than any other series. We avoid templates and tick-lists. Each guide is a one-of-a-kind expression of an expert author's interests, knowledge and enthusiasm for telling it how it really is.

And a commitment to wildlife, conservation and respect for local communities has always been at the heart of our books. Bradt Guides was **championing sustainable travel** before any other guidebook publisher. We even have a series dedicated to Slow Travel in the UK, award-winning books that explore the country with a passion and depth you'll find nowhere else.

Thank you!

We can only do what we do because of the support of readers like you – people who value less-obvious experiences, less-visited places and a more thoughtful approach to travel. Those who, like us, take travel seriously.

TRAVEL TAKEN SERIOUSLY